Assisted Suicide

Other Books in the Current Controversies Series:

Assisted Suicide

David Bender, *Publisher*
Bruno Leone, *Executive Editor*

Bonnie Szumski, *Editorial Director*
Brenda Stalcup, *Managing Editor*
Scott Barbour, *Senior Editor*

Laura K. Egendorf, *Book Editor*

CURRENT CONTROVERSIES

Library of Congress Cataloging-in-Publication Data

Assisted suicide / Laura K. Egendorf, book editor.
        p. cm. — (Current controversies)
    Includes bibliographical references and index.
    ISBN 1-56510-807-8 (lib. bdg. : alk. paper). — ISBN 1-56510-806-X
(pbk. : alk. paper)
    1. Assisted suicide—Miscellaneous. I. Egendorf, Laura K., 1973–   .
II. Series.
R726.A85   1998
174'.24—dc21   97-52277
                                                                                    CIP

Contents

Chapter 2: Is Assisted Suicide a Constitutional Right?

Yes: Assisted Suicide Is a Constitutional Right

No: Assisted Suicide Is Not a Constitutional Right

Chapter 3: Should Physician-Assisted Suicide Be Legalized?

Yes: Physician-Assisted Suicide Should Be Legalized

Currently, terminally ill patients who wish to end their suffering are at the
mercy of doctors who may refuse to help them die. Legalizing physician-
assisted suicide would respect the patients' freedom of choice while providing safeguards to protect their rights.

Physician-assisted suicide should be legalized, but strict guidelines
should be established to ensure that the practice is not abused. These safeguards should include counseling, consultation with doctors, and a convening of respected community leaders.

One argument presented by opponents of assisted suicide is that legalizing the practice would threaten the rights of the disabled by sending the
message that their lives are not worth living. These critics actually harm
disabled adults by treating them like children who need protection. Allowing competent disabled adults the option of assisted suicide would
empower them and improve their quality of life.

Opponents of physician-assisted suicide often argue that certain types of
patients—such as women, the disabled, or the uninsured—may be coerced into an assisted death if the practice is legalized. These critics do
not understand that abuse of the practice is less likely to occur if it is legalized. Coercion might not be completely eliminated, but legalized
physician-assisted suicide would protect patients by providing consistent
guidelines and safeguards.

No: Physician-Assisted Suicide Should Not Be Legalized

The drive to legalize physician-assisted suicide is based on several
misconceptions. Contrary to the beliefs of assisted suicide advocates,
physician-assisted suicide does not have strong support in the United
States. Furthermore, it is most often requested not because of uncontrollable pain, but because of depression and psychological distress. Keeping
the practice illegal is the correct moral course.

The Dutch example proves that legalized physician-assisted suicide is dangerous. In the Netherlands, where euthanasia is formally banned but is permitted if certain rules are followed, some doctors practice involuntary euthanasia or kill patients who are not terminally ill or competent. Legalizing physician-assisted suicide in the United States could lead to similar abuses.

Chapter 4: How Would Assisted Suicide Affect Individuals' Rights?

Assisted Suicide Would Threaten Individuals' Rights

they do not end their own lives. Instead of caring for, comforting, and learning from its dying members, society will encourage the use of assisted suicide in order to eliminate helplessness and deformities.

Assisted Suicide Would Not Threaten Individuals' Rights

Foreword

By definition, controversies are "discussions of questions in which opposing opinions clash" (Webster's Twentieth Century Dictionary Unabridged). Few would deny that controversies are a pervasive part of the human condition and exist on virtually every level of human enterprise. Controversies transpire between individuals and among groups, within nations and between nations. Controversies supply the grist necessary for progress by providing challenges and challengers to the status quo. They also create atmospheres where strife and warfare can flourish. A world without controversies would be a peaceful world; but it also would be, by and large, static and prosaic.

The Series' Purpose

The purpose of the Current Controversies series is to explore many of the social, political, and economic controversies dominating the national and international scenes today. Titles selected for inclusion in the series are highly focused and specific. For example, from the larger category of criminal justice, Current Controversies deals with specific topics such as police brutality, gun control, white collar crime, and others. The debates in Current Controversies also are presented in a useful, timeless fashion. Articles and book excerpts included in each title are selected if they contribute valuable, long-range ideas to the overall debate. And wherever possible, current information is enhanced with historical documents and other relevant materials. Thus, while individual titles are current in focus, every effort is made to ensure that they will not become quickly outdated. Books in the Current Controversies series will remain important resources for librarians, teachers, and students for many years.

In addition to keeping the titles focused and specific, great care is taken in the editorial format of each book in the series. Book introductions and chapter prefaces are offered to provide background material for readers. Chapters are organized around several key questions that are answered with diverse opinions representing all points on the political spectrum. Materials in each chapter include opinions in which authors clearly disagree as well as alternative opinions in which authors may agree on a broader issue but disagree on the possible solutions. In this way, the content of each volume in Current Controversies mirrors the mosaic of opinions encountered in society. Readers will quickly realize that there are many viable answers to these complex issues. By questioning each author's conclusions, students and casual readers can begin to develop the critical thinking skills so important to evaluating opinionated material.

Current Controversies is also ideal for controlled research. Each anthology in the series is composed of primary sources taken from a wide gamut of informational categories including periodicals, newspapers, books, United States and foreign government documents, and the publications of private and public organizations. Readers will find factual support for reports, debates, and research papers covering all areas of important issues. In addition, an annotated table of contents, an index, a book and periodical bibliography, and a list of organizations to contact are included in each book to expedite further research.

Perhaps more than ever before in history, people are confronted with diverse and contradictory information. During the Persian Gulf War, for example, the public was not only treated to minute-to-minute coverage of the war, it was also inundated with critiques of the coverage and countless analyses of the factors motivating U.S. involvement. Being able to sort through the plethora of opinions accompanying today's major issues, and to draw one's own conclusions, can be a complicated and frustrating struggle. It is the editors' hope that Current Controversies will help readers with this struggle.

Greenhaven Press anthologies primarily consist of previously published material taken from a variety of sources, including periodicals, books, scholarly journals, newspapers, government documents, and position papers from private and public organizations. These original sources are often edited for length and to ensure their accessibility for a young adult audience. The anthology editors also change the original titles of these works in order to clearly present the main thesis of each viewpoint and to explicitly indicate the opinion presented in the viewpoint. These alterations are made in consideration of both the reading and comprehension levels of a young adult audience. Every effort is made to ensure that Greenhaven Press accurately reflects the original intent of the authors included in this anthology.

Introduction

He may be its most recognized practitioner, but Jack Kevorkian did not invent assisted suicide. The practice of assisted suicide is not a modern phenomenon. In ancient Greece, the government gave hemlock to those who wanted it. William Shakespeare memorialized the Roman practice in *Julius Caesar* by depicting Brutus running into the sword held by Strato. Opposition to the practice is also not new, including in the United States; by 1868, more than half of the thirty-seven states in the nation prohibited assisted suicide.

In ancient days, assisted suicide was frequently seen as a way to preserve one's honor. For the past twenty-five years, on the other hand, the practice has been viewed as a response to the progress of modern medicine. New and often expensive medical technologies have been developed that prolong life. However, the technologies also prolong the dying processes, leading some people to question whether modern medicine is forcing patients to live in unnecessary pain when there is no chance they will be cured. Passive euthanasia—disconnecting a respirator or removing a feeding tube—has become an accepted solution to this dilemma. Active euthanasia—perhaps an overdose of pills or a deadly injection of morphine—remains controversial. Assisted suicide is most widely defined as a type of active euthanasia in which a doctor provides the means of death—usually by prescribing a lethal dose of drugs—but the patient is responsible for performing the final act.

Despite the changes in modern medicine, the attitudes toward assisted suicide in America's courts and legislatures have not altered considerably. For instance, in June 1997, the U.S. Supreme Court ruled that people do not have a constitutional right to assisted suicide. Although a constitutional right was not established, the ruling did not preclude states from passing laws prohibiting or permitting assisted suicide. However, similar to its status 130 years ago, assisted suicide is not widely supported in America's state legislatures. As of 1997, physician-assisted suicide was legal in only one state—Oregon. Moreover, that law faced challenges from right-to-life opponents and the Justice Department, which was trying to decide whether the Oregon statute violated any federal law. The other states remained strongly opposed to assisted suicide. As of this writing, thirty-five states have statutes that prohibit assisted suicide, nine states and the District of Columbia have common-law prohibitions, and five states have unclear laws. The common-law prohibitions are not always enforced;

Kevorkian, who has been present at over seventy assisted suicides, has never been convicted in any of several trials held in Michigan, despite that state's common-law ban.

Debate over assisted suicide nearly always centers on the "slippery slope" argument. This argument holds that permitting one behavior will lead to a series of increasingly dangerous behaviors. Critics argue that if voluntary assisted suicide is legalized for competent, terminally ill adults, the acceptance of involuntary euthanasia for incompetent, elderly, or uninsured people will follow. This view is reflected in an amicus curiae brief that was presented to the U.S. Supreme Court when it considered *Washington v. Glucksberg* and *Vacco v. Quill* (the two cases in which the Supreme Court decided there is no constitutional right to die). Written by a collection of doctors and nursing home staff, the brief states: "Any new constitutional right to suicide will extend to persons who are not terminally ill, persons who are merely disabled and/or suffering physically, and persons who are comatose, in a persistent vegetative state, or otherwise incompetent."

Assisted-suicide advocates contend that the slippery-slope argument is fallacious. They argue that legalizing assisted suicide would not place patients' right to life at risk because America is founded on democratic values that would ensure the rights of all citizens. Derek Humphry, founder of the Hemlock Society, a group that seeks to legalize physician-assisted suicide, writes:

> Is this the start of the slippery slope toward killing off the burdensome—our expensive elder folk, our physically and mentally handicapped, our citizens on welfare? If you believe that, it would be best to leave the country now, because you have no faith in the goodness of human nature or the ability of the American democratic system to protect the weak.

The use of euthanasia in the Netherlands, which was first permitted in 1973, can be examined in order to gain insight into whether legalized assisted suicide would threaten the weaker segments of American society. Although the practice is technically illegal, Dutch physicians are permitted to assist a patient's suicide if certain guidelines are followed. These guidelines require that the patient make a voluntary, informed, and repeated request for euthanasia because of unbearable suffering and that the doctor consult at least one colleague and write a report. Studies suggest that these regulations are not always followed faithfully. For example, the 1996 Remmelink report shows that one thousand cases of involuntary euthanasia occur in a typical year and that guidelines are not followed completely in nearly 60 percent of euthanasia and assisted suicide cases.

The inefficacy of the Dutch guidelines, as suggested in the Remmelink report, raises concerns among many opponents of assisted suicide. However, supporters of the practice argue that similar guidelines in the United States—such as the ones in Oregon that include waiting periods and confirmation from two doctors that the patient has less than six months to live—will actually protect patients by increasing physician accountability. They contend that the present underground system of assisted suicide, with doctors adhering to individual guidelines, is more problematic. Betty Rollin, who assisted in the suicide of her terminally ill mother, writes, "The current non-system is particularly troubling in cases where patients are helped to die by relatives, not doctors. . . . No legalization means no safeguards are in place to ensure these patients really wanted to die!"

The debate over whether assisted suicide should be legalized in the United States—a nation considerably larger and more diverse than the Netherlands—is not likely to be resolved in the near future. People on both sides of the issue will undoubtedly pay close attention to developments in Oregon, and perhaps other states, in an effort to bolster their side of the slippery-slope argument. The legalization of physician-assisted suicide is just one of the topics discussed in *Assisted Suicide: Current Controversies*. Other issues addressed by authors in this anthology include the ethics of assisted suicide, whether a constitutional "right to die" exists, and the effect that assisted suicide has on society as a whole.

Chapter 1

Is Assisted Suicide Ethical?

Chapter Preface

On March 30, 1995, in his *Evangelium Vitae* (*Gospel of Life*), Pope John Paul II declared assisted suicide unethical. "Suicide is always as morally objectionable as murder," he maintained. "'Assisted suicide' means to cooperate in and at times be the actual perpetrator of an injustice that can never be excused, even if it is requested." The pope's view is shared by many religious leaders, ethicists, and other people who feel that assisted suicide is unethical because it usurps what they consider to be God's right to determine a person's lifespan. Many also oppose assisted suicide because they believe it devalues life and sanctions killing.

However, others argue that assisted suicide is ethical because it respects a person's choice to end a life that lacks physical, emotional, or spiritual meaning. A 1995 editorial by the Hemlock Society, stating its opposition to the pope's encyclical, reflects this opinion. The organization, which seeks to legalize physician-assisted suicide, wrote that the pope's viewpoint does not respect individual autonomy: "[The pope] might recall that the U.S. was formed in the name of democratic religious freedom, where people are free to worship as they want (or not at all), to base their lives on whatever ethic they choose, and to have a say in governmental issues."

The disagreement between Pope John Paul II and the Hemlock Society presents an accurate reflection of the debate over the ethics of assisted suicide. The debate hinges on which belief should take precedence—the belief that it is immoral to intentionally end a life or the belief that terminally ill individuals should have freedom of choice regarding how and when they die. The following chapter will consider these and other ethical questions surrounding the issue of assisted suicide.

Assisted Suicide Shows Compassion for the Dying

by Arthur Rifkin

About the author: *Arthur Rifkin is a professor of psychiatry at the Albert Einstein College of Medicine in the Bronx, New York.*

Physician-assisted suicide in a concrete fashion forces us to consider and act on what we consider ultimate. It not only makes us question whether someone should commit suicide, but whether another person should help.

Advantages and Disadvantages of Technology

Do we "play God" when we seek to end life? The typical instance concerns someone terminally ill who considers life meaningless because of pain and mental and physical impediments. Technology, as in many areas, creates advantages and disadvantages. We live longer and more comfortably because of medical advances, such as renal dialysis, organ transplantations, joint replacement, and antidepressants. But technology, as well, can simply prolong dying. Where pneumonia, "the old man's friend," would kill a debilitated person relatively quickly, we, often, can prevent this. Mechanical ventilation and parenteral nutrition extend life, even for long periods of unconsciousness or stupor.

We can reduce suffering. Optimal treatment of pain can remove much discomfort, although many patients don't receive optimal pain management because of the mistaken concern that tolerance will develop to the analgesic effect or worry about addiction. Much suffering comes from unkind treatment, from insensitive caregivers, neglect from family and friends, and unpleasant surroundings. Much suffering comes from the narrowing of areas that sustain interest and pleasure, by sensory loss, invalidism, and lack of intellectual and social opportunities. Compassionate, intelligent care in pleasant surroundings would alleviate much suffering.

However, for many people we cannot mitigate the suffering. We think unrealistically if we expect to make all dying free of severe suffering.

The situation is not hopeless: some very painful conditions remit, even if the

Reprinted, with permission, from Arthur Rifkin, "Spiritual Aspects of Physician-Assisted Suicide," *Friends Journal*, October 1997.

patient does not recognize that this can occur. This raises the very difficult question of determining if the dying person has the mental capacity to make the decision to end his or her life. We would not honor the decision to commit suicide by minors or people with mental disorders, which includes everything from alcohol intoxication to Alzheimer's Disease. The difficult issue is assessing depression. We rightly protect a depressed person from committing suicide because his or her judgement is impaired, and most depressions eventually lift.

Depression and Dying

How do we distinguish depression from existential despair in the dying?

If the dying person no longer enjoys usual activities, has a poor appetite, sleeps poorly, cannot concentrate well, feels hopeless, and wants to die, are these symptoms of a mental disorder (depression) or understandable and reasonable responses to the illness and its treatment, and/or the result of the illness or treatment? Can we make the case for a mental disorder? Do the symptoms hang together, are the course, family history, and response to treatment predictable? Several studies have shown that depression associated with physical illness does respond to antidepressant drugs, but no studies have included terminally ill patients.

Some psychiatrists aver that the wish to die in a terminally ill patient always represents a treatable mental disorder: if not depression then demoralization—a sense of unrealistic pessimism. This assumes that the realistic suffering of dying can be ameliorated, a questionable assumption.

> *"We think unrealistically if we expect to make all dying free of severe suffering."*

As I assess the situation, there are inadequate psychiatric reasons for considering all instances of suicidal desires instances of psychopathology, and we cannot ameliorate all terrible suffering and lack of dignity in dying persons, although we can do a lot more than we have. The hospice movement shows that much can be done.

Altering Nature's Course

Do we play God by terminating a natural process? I think not. We hardly live in some pure state of nature. In small and large ways we don't "let nature take its course." We foster death by many unhealthful practices. We forestall death by healthful living, environment changes, and medical treatment.

Most people, and all courts, recognize that patients can request discontinuation of life support measures. Do we cross some qualitative bridge between ending life support measures and assisting in suicide, or is this more a quantitative difference, or is it no difference? It seems very late in the day to concern ourselves with altering nature. For better or worse, we have grasped the helm of much that determines our lives. It seems like cowardice and hypocrisy to lift our hands away from the rudder and say, "Now God, you take over."

Is opposition to physician-assisted suicide the last gasp of the "God of the gaps," pinning on God what we remain ignorant of, namely how to make our deaths a deeply spiritually meaningful event and not horrendous torture we would never think of inflicting on anyone? Does it serve God's purpose for us to lose, at the ends of our lives, that which characterizes us at our spiritual best: intentionality, seeking the Light Within to lead us to our culmination? This should be our time of letting go and deepest insight, not a time of agony, stupor, undignified dependence, a prisoner of tighter restrictions than inmates of a maximum security prison endure. Must we become slaves to our failing bodies?

The Shepherd's Rod

The 22nd Psalm aptly describes a horrible death:

> I am poured out like water,
> and all my bones are out of joint;
> my heart is like wax;
>   it is melted within my breast;
> my mouth is dried up like a potsherd,
>   and my tongue sticks to my jaws;
>   you lay me in the dust of death.

This psalm then leads to the magnificent, stately 23rd, filled with peaceful gratitude:

> Even though I walk through the darkest valley,
>   I fear no evil;
> for you are with me;
>   your rod and your staff,
>   they comfort me.

Is it stretching too far to say that the shepherd's rod at the time of death could be the physician's lethal dose of medication?

A treatment of ultimate finality—physician-assisted suicide—must have the most stringent safeguards against misuse. Although distinguishing reversible depression from nonreversible existential anguish is difficult, psychiatrists should use care to recognize and treat reversible depression. We should try to create an ambience most conducive to a meaningful death. We should have a method of paying for healthcare that does not drain away remaining resources. We should provide caretakers who view it as a privilege to competently and compassionately use technical skills and understanding to assist the dying patient.

We should not permit our hubris of thinking we can overcome the suffering of dying to keep the physician from acceding to the patient's request for a lethal dose. We hear misguided claims that following the Hippocratic Oath would keep physicians from assisting in suicide. The spirit of the Hippocratic Oath says the physician should be devoted to the patient's interests. How we define those interests today should not be limited by our understanding of medicine over two millennia ago.

What of the slippery slope? Does physician-assisted suicide open the door to unethical practices of killing people without consent and without good cause? The answer to unintelligent, unscrupulous behavior is intelligence and scrupulous concern for the patient's interest and not manacles to prevent ethical, useful acts. The history of humankind is a widening circle of compassionate and just concerns. We have recognized the need to free ourselves from the injustice of slavery, mistreatment of children, unequal treatment of women, and ethnic and religious bigotry. Now the horizon of concern has reached a group often treated as unfairly and sadistically as any of the foregoing groups: the dying. Let us grasp the chance boldly.

Assisted Suicide Is Consistent with Christian Beliefs

by John Shelby Spong

About the author: *John Shelby Spong is the bishop of the Episcopal Diocese of Newark, New Jersey. He is also the president of Churchman Associates, Inc.*

What gives life its value? What gives life its meaning? If value and meaning are removed from life before life ceases to exist, is it then still life? Do potential value and potential meaning attach themselves to fetal life that is so embryonic as to be only potential, not actual? Who has the right to make decisions about life that is only potential? Is it the society? Is it the affected individuals or the bearer of that life? Does the sacredness ascribed by religious systems through the ages to human life reside in our biological processes? Is biological life itself sacred whether it be human or otherwise?

Modern Ethical Issues

It is around these questions that debates swirl in this century on such ethical issues as euthanasia, assisted suicide, birth control, abortion, animal rights, the use of animal organs and parts in human attempts to combat diseases, vegetarianism and many environmental concerns. In most of these debates the emotional content is high. The person operates on the basis of an unstated but assumed answer to these questions that is passionately held. Frequently that answer is so deeply related to the core of the person's being that it allows no opposition. So the result is argument, not dialogue, and heat, not light.

One of these issues is today coming before our society with increasing rapidity and it requires of the Christian Church a response. Is active, as well as passive, euthanasia an acceptable practice within the ethics of Christian people? To state it more boldly, is assisted suicide an ethical option for Christians and, if so, under what circumstances? . . .

Reprinted, with permission, from John Shelby Spong, "In Defense of Assisted Suicide," *Human Quest*, May/June 1996.

The first thing that must be noted is that these issues are peculiarly modern ones. A century ago and, in most cases, even fifty years ago, these issues would hardly ever have arisen. Throughout western history, society in general, and the medical profession in particular, has been passionately dedicated to the preservation of life. The assumption commonly held was that life was sacred, that it bore the image of God and that its limits had been set by God. So deep was this conviction in the Judeo/Christian world, that murder was not only prohibited among members of the same tribe, but it was also surrounded by powerful disincentives.

Biblical Responses to Murder

In the biblical code, when murder occurred, blood retribution was the legal right and moral duty of the victim's nearest of kin. To escape immediate vengeance and to determine whether or not extenuating circumstances existed, cities of refuge were set up for those who accidentally killed a fellow Jew. In these centers the killer could find temporary sanctuary until the case could be decided and the verdict rendered by the society. If the murder was in fact accidental, then innocence and freedom was established. But if not, then guilt and the delivery of the killer to the family of the victim could be pronounced.

Of course the killing of an enemy was not covered by this prohibition. Thus the Hebrew scriptures had no conflict in proclaiming that the same God who said "You shall not kill" as part of the Ten Commandments could also order Saul to slay every "man, woman, infant and suckling" among the Amalekites (I Sam. 15:3). Even

> *"Is active, as well as passive, euthanasia an acceptable practice within the ethics of Christian people?"*

suicide was rare indeed in this religious tradition, so deep was this sense of the sacredness of life.

But in that world surgery was limited to the sawing off of a limb. Antibiotics were unknown. Blood transfusions could not be given. Organ transplants were inconceivable. Intravenous feeding was unheard of. Finally, machines or medicines that could stimulate the heart and lungs could not be imagined. The time of death did seem to be in the hands of God. Human skill could do little to prolong it. So the idea grew and became deeply rooted in the psyche of the whole society that the sole task of medical science was to prolong life. That was a noble value then and it remains so today.

Medical Complexities

The realities of our world, however, have changed dramatically. That which was inconceivable, unimaginable and unheard of is now a part of our contemporary experience. We have extended the boundaries of life to where the values and definitions of yesterday collide with the technology and skill of today. That is why the debate on assisted suicide now looms before us and that is why this generation must question the conclusions of the past.

Let me pose the complexities of this issue by asking a series of questions. In what does the sanctity of life reside? Is life sacred when pain is intense and incurable? Is it a value to drug a patient into insensibility for pain while continuing to keep him or her alive biologically? At what point does the quality of life outweigh the value found in the quantity of life? Is life's meaning found in the physical activities of the body or in the relationships that interact with the person whose physical body is alive? If those relationships

> *"Is life's meaning found in the physical activities of the body or in the relationships that interact with the person whose physical body is alive?"*

can no longer exist, should the body be allowed to continue functioning? Who should make the life and death decisions in this world? Should that power be given to doctors? But doctors today are less and less involved with patients as medicine becomes more and more impersonal and complex.

The Economics of Health Care

Since doctors still profit from hospital visits to their patients, we must recognize that there is a financial incentive to doctors to keep lingering patients alive. Should this decision be left to the family members? But there are cases in which family members have profited from the death of a relative. Family members have been known to kill a parent or a spouse when they had a vested interest in that person's demise. Should that decision then be left to chaplains, rabbis, pastors or priests? But the religious institutions today are too weak to carry such a responsibility, since perhaps half of the population of our nation is today not related to any religious institution. It might also need to be said that even members of this professional group of "God bearers" have not always been strangers to self-serving corruption. Can the decision be left to the individual involved? Certainly that person needs to be involved in that decision if at all possible, but can it be solely the decision of one person? Should extraordinary care for terminally ill persons be allowed to bankrupt families? Where is the point where such care becomes destructive to the economic well-being of the remaining family members? Because this generation is now capable of certain procedures, is there some moral necessity to use those procedures?

Given the interdependence today of the health of the whole society through insurance rates, Medicare and Medicaid, extraordinary measures to prolong life universally applied would bankrupt the whole nation. Already this nation spends more than 80 cents of every health care dollar in the last year of the person's life. Should such life supports then be available only to those who can afford them? Would we then be equating the sacredness of life and the values that grow out of that concept with wealth? If health care has to be rationed, as it increasingly is in the managed care contracts, on what basis are extraordinary procedures to be withheld?

The values of yesterday are colliding with the technological and medical expertise of today, rendering the conclusions of the past inoperative for the future. That is why questions abound and debate rages around the issues of life and death at both ends of life's spectrum. Even the word "murder" is being redefined in this debate. Is a doctor who performs an abortion a murderer? Is Dr. Jack Kevorkian a murderer? Should he be prosecuted for assisting people into death when hope for those persons had expired? Is it murder for a father who can no longer bear to see his child in intense pain or lingering malaise when all conscious function has been lost, to take matters into his own hands? Is it murder for a wife of long years to order no further food to be given to her dying husband in order to speed his death? Would it be different if she placed a plastic bag over his head? Would one be more moral than the other?

The lines are so vague, the decisions so awesome, the fear so great, the values of the past so compromised by the technology of today, that by not facing these issues consciously society will drift into decisions by default and a new uncritical consensus will become normative. The debate must be engaged and Christians must be part of it.

I, for one, am no longer willing to be silent on this issue. I, as a Christian, want to state publicly my present conclusions. After much internal wrestling, I can now say with conviction that I favor both active and passive euthanasia, and I also believe that assisted suicide should be legalized, but only under circumstances that would effectively preclude both self-interest and malevolence.

Created in God's Image

Perhaps a place to start would be to require by law that living wills be mandatory for all people. A second step might be to require every hospital and every community to have a bioethics committee, made up of the most respected leadership people available, to which a patient, family members, doctors or clergy persons could appeal for objective help in making these rending decisions.

My conclusions are based on the conviction that the sacredness of my life is not ultimately found in my biological extension. It is found rather in the touch, the smile and the love of those to whom I can knowingly respond. When that ability to respond disappears permanently, so, I believe, does the meaning and the value of my biological life. Even my hope of life beyond biological death is vested in a living relationship with the God who,

> *"My conclusions are based on the conviction that the sacredness of my life is not ultimately found in my biological extension."*

my faith tradition teaches me, calls me by name. I believe that the image of God is formed in me by my ability to respond to that calling Deity. If that is so, then the image of God has moved beyond my mortal body when my ability to respond consciously to that Divine Presence disappears. So nothing sacred is compromised by assisting my death in those circumstances.

So into these issues Christian people must venture. It is a terrain fraught with fear and subject to demagoguery by the frightened religious right. That is why the mainline churches must consider these issues in the public arena where faith, knowledge, learning and tradition can blend to produce understanding.

Christian Arguments Against Assisted Suicide Are Misguided

by John A. Pridonoff

About the author: *John A. Pridonoff is a former executive director of the Hemlock Society, an organization that works toward legalizing physician-assisted suicide.*

The Roman Catholic Church and the fundamentalist extreme-right wing of the Protestant Church have been among the most vocal opponents of 'right to die' groups. Using 'God' and the 'Name of God' as their invocation and justification, they pontificate about the sins of those who advocate the option of physician aid-in-dying for the terminally ill. As an ordained Christian minister I have come to the conclusion that these misguided zealots must be answered. Below, I have listed the major complaints, accusations, and exclamations of the radical dimension of Christianity, and my responses:

Which Bible? Which God?

The Bible condemns suicide. The Bible does not take any moral, religious or ethical stand on suicide. Some of the writers of books of both the Old and New Testaments have acknowledged the existence of suicide (such as when Judas committed suicide after betraying Jesus). Neither God nor Jesus make any judgments on the taking of one's life. Recognizing that there are scores of translations and revisions of the various texts and scriptures of the books of the Bible, if one were to 'quote' the Bible, one would also have to prove that the version, translation or revision used was the 'authentic' one. Such proof has been impossible throughout the hundreds of denominations within the Christian Church—not to mention the varied approaches in the Jewish faith.

Physician aid-in-dying is against 'God's Will'. Humankind has been invoking 'God's Will' since the beginning of organized religion. First, we must ask,

Reprinted, with permission, from John A. Pridonoff, "How 'Right' Is the Religious Right?" *Hemlock Quarterly*, April 1993.

'Which God?' The God of the Jews? The Christians? The Moslems? The Buddhists? The Hindus? What about the major religions of the world that don't have a single God, but multiple Gods? Operating on the myth that ours is a 'Christian Nation', I will limit the discussion to the 'Christian God'. Change, whether by an individual or by a society, is always difficult—especially when it goes against long held beliefs, regardless of historical accuracy or honesty. The same people who argue that we are violating 'God's Will' with our Hemlock Mission Statement, also argued that it was against

> *"The Bible does not take any moral, religious or ethical stand on suicide."*

'God's Will' to develop the Durable Power of Attorney for Health Care a few years ago, and before that, to enact the 'Living Will'. In earlier years, when antibiotics were discovered and developed, these religious power brokers maintained that these too, were against 'God's Will', as was the art and science of surgery. These religious mind-controllers would have us believe that any progress in taking control (or maintaining control) of your life would be acting in the 'Place of God'. Only recently the Roman Catholic Church reluctantly condoned the use of medication to effectively control or eliminate pain. (Previously, if such measures hastened the death of a person, the Catholic Church would have had the person remain in intractable pain or suffering.) Only after significant pressure from medical and other groups did the Vatican change their 'official policy'.

Do Not Impose Beliefs

Suffering is a 'good' and 'right' thing to do. The Roman Catholic Church historically has taught that a major purpose in this life was preparation for the Life to Come (that life which comes after death and resurrection). Suffering was seen as a noble experience and as a means of preparation for the 'bearing of one's cross.' Through suffering, a believer could more closely experience what Christ did upon the Cross. Believers who truly want to achieve redemption (the ultimate goal of a true believer), should relish the idea of suffering to better understand the Gift of Sacrifice that Jesus gave them. For the true believer an important part of Personal Salvation has been suffering—the more, the better. Therefore, in end-of-life experiences, to remove suffering from illnesses, would be to rob the person of the opportunity to 'prepare' for death and ultimately, resurrection. While I disagree with it, I have no problem with this 'theology' for such believers. Where I have a problem is when religious organizations try to thrust or impose their belief system on non-believers, or try to make people who have different belief systems feel guilty or unequal in 'the eyes of God' because they do not affirm their particular belief system.

God gives. God takes away. A person who truly accepts this belief would not make any decisions. All decisions would have already been made by a predestined, preordained God. But, for the sake of discussion, what about 'Gifts' from God? Are they 'conditional'? Do they require 'right behavior'? If they do, then are they truly 'Gifts'? My understanding of a gift is that it is given without strings or attachments. If God has truly 'given me a gift of life', then it is mine to do with as I wish.

Aren't you suggesting anarchy? No. God gave us each a *mind.* We have the ability to *think* and to *understand* the relationship between cause and effect, action and reaction, freedom and responsibility, choice and consequence. We have *feelings*—love, guilt, happiness, sadness—that guide us in decision-making and help us establish parameters within which to live our lives, as well as to live our lives within a society and a society within societies.

Society Has Changed

What about the people of the Bible? The writers of the 66 books of the Bible (more books, if you are Catholic) lived and wrote in a time when medical science did not exist. People often died from the first major illness or disease they acquired. Antibiotics had not been discovered and germs were unknown. *Infection was a way of life.* People didn't die because they disobeyed God. They died because they were sick. Behavior resulting from depression, emotional problems or mental illness, was seen in the Middle Ages as the actions of the devil, of Lucifer, of moral corruption and decay. What we now understand as the actions of geography and astronomy were considered actions of good and evil gods, of rewards and punishments by giving and vengeful deities.

So, where is the place of religion? Of the Bible? In the hearts, minds and lives of believers—where it should be. Our purpose is not to take any religious or spiritual belief system away from anyone. Mutual respect for all religions is essential, and no single religion should dictate end-of-life decisions. Physician aid-in-dying is a personal issue that should be reserved for the interactions and trust between patients and physicians. No person, no institution—political or religious—should interfere with that sacred bond.

'Sacred bond'. Are you saying that life is sacred? Yes! We believe that life is sacred as is death and the dying process. Personal beliefs, decisions and desires should be respected. What is 'right' for me may not be 'right' for you. Each of us should be able to determine what is appropriate for ourself. The right to self-determination is a most sacred right—in living, in dying, and in death.

Allowing Competent People to Commit Suicide Is Ethical

by Julian Savulescu

About the author: *Julian Savulescu teaches philosophy at the Centre for Human Bioethics at Monash University in Australia.*

Do-gooders do unwanted good. The trouble with do-gooders is that, despite the best intentions, they often fail to do good. . . . Sometimes, do-gooders do some good. Yet the trouble is that this good is not wanted. My object is the do-gooder in general. However, my focus will be the medical do-gooder: the doctor who helps a patient out of a sincere desire to do the best for him or her, when the patient does not want help.

One example of doing-good in medicine is the treatment of suicidal patients against their wishes. A patient takes an overdose of tablets, such as paracetamol, and arrives in the emergency department alert. The patient refuses to have a nasogastric tube inserted or to cooperate with treatment. She wants to die. If her life is to be saved, a nasogastric tube must be forcibly inserted and intravenous access established in the face of violent opposition. In other circumstances, this would constitute assault. Should it be done?

The Elizabeth Bouvia Case

One much publicised case of doing-good is that of Elizabeth Bouvia. In September 1983, Bouvia entered the casualty department [emergency room] of Riverside [Calif.] Hospital, stating that she wanted to be admitted and allowed to starve herself to death. She was almost totally paralysed in both her legs and arms, and suffered from painful arthritis. In the preceding year, she had married an ex-convict, Richard Bouvia, whom she had corresponded with by mail. She had also had a miscarriage, been refused financial support by her father and sister-in-law, and then been deserted by her husband. She wanted to die because of

Adapted from Julian Savulescu, "The Trouble with Do-Gooders: The Example of Suicide," *Journal of Medical Ethics*, vol. 23, pp. 108–13 (1997), by permission of the author and the BMJ Publishing Group.

her physical disability and mental suffering.

The hospital refused to allow her to die. She was force fed. The case came before John Hews, a California probate judge. He found her to be rational, sincere and fully competent. However, he permitted the hospital to force feed her because of the effect her death might have on the medical personnel caring for her and other handicapped persons.

Bouvia was committed to living a life she did not want to live. She tried two further times to starve herself to death but was unsuccessful. Not all patients who want to die are treated against their wishes. Mrs N was 45 when she developed respiratory failure requiring artificial ventilation. A diagnosis of atypical motor neuron disease affecting her intercostal muscles was made. The disease spread to involve other muscles. She wanted to die. Repeated psychiatric examination found her to be sane. Mr Nicholas Tonti-Filippini, a hospital ethicist in a Roman Catholic hospital, was involved in Mrs N's case. He and the nursing staff involved in her care formed the opinion that "she was competently, freely and informedly refusing treatment, and that opinion was recorded by several independent consultants". He argued that she was not morally obliged to have treatment that she found burdensome and that she had a moral right to refuse medical intervention. Her treatment was withdrawn and she died.

Refusing Burdensome Treatment

Suicide is intentional self-killing; homicide is the intentional killing of one person by another; euthanasia is the intentional killing of one person by another for the former's benefit. Bouvia's starvation diet was attempted suicide; the withdrawing of artificial ventilation of Mrs N was a case of euthanasia.

There was broad-based agreement from both religious and secular groups that Mrs N ought to be allowed to die. Indeed, based on her case and others like it, the Victorian [Australia] Parliament passed the Medical Treatment Act 1988. This act provides legal protection and mechanisms for patients to refuse life-prolonging treatment and doctors to respect these refusals. Why was Mrs N allowed to die but Bouvia was not? If Mrs N was allowed to refuse the provision of air her body needed, why was Bouvia not also allowed to refuse the provision of food that her body needed?

One reason has to do with the nature of the treatment which each was refusing. Mr Tonti-Filippini described life on the ventilator as "a precarious, burdensome existence

> *"The trouble with do-gooders is that, despite the best intentions, they often fail to do good."*

that demands great fortitude on the part of a conscious, competent patient". It was his opinion that people requiring long-term artificial ventilation have no obligation to have such burdensome treatment, although he believed that each person should try. This position implies that if Mrs N had not had to endure burdensome treatment, she ought to have been compelled to live.

We can imagine a patient like Mrs N, who has severe motor neuron disease but who does not require treatment with a ventilator. In some ways, this patient's life is worse. He cannot speak. He can only move his eyes. According to standard Roman Catholic doctrine, not only would such a life be worth living, but such a person ought to be compelled to live that life, even if he preferred to die. Today, there is emerging secular agreement that some human lives are not worth living. And Mrs N's life seems just one instance of that.

> *"Today, there is emerging secular agreement that some human lives are not worth living."*

It is misleading to focus on the burdensome nature of treatment and to equate a person's good with the level of medical treatment she requires. It is not merely treatment which can be burdensome, but life with serious disability and suffering. The reason why many people now believe that a patient such as Mrs N ought to be allowed to die, and *a fortiori* to commit suicide, is because her life is so bad. If this is the reason, then one reason why Bouvia was compelled to live may have been that those involved in her care believed that her life was worth living. Certainly, many disabled groups argued vocally to this effect. (One lawyer at the Law Institute for the Disabled said: "She needs to learn to live with dignity".)

Preference Toward Jehovah's Witnesses

After a complicated series of events and admission to another hospital and another court hearing, the decision to permit the force feeding of Bouvia was overturned by the California Court of Appeals on April 16, 1986. The trial justices noted that a competent person has a right to refuse life-sustaining treatment. We will return to this. They also noted: ". . . in Elizabeth Bouvia's view, the quality of her life has been diminished to the point of hopelessness, uselessness, unenjoyability, and frustration. She, as a patient, lying helplessly in bed, unable to care for herself, may consider her existence meaningless. She is not to be faulted for so concluding . . .". [Elizabeth Bouvia later changed her mind. Despite the court's ruling, she opted not to have the nasogastric tube removed.]

Why was Bouvia prevented from dying? One reason is that do-gooders misjudged what was good for her. The Court of Appeals concluded that she was not making a mistake in considering her life meaningless.

Bouvia was no doubt a difficult patient who engendered little sympathy from her doctors. Compare the way Bouvia's physicians tied her down against her will and force fed her, with the way physicians behave towards Jehovah's Witnesses. Not only are Witnesses allowed to refuse life-saving blood transfusions, but they are given special treatment: extra care is taken to make sure that they do not lose much blood, small bleeding vessels are closed off at operation, they are given other forms of fluid replacement. There is an extraordinary amount of good will towards Jehovah's Witnesses, which was conspicuously lacking in the case of Bouvia. One physician said of Bouvia: "Since she is occupying our space, she must accede to the same care which we afford every other patient here . . .".

This difference in treatment is important. It might be argued that Bouvia was not as disabled as Mrs N. Her life was not as bad. That was the reason for the difference in their treatment. This argument cannot be used when comparing the treatment of Bouvia with that of Witnesses. In some cases, Witnesses are allowed to refuse life-saving transfusions when, if they had one, they would not be left with any disability. Why, then, are healthy Witnesses allowed to die but the disabled Bouvia was not?

The reason again has to do with how we construe what is good for others. The reason why many people believe that Jehovah's Witnesses ought to be allowed to refuse life-saving blood transfusions (and die) is because they believe that it is good to lead one's life according to one's values, particularly religious values. They have legitimate reasons to die (Bouvia apparently did not). Michael Wreen puts it this way: "[R]eligion has to do with (i) describing and explaining the human condition at its most fundamental level; (ii) providing a person with a unique concept of personal identity . . . (iii) making sense of ourselves and the world around us in a complete and satisfying way".

Wreen believes that religious values are special. It is because of these special qualities that people should be allowed to die for them. . . .

Judging One's Life

Mr Tonti-Filippini argues that when suicide appears to have been attempted, "[t]he problem is to separate suicidal refusal of medical treatment from refusal of medical treatment because the patient considers the treatment overly burdensome or contrary to his or her religious or cultural beliefs".

On the one hand some Christian ethicists claim that quadriplegics and other severely disabled people should not be allowed to die on the basis of their judgment of the value of their own lives unless they are being subjected to "burdensome treatment", but on the other hand claim that Jehovah's Witnesses should be able to die because this is in accordance with their religious values (and so treatment is burdensome to them). Is this consistent?

"[People] may have personal ideals, ends which they take to be the point of their own lives."

People may have commitments to ends other than religious or cultural ends. Most importantly, they may have personal ideals, ends which they take to be the point of their own lives. These judgments of what is important may extend to the kinds of lives they think are worth living for themselves. If Jehovah's Witnesses ought to be allowed to die for what they think is important, so, too, ought Bouvia have been allowed to die according to her conception of what is important. On this way of thinking, the fact that Bouvia was severely disabled was not in itself paramount in determining that she had good reason to die; what was paramount was that she judged that these difficulties made her life not worth living. That judgment, in the face of real difficulty, provides her with as much reason to refuse lifesaving treatment as the Jehovah's Witness.

> *"Do-gooders may do good. . . . [But] people have the right to choose a course which is less than the best."*

In one way there is more reason to respect the quadriplegic's desire to die, or the cancer patient's desire to stop suffering, than there is to allow Witnesses die. The Jehovah's Witness's desire is based on the following belief: "If I refuse blood and die, I'll be resurrected". The former's refusal of treatment may be based on this belief: "Future life in a dependent and undignified state is not worth living for me". How we should interpret religious belief is a complicated question. On one view, Jehovah's Witnesses mistakenly believe that the Bible forbids blood transfusion, when the Bible is only referring to certain dietary practices. If this were so, a Witness's refusal of blood transfusion would be based on a false belief. Bouvia's desire to die was not based on any false belief.

The Harm Principle

Do-gooders often fail to do good. They choose the wrong way to go about achieving good and sometimes are aiming at what is not good at all. But there is a more important problem with do-gooders. The good that do-gooders do is unwanted.

Unwanted good may be intrinsically or instrumentally of less value than good that is desired. An example of the instrumental value of desiring good is that good is more likely to be achieved in a patient who diligently takes his medicine, eats well, monitors his symptoms and attends clinic regularly than in one who is non-compliant and aggravates his condition with various excesses.

The unwantedness of the good do-gooders do is important for a more significant reason. People have the right, or at least are allowed in this society, to refuse benefits or to engage in risky ventures. We do not believe that a person ought to be compelled to do what is best for himself. As [John Stuart] Mill put it, "the only purpose for which power can rightfully be exercised over any member of a civilised community, against his will, is to prevent harm to others. His own good, either physical or moral, is not a sufficient warrant". This is Mill's harm principle.

A person is not compelled to accept money he has won in a lottery, or social security benefits he is due from the state, even if he is particularly destitute. Perhaps a destitute person ought to accept money. But it is not true that he ought to be compelled to accept money.

There are two exceptions to Mill's harm principle. Firstly, choice based on inadequate or wrong information need not necessarily be respected. Secondly, some people are incompetent to make an informed choice. In these two cases, doing-good can be justified.

The principle of respect for competent, informed choice has crystallised in common law. In the case of *Schloendorff v New York Hospital*, Justice Benjamin Cardozo observed in 1914: "Every human being of adult years and sound mind has a right to determine what shall be done with his own body". This common law principle grounds the requirement that a competent person must give informed consent before a medical procedure is performed upon him, even if that procedure is life-saving. Whether we should prevent a person attempting or completing suicide depends on whether that person is misinformed or incompetent. If she is informed and competent, as both Bouvia and Mrs N were, then she ought to be allowed to die.

> *"The freedom to finish one's life when and how one chooses is, it seems to me, about as important as any freedom."*

This was the finding by the final court, the Appeals Court, in the case of Bouvia.

"The right to refuse medical treatment is basic and fundamental. It is recognized as a part of the right of privacy protected by both the state and federal constitutions. Its exercise requires no one's approval."

Do-gooders may do good. Bouvia's life may have been worth living. But, as Mill's harm principle makes clear, people have the right to choose a course which is less than the best. Perhaps it is true that they ought to pursue the best course. But it is not true they ought to be compelled to pursue that course, no matter how attractive it is to others. . . .

Possible Objections to Assisted Suicide

The do-gooder offers two important objections. "If we are to respect what a person values, we might end up allowing patients to die for some very bizarre reasons." The difficulty with this objection is that a definition of what constitutes a life which is objectively worth living has been elusive. Even if it were possible to come to a defensible judgment, it is hard to see how the Jehovah's Witness's belief that if he refuses a blood transfusion and dies, he will be resurrected, is worth dying for, and beliefs like those held by Bouvia and Mrs N are not. Current practice seems committed to allowing people to act on subjective values. (I think that this is problematic. But even if what is objectively good could be settled, this would not imply that a person ought to be *compelled* to promote it.)

The second objection is that there will be flow-on effects if we allow suicide. Others will be harmed.

This is perhaps the best argument for a blanket prohibition of allowing people to suicide. But do we really believe that allowing competent people to kill themselves will cause hordes of innocent bystanders to be sucked into a frenzy of self-destruction?

If we set the level of competence required to be allowed to die high, then few people will meet the requirement of competently desiring to die. Indeed, I believe that most desires to die are associated with either lack of information or an evaluative error. If this is true, the numbers who are allowed to die will be small. *A fortiori*, harm to others in the form of death of innocent bystanders will be small.

Assume that my suicide does encourage others to suicide. Unless we believe that seeing my suicide has such catastrophic effects on their psyche that it renders them incompetent, then it is questionable whether societal interference is justified. X seeing Y getting drunk encourages X to get drunk. This observation is not a reason to prohibit people getting drunk.

In a society in which freedoms exist, there will always exist the risk of abuse of these freedoms. But the mere risk, and even actual cases, of abuse, is not sufficient grounds for the abolition of those freedoms. Similarly, nearly all freedoms have some societal cost. The freedom to move from one place to another easily by car is associated with the many costs of motor vehicle accidents, even to innocent pedestrians. Yet the fact that this exercise of freedom has some cost does not justify its abolition. Some freedoms are worth the cost in innocent life. The freedom to finish one's life when and how one chooses is, it seems to me, about as important as any freedom.

Letting Competent People Decide

Do-gooders often fail to do good. They often hold mistaken conceptions of what is good. More importantly, the good do-gooders do is unwanted. Competent people sometimes choose to pursue the less than the best course. Perhaps they ought to pursue the best course. But it does not follow that they ought to be compelled to pursue the best course. Do-gooders fail to appreciate this distinction.

If a person is competent and knows all the relevant facts, including facts about himself, and wants to die and takes steps to effect that desire, we ought not to interfere. His choice may be unusual. There is a place for talking with him, evaluating his competence, the way he is thinking, whether his decision is the result of coercion by others, trying to convince him that he is wrong, but not, ultimately, for interfering with him.

It is difficult to stand by and watch people die. But an active response need not take the form of coercion. We ought to try to convince competent people whom we believe have an unjustified desire to die to change their minds. But we ought not to compel them. It can be difficult to understand why a person desires some course that is less than the best. It can be even more difficult to convince him that he is mistaken. These are topics for another paper. But this is where do-gooders should be directing their energy, not in devising new ways of doing-good.

Physician-Assisted Suicide Undermines Medical Ethics

by *American Medical News*

About the author: American Medical News *is a weekly newspaper published by the American Medical Association (AMA).*

Wrong messages about physician-assisted suicide were delivered in two courtrooms during spring 1996.

A Pontiac, Mich., jury came to the incredible conclusion that Jack Kevorkian, MD, was innocent on charges that he assisted in two suicides. A few days later, a federal appeals court in San Francisco struck down Washington state's ban on physician-assisted suicide. The panel also telegraphed plainly that it will approve an Oregon law that allows the practice. That law is on hold while on appeal. [On October 14, 1997, the U.S. Supreme Court upheld the Oregon law. On November 4, 1997, an effort to repeal the law was rejected by voters.]

Damage to Medical Ethics

We can't recall a time when medical ethics has suffered such a damaging series of blows in rapid succession. However well-intentioned, these courtroom decisions undermine medicine's most fundamental ethical tenet: First, do no harm. Anyone pondering this issue seriously should think twice before accepting these determinations and the reasoning behind them at face value.

That's especially true of the odd trial of Dr. Kevorkian. It featured confusing jury instructions from both the trial judge and Michigan Court of Appeals, as well as a revelation that the jury foreman was a published advocate of assisted suicide.

The ruling on the Washington state law by the 11-member federal appeals panel quickly reduced Dr. Kevorkian's legal problems to a sideshow anyway. The 8-3 decision is the highest court ruling so far on physician-assisted suicide. It is a strong contender for appeal to the Supreme Court. Dr. Kevorkian's lawyer has said he will cite it in an attempt to get the remaining charges against his client dismissed. [On June 26, 1997, in the cases of *Vacco v. Quill* and

Washington v. Glucksberg, the Supreme Court refused to give Americans a constitutional "right to die." However, states are not precluded from passing laws that would establish this right.]

A Dangerous Leap

The appeals court ruling revealed a strange and troubling understanding of both physician-assisted suicide and the value of medical ethics. Judge Stephen Reinhardt, writing for the majority, characterized physician-assisted suicide as the logical extension of other ethically sound actions.

The judge cited examples such as the fully ethical administration of pain relievers knowing that unintentional death might result or withholding treatment at the request of a patient. But it is a wrong and dangerous leap to suggest that intentionally causing the death of a patient is in the same league.

Not a Decision for the Courts

What also gives us pause is Judge Reinhardt's implication that medical ethics rests on a judicial interpretation. "Following the recognition of a constitutional right to assisted suicide, we believe that doctors would engage in the permitted practice when appropriate, and the integrity of the medical profession would survive without blemish," he writes.

It is disconcerting to hear medical ethics treated as a simple matter for the courts to decide. The concept of "First, do no harm" has served patients well for many years. It deserves more than the split vote of an appeals court before it's abandoned or recast.

All of this comes at a time when profits and cost containment are already putting pressure on other ethical standards in medicine. If anything, patients need to know now that their physicians will remain advocates on their behalf and not be party to the inevitable claims that some patients are needlessly "taking up space."

Judge Reinhardt dismissed such "slippery slope" arguments. But in a dissenting opinion, Judge Robert R. Beezer, citing the ongoing experience of euthanasia in the Netherlands, was not so sanguine: "If physician-assisted suicide for mentally competent, terminally ill patients is made a constitutional right, voluntary euthanasia for weaker patients, unable to self-terminate, will soon follow. After voluntary euthanasia, it is but a short step to a 'substituted judgment' or 'best interests' analysis for terminally ill patients who have not expressed their constitutionally sanctioned desire to be dispatched from this world."

> *"The acceptance of physician-assisted suicide is a sign of failure to help patients in need—not a victory to be celebrated."*

The acceptance of physician-assisted suicide is a sign of failure to help patients in need—not a victory to be celebrated. It is sadly true that medicine could do much more for patients at the end of life than it has. The AMA has responded to the growing awareness of this problem with more than an opinion in an ethics book. It is doing more to promote advance directives, to improve physician knowledge of palliative care and to protect physicians so they can prescribe pain medication without fear of prosecution. It's not as simple or dramatic as helping patients kill themselves, just better.

Assisted Suicide Distorts the Meaning of Mercy

by Charles J. Chaput

About the author: *Charles J. Chaput, a member of the Order of Friars Minor, Capuchins, is the archbishop of Denver.*

See if this story sounds familiar: A happily married couple—she is a pianist; he a rising scientist—have their love suddenly tested by a decline in the wife's health. Diagnosed with multiple sclerosis, she falls victim to a steady loss of muscle control and paralysis. The desperate husband uses all his professional skills to save her. But ultimately he must watch her deteriorate in hideous pain. The wife worries that she will soon no longer be "a person anymore—just a lump of flesh—and a torture" for her husband. She begs her husband to kill her before that happens. And eventually, worn down, the reluctant husband releases his wife from her misery with poison.

The husband is indicted for murder. But the understanding judge and jury soon agree that, given the circumstances, the husband is not a killer, and the law needs to be reformed. Meanwhile, in impassioned public comments, the husband attacks "the proponents of outmoded beliefs and antiquated laws" who inflict unnecessary anguish on the terminally ill, "who suffer without hope and whose death would be deliverance for them."

Euthanasia and Propaganda

The story fits comfortably with today's medical headlines. It could easily be a *20/20* segment or a page from Jack Kevorkian's latest trial. But it comes from another era. Produced in 1941, it's the plot line of *I Accuse,* one of the Third Reich's most effective propaganda films. *I Accuse* was created for one reason only: to advance the Nazi campaign of euthanasia for the mentally and physically handicapped, "antisocial elements," and the terminally ill. And it worked. It was a big box-office success. It's also the classic example of how compassion can be manipulated to justify mass killing—first in the name of mercy, then in the name of cost and utility.

Reprinted from Charles J. Chaput, "Eugenics to Euthanasia," *Crisis*, October 1997, with permission from *Crisis* magazine. For subscriptions, call 800-852-9962.

Obviously, America in 1997 is not Germany in 1941. Americans have a practical sense of justice that favors the weak and the little guy. But if we want to keep it that way, we shouldn't assume that merely knowing about a past tragedy prevents us from repeating it. We need to learn from history. And in reflecting on physician-assisted suicide, the first lesson for our lawmakers is that any killing motivated by a distorted sense of mercy—no matter how many reasonable and honeyed words endorse it—leads to killing that has nothing at all to do with the best interests of those killed.

Let's examine a few simple facts.

Three Misconceptions

First, every one of us fears the image of a dying patient stripped of dignity and trapped in a suffering body. But today, no one needs to suffer excruciating pain in a terminal illness. Modern pain-suppression drugs can ensure the comfort of persons even in the final stages of dying. Hospice care, focused on ensuring a natural death with comfort and dignity, is increasingly available. It's true that some doctors underprescribe pain medication or seek to artificially prolong life beyond reasonable hope of recovery. But that is an issue of training. Patients have the right to decline extraordinary means of treatment. They also have a right to be free of mind-numbing pain. Both these goals can be accomplished without killing them.

Second, terminally ill persons seeking doctor-assisted suicide usually struggle with depression, guilt, anger, and a loss of meaning. They need to be reassured that their lives and their suffering have purpose. They don't need to be helped toward the exit. We should also remember that in helping the terminally ill to kill themselves, we're colluding not only in their dehumanization, but our own. Moreover, the notion that suffering is always evil and should be avoided at all costs is a very peculiar idea. Six thousand years of Judeo-Christian wisdom show that suffering can be—and often is—redemptive, both for the person who suffers and for the family and friends of the one in need. In any case, it is very odd to try to eliminate suffering by killing those who suffer.

Third, the Hippocratic Oath has very good reasons for binding physicians to "do no harm." Doctors wield enormous power over their patients. And that power quickly corrupts the profession unless it is rigorously held in check. That is one of the reasons

> *"[I Accuse is] the classic example of how compassion can be manipulated to justify mass killing—first in the name of mercy, then in the name of cost and utility."*

the American Medical Association has rightly, and so strongly, opposed physician-assisted suicide.

The alternative is immensely dangerous. The doctors who killed their patients in Nazi Germany may be written off as the product of a special and terrible time. But what about the doctors in the Netherlands—right now, today—who admit to killing patients without their approval?

Physician-assisted suicide among the Dutch has been quietly tolerated for some time. But no one was prepared for the number of Dutch doctors who have taken it beyond that, proactively dispatching the terminally ill without their knowledge. The point is: The logic behind doctor-assisted suicide naturally expands. Can anyone honestly argue that physician-assisted suicide will limit itself to voluntary candidates in an era of ruthless medical cost-efficiency? And do we really want a society where patients aren't sure they can trust their physicians? . . .

"In helping the terminally ill to kill themselves, we're colluding not only in their dehumanization, but our own."

Missing from too much of today's discussion of doctor-assisted suicide is the presence of God. Yet God, in the view of the great majority of Americans, is the author of life and its only true "owner." Life is God's gift, and he alone is its Lord. However wounded or attenuated it may seem, life is precious. Every life is sacred, from conception to natural death. We rarely understand life. We certainly don't own it. But if this sad century has taught us anything, it's that we have no right to dispose of it—however good the alibi.

Assisted Suicide Violates Christian Beliefs

by Diane Komp

About the author: *Diane Komp is an oncologist and a professor of pediatrics at Yale University's School of Medicine in New Haven, Connecticut.*

Nine-year-old Mikey came to see me today. His parents wanted a second opinion about the tumor that is growing out of control a hair's breadth from part of his brain that tells his lungs to breathe, his heart to beat. Mikey sat in a wheelchair during our visit, his eyes closed against the light, ears plugged to mute the ambient noise. This helps his headache.

"What do you want, Mikey?" his mother asked, softly.

"I want to live," Mikey said.

Treating a Dying Child

Mikey is not afraid of death itself. He knows Jesus, and the two of them have discussed this matter thoroughly. His oncologist gave him only four more days to live, but Mikey and Jesus don't agree. That was weeks ago. Like most dying children, Mikey will make a fool out of any doctor who pretends to be a prophet.

The team at the hospital who treated Mikey had their own nurses to follow terminally ill children through to the end at home. But managed care has changed all that. The family's insurance offers hospice services, but only through a provider of the company's choice. The first day the "hospice" nurse came to Mikey's home, she criticized the oncologist's prescriptions.

"We need to get him off Decadron," she said to his mother, about the steroid used to reduce the swelling in his brain.

"But it helps with his headaches," his mother pointed out.

"We'll use morphine for that," the nurse informed.

"But Decadron has helped the headaches before, and it doesn't depress his breathing," his mother responded (correctly).

"Decadron will only prolong things," said the nurse of the child who does not yet intend to die.

Reprinted from Diane Komp, "Life Wish," *Christianity Today*, March 3, 1997, by permission of the author and *Christianity Today* magazine.

Killing Is Not Caring

Even before the Supreme Court has spoken its piece on physician-assisted suicide (PAS), the merchants of managed death are recasting the name *hospice* into their own cost-effective, choice-limited toboggan ride down the slippery slope. While the country's focus has been riveted on highly vocal sufferers who want to cut their own lives short, few are listening to dying people who do not want to shorten their lives, even by a day.

Joseph Cardinal Bernardin is one voice that may be heard. "There can be no such thing as a 'right' to assisted suicide," he wrote during the last week of his life. The most straightforward and pastoral of the 62 amicus curiae briefs filed with the Court came from a saint who had already finished his race before the honorable justices began hearing arguments on January 8, 1997, to permit states to allow physician-assisted suicide. [On June 26, 1997, the Court ruled that the Constitution does not grant people a "right to die." However, states are not precluded from passing laws that would establish this right.]

> *"Few are listening to dying people who do not want to shorten their lives, even by a day."*

"Creating a new 'right' to assisted suicide will endanger society and send a false signal that a less than 'perfect' life is not worth living," wrote Bernardin. PAS "introduces a deep ambiguity into the very definition of medical care, if care comes to involve killing."

On the opening day of arguments in the Supreme Court, several wise justices verbalized their misgivings about such a right. Justice Ruth Bader Ginsburg expressed her concerns about giving such a dangerous power to the medical profession. The Clinton administration weighed in as opposed to PAS as well, but polls continue to demonstrate that the majority of the American public supports its legalization.

Today we struggle with issues of life and death in a culture that denies the existence of a common ethic. For many years, the first principle of the medical ethic was that of beneficence—generosity of the healer toward one's fellow beings. But relying on physician beneficence was not an adequate safeguard for Jews in Nazi Germany. In the wake of the Holocaust and disclosure of the role that physicians played in the carnage, society turned to the law to bridge that ethical gap. Thus, the Geneva Convention and the Nuremberg Code, with their emphasis on the rights of individuals and autonomy, supplanted the Hippocratic tradition. Today the debate over physician beneficence and patient autonomy is carried out in the courts.

As the elderly, infirm, and the terminally ill struggle to maintain control over their lives, they come to realize that at some level we are all dependent on others. The ethical principle of beneficence requires a benefactor. Autonomy is neither truly autonomous nor wholly automatic.

A Matter of Conscience

Today, not only the American Medical Association but also the American Nurses Association continue to stand officially opposed to assisted death as a violation of the professional ethic. Similarly, the Hippocratic cult of medicine deposed the sorcerer and separated the power to kill from the power to cure. In accepting this separation, Hippocratic healers defied the norms and ethics of their times. But surveys of individual nurses and doctors today show an increasing erosion of consensus. Some nurses admit privately or in anonymous surveys that they have hastened patient demise, even in the absence of patient consent or family demand. Not even all hospice professionals are opposed to assisted death.

Neither the lay health movement nor current health policy planners seem to have considered adequately the critical role that nurses and other nonphysician health-care workers may have in implementing lethal orders that physicians might prescribe for patients in hospitals, hospices, and in private homes. For this reason Nurses Christian Fellowship, Fellowship of Christian Physician Assistants, and Christian Pharmacists Fellowship International joined the Christian Medical and Dental Society and the Christian Legal Society in a brief that highlighted the limitations that would be placed on conscientiously objecting health-care providers if PAS is legalized.

While each side in the debate acknowledges the right of individual health practitioners to dissent as a matter of conscience, little attention has been paid to the conscience of institutions. Here, as both sides of the argument would admit, there are parallels in the abortion issue.

> *"Today we struggle with issues of life and death in a culture that denies the existence of a common ethic."*

Medical students in support of abortion rights are now demanding education in abortion, imperiling accreditation of institutions that, for reasons of conscience, do not provide abortion services. Abortion supporters are bringing pressure on medical accrediting bodies to require abortion training for certification in obstetrics/gynecology, and even family practice.

Similar requirements could be sought to support assisted-death education in a variety of specialties, including geriatrics, oncology, anesthesiology, neurology, palliative care, and even primary care. Although abortion services are limited to certain hospital wards, operating rooms, and specific outpatient facilities, assisted death, if legalized, will be requested in a wide variety of hospital, hospice, home, and outpatient settings.

Christian Actions

Christians who want to pull the toboggan back from the slope on which it is precariously perched need to engage effectively in community conversations. Here are some concrete actions you and your church can take:

1. *Speak the truth in love.* Too much of the abortion debate has been delivered in shrill and sarcastic tones more attuned to ventilation than genuine engagement and effective persuasion. Let's frame this conversation with those who hold opposing views as compassionate dialogue rather than serial monologue.

2. *Express your concern about "managed death" to your members of Congress.* Public involvement helped stem the tide against other nefarious managed-care practices such as gag rules on physicians and ultrashort hospital stays after births ("drive-through deliveries"). Tell your legislators your concerns about "drive-through dying."

3. *Expand your church's services to the elderly.* Most of the surveys show strong support for PAS amongst the elderly who are frightened about the ends of their lives. Adopt an elderly person without family in your area. Try bringing music and young life to nursing homes.

4. *Support Christian health-care facilities.* Help Christian nursing homes, hospices, hospitals, and agencies that assist the dying stay in business. If you want a Christian option for yourself when your turn comes, support those options financially now.

5. *Support your community nonprofit hospice.* Many legitimate hospices who bring honor to the Christian origins of the movement are floundering financially as they are unable to compete against their leaner competitors. Be a volunteer. Get involved on the board. Help raise funds.

6. *Develop resources in your church to inform your congregation.* A packet of resources is available through the Christian Medical and Dental Society. This collection includes a video narrated by actor Joseph Campanella that focuses on compassionate caring for the dying.

7. *Speak to your own physician about PAS.* I strongly believe in the power of a patient to educate a doctor. Share your concerns about PAS with your doctor. Discuss your own views and ask about your doctor's as well.

A Daughter's Realization

In early 1996, I faced the death of my elderly father from cancer. I was not pleased with what I learned about the luck of the medical draw in a quiet, heartland community. I came to realize why some elderly people might entertain the notion that even suicide might be better than lingering life. As I sat at my father's bedside in an intensive care unit (ICU) waiting for the reluctant doctor to translate Dad's advanced directives into an order not to resuscitate, I was struck by the thought: What if my father asked his oncologist daughter to bring his life quickly, now, to a pain-free end?

The question is moot—my father never asked. But in my heart I realized that my first response came not from my Christian morality, but from what it means to me to be a physician. In that moment by his bed I understood that if I were to cross that line, even once, even for someone I loved, I would never be able to practice medicine again. That's how treacherously slippery this slope really is.

Assisted Suicide Violates the Dignity of Patients

by John Bookser Feister

About the author: *John Bookser Feister is an assistant editor for* St. Anthony Messenger, *a monthly Catholic periodical. He is also the managing editor of* Catholic Update.

When I first saw my 39-year-old friend Jim lying in a nursing-home bed, he was barely responsive. I didn't know what to think. He was emerging from a coma a month after a car wreck near the parish where he served as pastor. He had experienced a terrible blow to the head. His passenger had died. After a disappointing few weeks at a rehab center in 1997, life seemed to offer a bleak and painful future for this young priest.

Consecrated to serve the needs of others, would he now become merely an expensive burden on his small religious order and his family? Or on the Medicare system? He could not speak and it was unclear how much he understood what was going on around him. He was being fed by a tube. I couldn't help but think that, were assisted suicide or euthanasia allowable options, someone in a prolonged coma or even in Father Jim's severely disabled condition might well be a candidate. That is not even to mention very old people or those who know they will die soon from illness.

States Could Determine Legality

Physician-assisted suicide could become a legal option in the near future in some states. True, 15 state legislatures have defeated measures to allow the practice since Oregon's voters accepted assisted suicide in 1994. But opinion polls show a closely divided public.

In June 1997 the U.S. Supreme Court is expected to hand down a ruling that will likely set the stage for upcoming political battles nationwide. Considering cases from Washington and New York, the Court will decide whether these states' prohibition of physician-assisted suicide violates the U.S. Constitution. [On June 26, 1997, the Court ruled that the Constitution does not guarantee a

Reprinted from John Bookser Feister, "'Thou Shalt Not Kill': The Church Against Assisted Suicide," *St. Anthony Messenger*, June 1997, by permission of the *St. Anthony Messenger*.

"right to die." However, states are not precluded from passing laws that would establish this right.]

While Catholic organizations scramble to keep the Oregon pro-assisted-suicide law from going into effect and to prevent such legislation elsewhere, a privacy clause in the Florida Constitution may be what "opens the floodgate," according to attorney Robert Castagna, lobbyist for the Oregon Catholic Conference. The legal case based on Florida's Privacy Amendment will set a precedent for the 12 other states which have similar language in their constitutions. Short of an outright Supreme Court ban on physician-assisted suicide, state constitutions will weigh heavily in determining whether or not assisted suicide can be legalized.

The Church—both officially and through lay efforts—is in the midst of the emerging fray as moral teacher and advocate for justice. In this viewpoint you will hear from some people who have taken on the struggle against physician-assisted suicide as a pro-life cause.

The Basics of Assisted Suicide

Dr. William Toffler and attorney Robert Castagna are in Oregon, the state that narrowly legalized assisted suicide in 1994 but, until April 1997, had been stopped from implementing the law by the federal appeals court. Now a coalition of groups including the Oregon Catholic Conference has worked to place a repeal referendum on Oregon's November 1997 ballot. Attorney Lisa Gigliotti is a disability-rights advocate in Michigan, where Jack Kevorkian has admitted assisting in at least 45 suicides, yet has been acquitted in each of three prosecuted cases. [A fourth trial was declared a mistrial during opening statements on June 12, 1997.] Richard Doerflinger, a layman, leads the U.S. bishops' efforts to fight assisted suicide. . . .

First, though, it might help to review some basics. Assisted suicide happens when a person commits suicide with the help of someone else. Jack Kevorkian, disbarred from medical practice in 1991, is the best known of these helpers. He sets up a machine and the person who wishes to die operates it. Voluntary euthanasia, on the other hand, occurs when someone kills another person at that person's request, presumably to end suffering or some other undesirable condition. Withdrawal of medical equipment which is creating more burden than benefit is neither suicide nor euthanasia: The Church teaches that it is ethical to withdraw useless medical intervention and accept natural death. The Church also teaches that drugs used to eliminate pain are desirable, even if they hasten inevitable death.

> *"The Church—both officially and through lay efforts—is in the midst of the emerging fray as moral teacher and advocate for justice."*

The current campaign to legalize physician-assisted suicide in the United

States began with the Hemlock Society and Compassion in Dying, two groups which started in the West but now operate nationally. These suicide advocates organized a ballot campaign in Washington that was narrowly defeated in 1991. They then turned their sights on California and narrowly failed again in 1992.

After they adjusted their strategies, their efforts paid off in Oregon's becoming the first jurisdiction anywhere in the world ever to legalize assisted suicide. In a 1994 ad campaign pro-suicide groups characterized the debate over Oregon's Ballot Measure 16 as the Catholic Church against the people of Oregon. The measure won 51 percent to 49 percent—by about 16,000 votes. A referendum to repeal Measure 16 appeared on Oregon ballots in November 1997. [The repeal effort failed by a 60 percent to 40 percent margin.]

Anti-Christian Advertising

William L. Toffler, M.D., is a family physician and faculty member at the Oregon Health Sciences University in Portland, Oregon. He teaches medical students, interns and physicians when he is not treating patients or caring for his family of seven children. He is cofounder and president of the fledgling Physicians for Compassionate Care—a multistate group vocally opposed to assisted suicide. Membership is 900-strong and growing. He is a committed Catholic and was a leader in the unsuccessful drive to defeat Measure 16 in 1994. It was Dr. Toffler who appeared on a CBS *60 Minutes* program preceding the 1994 vote on assisted suicide and who debated Hemlock Society president and "how-to" suicide author Derek Humphry on Oregon TV.

> *"Withdrawal of medical equipment which is creating more burden than benefit is neither suicide nor euthanasia."*

Advertising swayed Oregon's voters, though, insists Dr. Toffler: "The average ballot-measure campaign depends upon advertising totally—mostly 15- to 30-second TV sound bites," he says. Radio played an important part, too, he adds. "There were literally radio pieces that said, 'Don't let those Christians impose their morality on you. Don't believe that garbage the Catholic Church is telling you.' That's a quote," he insists. These ads that stirred anti-Catholic sentiment were well documented by national news programs.

The Church, indeed, had taken the lead role in opposing the ballot measure. Robert J. Castagna has held the job of general counsel and executive director of the Oregon Catholic Conference for the past 13 years. On behalf of Oregon's Catholics, he leads official Church efforts against suicide legislation. He says that assisted suicide not only flouts Catholic convictions about the sanctity of life, but also goes to the very heart of who we are as a society.

"I believe this is the most dangerous issue confronting this nation today," he says. Castagna sees physician-assisted suicide's acceptance as driven by our inability to provide medical care for all citizens. This attorney and lobbyist sees freedom of choice in dying as a surface issue: "I think the stronger public policy issues revolve around demographics and the economics of health care." As Baby Boomers enter the senior population, their medical needs will increase, he observes. That will place a growing burden on our health-care system.

The Vulnerable Will Be at Risk

Castagna notes that this social aspect of assisted suicide is what drove a diverse panel of New York leaders in 1994 to recommend unanimously against physician-assisted suicide as "unwise and dangerous public policy." The panel found that poor, weak and vulnerable people, people without access to health care, people who had been discriminated against in society in the past, would be the ones whose lives would be at risk in the face of such a public policy.

Castagna's legal sensibilities are offended by the Oregon law, too. "This one precedent would pollute and corrupt the entire English-American legal system," he says. He cites the British Parliament's select committee on medical ethics: "They called the prohibition against intentional killing a cornerstone of law and of social relationships."

Both Castagna and Dr. Toffler are gearing up for a major effort to sway the small percentage of Oregon voters who will make the difference in the campaign to repeal Measure 16 in November. Toffler thinks that some people will take the campaign far more seriously this time than they did in 1994. "I wish I had a nickel—or a dollar—from everyone who came up to me afterward and contritely said, 'I never thought it had a serious chance!' They had no idea of the depth of darkness that pervades our society," he says. Toffler credits disrespect for life to poor moral formation and a deeper rejection of God.

A Disabled Woman Speaks Out

Lisa K. Gigliotti is an attorney and policy adviser for the Michigan Senate Majority Policy Office in the areas of physician-assisted suicide, mental health, welfare and Medicaid. She was one of a group of leading anti-suicide and anti-euthanasia advocates who gathered for an April 1997 conference in Washington, D.C. The conference was sponsored by the National Conference of Catholic Bishops, The Catholic University of America and the Center for Jewish and Christian Values.

"Assisted suicide not only flouts Catholic convictions about the sanctity of life, but also goes to the very heart of who we are as a society."

Gigliotti herself has chronic rheumatoid arthritis and myasthenia gravis, a neuromuscular disease that can be fatal. Citizens with disabilities, like Gigliotti, have been some of the most outspoken against physician-assisted suicide. One group, called Not Dead Yet, brought pickets, wheelchairs and speeches to the Michigan legislature and even to the front of the U.S. Supreme Court as oral arguments were being heard in the Washington and New York cases.

Lisa was a college student preparing for medical school when she first became ill with rheumatoid arthritis. Before the illness, she ran three miles daily. "I lived to run," she says. As she became increasingly disabled, she was cared for by her mother and grandmother: "It hit really hard really fast. I was totally incapacitated. I needed someone to lift my head and hold a glass for me to drink, and I needed to use a bedpan and had to be cleaned."

Then worse things happened. Her mother and grandmother were killed in an auto accident, leaving no one to care for Lisa. Two weeks later she was diagnosed with the neuromuscular disorder. She was admitted to a nursing home. But her condition improved and gradually she was able to gain independence again. She spent three years using a wheelchair.

Loss of Dignity

When Lisa heard that Jack Kevorkian helped to kill another woman with rheumatoid arthritis, she became alarmed. Now her passion is to protect the dignity of vulnerable people. "I know there can be dignity in infirmity," she insists. "My mother and grandmother valued my life. I could tell that. They kept encouraging me to keep preparing for medical school."

Unfortunately she's seen the undignified side, too. With a touch of sarcasm she recalls bitter memories of her nursing-home years: "They were nice enough there to put me in a room with a woman 10 years older than me who was in a persistent vegetative state," she says. "Here I was wanting to be in medical school so badly, and grieving so deeply for Mom, who was my best friend, my advocate. I would wake up and open my eyes and here would be someone staring right at me, a woman in a coma." There were 45-minute waits for a bedpan, "and then they were so impatient and rude," she recalls. There were times when mistaken nurses would try to get her to take someone else's medicine. She could scarcely argue with them because they didn't speak English. "Even the strongest of human psyches is affected when treated as a burden rather than treated with dignity," she laments.

Gigliotti thinks that people are attracted to physician-assisted suicide because they fear their own pending weakness. "But how do you know until you get there? Running was so important to me. It was something I did every day," she recalls. She would have emphatically denied that she could ever be happy without running,

> *"Even the strongest of human psyches is affected when treated as a burden rather than treated with dignity."*

she recalls. "Yet who would ever have known that I would be in the position I am in now, as a policy adviser to our state senators, in Michigan of all places! And I know both sides!"

She also knows that people facing terminal illness fear a loss of dignity. Yet "*we* are the ones who take away each other's dignity," she emphasizes, with the compassion of someone who has suffered. "If my caretakers had treated me with patience and respect, it would have made things so much different!"

Creating a Compassionate Society

Lisa sees encouraging signs of the Church in Michigan opposing physician-assisted suicide, but she says she wishes Church leaders in her state would take a stronger lead. That's all the more true in light of efforts to put a pro-assisted-suicide referendum on the Michigan ballot for 1998, assuming that the U.S. Supreme Court will leave the matter up to states. "We need to start taking charge now," she says. "Kevorkian and others have desecrated that beautiful gift of truly giving and receiving compassion." Euthanasia advocates view helping a disabled person to die as the paramount act of compassion, she says, quoting Hemlock Society literature. "Yet a truly compassionate society would provide whatever ongoing support is necessary to embrace members of the society with disabilities."

Attorney Lisa Gigliotti was just one of several hundred anti-suicide advocates who gathered at Catholic University to share strategies in April 1997. Massachusetts State Senators John H. Rogers and David T. Donnelly were there, gathering information on the issue which already is cropping up in their state. "We think it's important to get out on this issue early and frame the debate," says Senator Donnelly, chairman of the Ethics Committee for his legislature. . . .

> *"Could it be a coincidence . . . that managed care and managed death appear at the same time?"*

The common prediction among the lawyers, doctors and other Church advocates gathered at Catholic University was that the High Court will step cautiously into this new legal area and, at least for now, leave it to the states to decide.

A Duty to Die?

If state legislatures are permitted to ban assisted suicide, it seems likely that most will. That's the opinion of Richard M. Doerflinger, associate director for policy development in the pro-life activities office of the National Conference of Catholic Bishops. From 1994 to 1997 he has lent support of materials, advice and sometimes Church funds to help defeat 15 state legislative attempts to legalize the practice. "The more the legislators learn, the less support they lend to physician-assisted suicide," says Doerflinger. He predicts that the American public will follow suit. It was Doerflinger who organized the Catholic University conference, the first ever to bring together major experts from Canada, Britain, the United States and the Netherlands.

People are attracted to the slogan of freedom of choice, he observes. "But if you begin to tell them what this really entails, that it gives doctors a new power to distribute lethal drugs to their patients, that people could be pressured into this in a cost-conscious health-care system, that the most vulnerable people fear this the most, there's an opportunity to turn public opinion around.

"People need to learn a lot more about it," Doerflinger contends, and his small staff is doing what it can to help. Besides letters to Congress and the Supreme Court, and supporting the work of state Catholic conferences, the pro-life office publishes a monthly newsletter on euthanasia trends, called *Life At Risk*, which in June 1997 had a circulation of 8,000. He fears that "a right to die will soon become a duty to die." If the option is available, Doerflinger and others predict that those who would become a burden on their loved ones or on society would almost certainly feel pressured by societal or family expectations to end their lives. Several conference speakers told chilling tales of how that is happening already in the Netherlands.

Rabbi David Novak, from the University of Toronto, put the issue of assisted suicide into perspective when he quoted Communist dictator Joseph Stalin: "I solve social problems by eliminating the people who cause them: No people, no problems." Those who are fighting assisted suicide in this country fear that the same logic is at work behind the push towards physician-assisted suicide and euthanasia beyond. Could it be a coincidence, they ask, that managed care and managed death appear at the same time? . . .

Father Jim Recuperates

I visited Father Jim many times over the past several months. Against predictions, he rapidly progressed from a state of confusion along a path of dramatic recovery. One day he quit drooling. Another day he reached out and grasped my hand. Visited often by his loving family, he suddenly started speaking in sentences as he regained control of his mouth muscles. His thinking powers are intact, though he doesn't remember anything surrounding his injury. The feeding tube is gone. He walks, with some effort. On the 10th anniversary of his ordination in May 1997, he was able to concelebrate Mass, though he still will be in recuperation for some time.

True, his is an unusual case. But Father Jim is now a sign to those around him that God is the author of life, that we do better to trust even what we do not fully comprehend rather than to wrap things up neatly at any cost. Whether it be a person who will be severely disabled, or a person who is without a doubt in the final phase of life, none of us really know what physical and spiritual healings are in store for us before we die. The medical evidence is that, when pain is managed effectively, when depression is treated, people can encounter life's final passage with dignity, in God's hands.

Assisted Suicide Is Not Morally Equivalent to Letting Patients Die

by James F. Bresnahan

About the author: *James F. Bresnahan is a professor in the Medicine Department of Northwestern University Medical School in Chicago.*

Fundamental to the Roman Catholic moral theological tradition is a distinction we make in the practice of medical care of the dying. Many others who are neither Catholic, Christian nor religious also make it. We distinguish between *killing* and *letting die*. We consider it morally permitted—even, under certain circumstances, morally required—that at a patient's request we let the person die of lethal disease processes by foregoing cure-oriented treatments while continuing to provide relief of suffering in ways needed and wanted by the dying patient. But we consider it morally forbidden to initiate deliberately a new lethal process consciously intended to precipitate death, whether this is done by patients themselves with help from a physician or by a physician at the request of a patient. . . .

The Practical Uses of This Distinction

Using this traditional Catholic moral distinction, over the last 20 years we have been increasingly able to resist "medical vitalism"—a war against death that too often prolongs the suffering of the dying person. Instead we have promoted the practice of good palliative medicine in the care of the dying, especially by the hospice movement, with its basic commitment "neither to hasten nor to delay death." Our distinction was accepted as morally meaningful in shaping good care of the dying by the President's Commission for the Study of Ethical Problems in Medicine, in its March 1983 report, *Deciding to Forego Life-Sustaining Treatment.* The distinction subsequently gained wide, though not universal, acceptance among physicians and other health care practitioners

Reprinted from James F. Bresnahan, "Killing vs. Letting Die: A Moral Distinction Before the Courts," *America*, February 1, 1997, by permission of the author.

in the United States as they faced frequent moral dilemmas in the care of the dying brought on by the two-edged sword of high technology medicine.

Stopping cure-oriented treatment when its use becomes excessive and substituting appropriate palliative medicine and intensive personal support—these have gradually become accepted in the medical community as appropriate means of caring for the dying. Crucial to that acceptance, however, has been the understanding that, morally speaking, this approach does not involve killing. Rather, this way of caring for the dying accepts death as an unavoidable challenge to the dying and their caregivers to come to terms with suffering and grief.

> *"Over the last 20 years we have been increasingly able to resist 'medical vitalism'—a war against death that too often prolongs the suffering of the dying person."*

Indeed, this is a moral distinction that seems to remain persuasive even to many of the physicians who now advocate decriminalization of physician-assisted suicide for the terminally ill. The distinction remains morally meaningful, that is, for those who strictly limit such proposals by explicitly expressing moral disapproval of direct killing by doctors themselves—physician-effected euthanasia. This is true as well for those advocates who insist (as very many do) that a physician's assistance in the suicide of dying patients should be and will be rarely used, that it is a desperate measure justified only in exceptional cases where every effort has first been made to care adequately for the dying person by other means. Finally, this is a moral distinction that was *not* explicitly denied moral and legal validity by the 1994 Oregon ballot initiative that authorized, under certain constraining controls, physician-assisted suicide of competent dying patients who request it.

The majority opinions in two recent and widely discussed decisions by Federal courts of appeal, however, have explicitly rejected this distinction. They deny not only the legal (constitutional) validity but even the moral meaningfulness of our ethical distinction between letting die and inflicting death.

Two Court Rulings

In an eight to three decision, the Ninth Federal Circuit Court of Appeals sitting *en banc* in California affirmed a Federal district court decision declaring unconstitutional a Washington State statute making assistance of suicide a crime (*Compassion in Dying v. State of Washington*, March 6, 1996). This decision required that a previous contrary two to one decision by a panel of the Ninth Circuit be vacated; the majority opinion of that panel was written by Judge John Noonan and is well worth reading.

In the majority opinion of the "full bench" decision, Judge Stephen Reinhardt argues that, because the 1990 Nancy Cruzan case recognized a "due process liberty interest in terminating unwanted medical treatment," therefore "we conclude that Cruzan, by recognizing a liberty interest that includes the refusal of artificial provision of life-sustaining food and water, necessarily recognizes a liberty interest in hastening one's own death." He argues further that helping a patient hasten death by using a doctor's prescription of a lethal substance must be interpreted as simply extending the already accepted practice of stopping what he calls "life-sustaining" treatment. If dying patients request this "emergent right to receive medical assistance in hastening one's death," he says, they exercise a liberty interest protected by due process of law and guaranteed by the 14th Amendment of the U.S. Constitution. Since a state can have no reasonable interest in denying a dying patient the exercise of this right, to threaten criminal penalty against a doctor responding to this patient's request for help is judged a denial of constitutionally protected due process.

> *"[Two recent court decisions] deny not only the legal (constitutional) validity but even the moral meaningfulness of our ethical distinction between letting die and inflicting death."*

A month later a unanimous decision of a panel of the Second Federal Circuit Court of Appeals in New York overturned a contrary finding of a Federal district court and declared unconstitutional a New York State statute making assistance of suicide a crime (*Quill v. Vacco*, April 2, 1996). The leading opinion by Judge Roger J. Miner argues that since New York recognizes the right of a dying patient to refuse life-prolonging treatments (again, so-called!), therefore it has "placed its imprimatur upon the right of competent citizens to hasten death by refusing medical treatment and by directing physicians to remove life-support systems already in place." The judge concludes that New York "does not treat similarly circumstanced persons alike: Those in the final stages of terminal illness who are on life-support systems are allowed to hasten their deaths by directing removal of such systems; but those who are similarly situated, except for the previous attachment of life-sustaining equipment, are not allowed to hasten death by self-administering prescribed drugs." So Judge Miner judges such a denial of equal protection of the law to be constitutionally forbidden by the 14th Amendment.

In the view of both of these courts, then, one is "hastening death" whether one ceases to interfere with a dying process by medical interventions that merely prolong the dying or initiates a new lethal process using a medical prescription. In either case, these courts say, one simply hastens death. From a superficial, empiricist view of the matter, of course, death does follow a medical action in either case. But these courts are asserting that, whatever differences one may notice in the causal relationship of the act to the death, as long as doctors act "medically" no moral stigma and no legal penalty should attach. For them, a physician's aid in self-inflicted death is merely an "emerging" development of an already socially and legally accepted treatment of the dying by hastening death.

These judicial opinions envision, therefore, inflicted death as just another optional medical therapy—if wanted by a competent dying patient. Aiding the suicide of the dying (at least if done by physicians) is not correctly described as killing. If it were, one would have to justify it—by a claim, for instance, of the pressure of extraordinary circumstances—in the way we customarily justify killing when self-defense is proven. (In all fairness, it must be noted that Judge Guido Calabresi, concurring only in the result of the New York decision, expresses a reservation about the scope of the decision. He insists that the State Legislature might be able to justify re-enacting the very same statute now found to be unconstitutional if they presented persuasive reasons for doing so. He does not suggest what these reasons might be.) So these opinions make a physician's knowing act of assisting suicide at the request of a dying patient just another "standard treatment option"—though perhaps one whose use is to be specially limited by regulations designed to prevent abuse. [On June 26, 1997, the Supreme Court overturned both decisions and ruled that the Constitution does not grant Americans a "right to die." However, states are not precluded from passing laws that would establish this right.]

Doctors Make the Distinction

Justice Oliver Wendell Holmes stated in his classic, *The Common Law*, "The life of the law is not logic but experience." The legal reasoning of these appellate judges ignores the medical experience and the moral reasoning based upon that experience of the many physicians who maintain the validity of the distinction between killing and letting die. It ignores as well the medical experience of many physicians who have advocated "physician aid in dying"—many of whom argue that if good care of the dying (especially hospice-style care) is being provided, requests for aid in suicide will be very rare.

Some of these physicians (Sherwin Nuland, for instance, a surgeon and the author of the valuable book *How We Die*) explicitly concede that aiding a dying patient to commit suicide should be honestly acknowledged to involve *participation in killing*. But, they argue, it is killing that can be morally justified by what they view as rarely encountered, truly desperate circumstances. Nonetheless, many of these physicians also insist that while doctors should be allowed to provide the means of suicide to a dying patient who requests them, they should not actually administer the lethal agent themselves.

> *"Many physicians . . . argue that if good care of the dying (especially hospice-style care) is being provided, requests for aid in suicide will be very rare."*

In sharp contrast to these various expressions of medical experience in care of the dying, the opinions of the two circuit courts of appeal find no rational validity at all, neither in law nor in morality, for the distinction between killing and letting die. Doctors who assist suicide at the request of a patient are simply rec-

57

ognizing the patient's right to hasten death as the patient sees fit.

It is true that these judges do not deny that a claim of conscience based on this moral distinction will excuse "conscientious objectors" from helping the suicidal dying to inflict death on themselves. We can assume, I think, that they would admit a claim of conscience by religious believers who continue to hold this distinction between killing and letting die. By analogy with conscientious objection to war, this claim would be valid for anyone who for philosophic reasons of "ultimate concern" refuses to kill directly. But since these two appellate court opinions deny that hastening death is really killing, this religious or quasi-religious claim of conscientious objection would be allowed only as an irrational preoccupation that must be tolerated because our Constitution's First Amendment guarantees religious freedom.

> *"All medical treatments . . . must eventually be stopped when they bring the dying patient nothing but intensified and prolonged suffering."*

Stopping Useless Treatment

Thus, from the perspective of Catholic moral theology and of others who agree with it, these Federal judges give short shrift to widely shared moral experience that there really exists a profoundly felt difference between not persisting in futile, death-prolonging medical treatment against the will of a patient, as contrasted with doing an act that precipitates death. These caregivers experience something many in our society do not experience, or even deny: that the nearer death approaches, even the most sophisticated cure-oriented treatments commonly inflict more harm than benefit. Caregivers know that all medical treatments, however wonderfully life-saving for some patients, must eventually be stopped when they bring the dying patient nothing but intensified and prolonged suffering. A patient rightly considers such treatment useless and harmful because dying is now inevitable. The patient expects to receive and the doctor is obliged to provide intensified palliative medicine. By characterizing such decisions as aimed at hastening death, these two court opinions ignore the moral ingredient in the professional moral experience of letting die.

To characterize the refusal of so-called life-prolonging treatments as merely a hastening of death is, in my opinion, disingenuous at best. This conflation has been shaped by legal abstractions manipulated to justify the moral and legal conclusions favored by the judges. As a moral description it distorts rather than accurately reflects the widely shared clinical medical experience of those who try to care well for the dying in our high technology medical care system. As the basis for moral argument, such a description distorts the experienced meaning of foregoing excessively burdensome, therefore harmful and hence unwanted treatments.

No mention is made of palliative medicine and hospice care of the dying. Practitioners of such care testify that they can now control all kinds of pain.

They testify further that intensive personal response to psychological and spiritual suffering of the dying prevents requests for help with suicide. Indeed, it makes the dying experience precious for the patient, family, friends and caregivers. This experience is apparently irrelevant for these judges.

In neither of these decisions do the judges exhibit any awareness of the history of how difficult many caregivers have found it to renounce their unremitting war against death and to accept the moral appropriateness of not beginning and, even more, of stopping so-called life-sustaining treatment—even when they recognize that to continue these cure-oriented treatments would merely obstruct and so prolong, often torturously, an irreversible dying process. To describe their change of heart and practice as accepting an activity aimed at hastening death is to confirm the worst moral scruples of these caregivers, who have struggled mightily to shed their misguided medical vitalism. It undermines the moral insight that relief of suffering is a goal of medicine that can be achieved even when the goal of prolonging life cannot, and this *without killing*.

> *"To characterize the refusal of so-called life-prolonging treatments as merely a hastening of death is, in my opinion, disingenuous at best."*

Much less do these opinions acknowledge how very many medical caregivers feel about providing a lethal prescription for their patients. The idea is morally repulsive. These are professionals who are willing to stop excessively burdensome cure-oriented treatments, who are willing then to focus strenuous efforts on effective measures to eliminate pain and on demanding personal efforts to relieve the mental and spiritual suffering of the dying. They are willing to face death with the patient but are not willing to inflict death.

A New Medical Morality

I think this moral revulsion stems from the fact that these professionals see that the use of medicine for this end camouflages violence. It is especially felt by surgeons and others who do obviously life-endangering medical invasions of the body. These doctors and those who assist them are vividly aware of how such medical activity involves taking the life of a patient into one's hands and risking that life in a particularly dramatic way in order to achieve healing. These judicial opinions simply discount the felt moral difference between such risk-taking, which medical caregivers try to perform responsibly for their patients, and directly causing a death—even when the latter might be claimed to be an act of mercy. As medical professionals, they strive constantly to achieve a precarious balance of intention and action—to avoid undue risk, yet to take prudently calculated risks in doing what may nevertheless produce an unwanted death. Authorizing death as a treatment for the dying discounts and may even discourage such moral striving to take risks but avoid precipitating death.

In my opinion, the judges of the Ninth and Second United States Circuit Courts of Appeal have gone beyond mandating a new legal interpretation of a particular medical activity that they characterize as "emerging" in treatment of the dying under high technology health care. They have in effect decreed the abrogation in the public sphere of the intellectual, moral and legal respectability of traditional religious and medical thinking about the moral distinction between letting die and killing. Their decree legally establishes a new morality for medical practice—one with its own religious overtones.

This new medical morality has been advocated by those who emphasize patient autonomy—which patients may exercise no matter how harmful the acts chosen are to others and to their freedom. Some of these single-minded advocates of individual liberty also believe, in a quasi-religious way, that self-killing is really the morally best way to meet death when it approaches ("One ought not leave a mess for others to clean up"). What rights then, remain in the public square for those of us who believe, as a matter of ultimate moral integrity, that we must do everything possible to relieve suffering, but that we must not kill?

The Catholic Response

Catholic believers and many who agree with us will, of course, *not* cease to view an act of killing as a terrible and desperate measure, one to be taken only *fearfully* and *regretfully* and *mournfully*—and as an act morally justified only if it is a last resort in circumstances of necessary self-defense against unjust aggressors. But, we also have much sad experience with the historical aftermath of what we regard as morally justified killing in self-defense in war and domestic policing. This painful experience teaches us that every act of killing, even when claimed to be morally justified, appears inevitably to bring with it new forms of uninhibited violence. When we confront killing, our view of history tells us that we do not deal here with a fictional slippery slope.

We cannot be passive, therefore, when we contemplate the possibility that inflicting death may now be legally authorized as just another medical intervention—one that patients must be informed about, that doctors must be free to recommend to their patients, that families will be free to urge upon their dying members and that harried medical caregivers will be free to urge a suffering patient to consider seriously. It may even be one that administrators of managed care will eventually choose to make mandatory for some patients in some situations as a condition of payment for care. We have solid reason to doubt that constraining conditions such as those mentioned in the Oregon referendum will prevent frequent tragic abuse of this "treatment."

> *"Legal endorsement of homicide as one more optional treatment for the suffering of the dying ... threatens our Catholic, faith-inspired moral practices in caring for the dying."*

Chapter 1

Legal endorsement of homicide as one more optional treatment for the suffering of the dying thus threatens our Catholic, faith-inspired moral practices in caring for the dying. I foresee formidable obstacles to our ways of caring for the dying within a medical care system that increasingly practices death as a treatment. Done as a medical "quick fix" for the sufferings of the dying, assisted suicide will transform health care institutions into places of threatened violence and the moral danger of guilty cooperation with violence. Such a medical system will be ever more deeply suspect to many people in crisis. And it will be increasingly subjected to stress in its efforts to preserve its traditional moral ideals of self-risking altruism.

Chapter 2

Is Assisted Suicide a Constitutional Right?

Chapter Preface

In June 1997, in its rulings on *Washington v. Glucksberg* and *Vacco v. Quill*, the U.S. Supreme Court declared that the Constitution does not guarantee a "right to die" (although the Court's ruling does not prevent states from passing laws to establish or bar this right). In *Vacco v. Quill*, the Court overturned a 1996 ruling by the Second Circuit Court of Appeals declaring New York State's ban on assisted suicide unconstitutional. In the Second Circuit Court's decision, Judge Roger Miner had determined that the ban violated the equal protection clause of the Fourteenth Amendment, which declares that a state cannot "deny to any person within its jurisdiction the equal protection of the laws." Plaintiffs had charged that, in violation of the Fourteenth Amendment, New York State treated two similar classes of people unequally: Terminally ill people on life support systems were legally permitted to refuse treatment, thereby ending their lives, whereas terminally ill people who were not on life support systems were barred from taking measures to end their lives. Miner agreed that the law violated the constitutional rights of the terminally ill people who were not on life support systems.

In its reversal of the appellate court's decision, the Supreme Court maintained that the distinction between these two classes of terminally ill patients was widely recognized and logical. In its ruling, penned by Chief Justice William Rehnquist, the Court further explained this distinction, arguing that a patient who refuses treatment may not specifically wish to die, whereas a patient who takes lethal medication does intend to do so. Because refusal of treatment and assisted suicide are different acts, the Court asserted, "New York may therefore, consistent with the Constitution, treat them differently."

The debate over the constitutionality of assisted suicide is sure to continue. The Court's decisions left open the possibility of further debate within the states, so more assisted suicide cases may reach the Supreme Court in coming years. Therefore, while many of the viewpoints in the following chapter were written prior to the June 1997 decisions, they remain cogent arguments for and against the existence of a constitutional "right to die."

Bans on Assisted Suicide Violate the Fourteenth Amendment

by Stephen Reinhardt

About the author: *Stephen Reinhardt is a circuit judge for the U.S. Court of Appeals for the Ninth Circuit.*

Editor's Note: The following viewpoint is excerpted from the Ninth Circuit Court of Appeals decision in Compassion in Dying v. State of Washington *(1996).*

We are required to decide whether a person who is terminally ill has a constitutionally protected liberty interest in hastening what might otherwise be a protracted, undignified, and extremely painful death. If such an interest exists, we must next decide whether or not the state of Washington may constitutionally restrict its exercise by banning a form of medical assistance that is frequently requested by terminally ill people who wish to die. We first conclude that there is a constitutionally protected liberty interest in determining the time and manner of one's own death, an interest that must be weighed against the state's legitimate and countervailing interests, especially those that relate to the preservation of human life. After balancing the competing interests, we conclude by answering the narrow question before us: We hold that insofar as the Washington statute prohibits physicians from prescribing life-ending medication for use by terminally ill, competent adults who wish to hasten their own deaths, it violates the Due Process Clause of the Fourteenth Amendment. . . .

Under the Washington statute (RCW 9A.36.060), aiding a person who wishes to end his life constitutes a criminal act and subjects the aider to the possibility of a lengthy term of imprisonment, even if the recipient of the aid is a terminally ill, competent adult and the aider is a licensed physician who is providing medical assistance at the request of the patient. The Washington statute provides in pertinent part: "A person is guilty of promoting a suicide when he

Reprinted from the decision of Stephen Reinhardt in *Compassion in Dying v. State of Washington*, 96 C.D.O.S. 1507 (1996).

knowingly causes or aids another person to attempt suicide." A violation of the statute constitutes a felony punishable by imprisonment for a maximum of five years and a fine of up to $10,000. . . .

The plaintiffs do not challenge Washington statute RCW 9A.36.060 in its entirety. Specifically they do not object to the portion of the Washington statute that makes it unlawful for a person knowingly to cause another to commit suicide. Rather, they only challenge the statute's "or aids" provision. They challenge that provision both on its face and as applied to terminally ill, mentally competent adults who wish to hasten their own deaths with the help of medication prescribed by their doctors. The plaintiffs contend that the provision impermissibly prevents the exercise by terminally ill patients of a constitutionally protected liberty interest in violation of the Due Process Clause of the Fourteenth Amendment, and also that it impermissibly distinguishes between similarly situated terminally ill patients in violation of the Equal Protection Clause. . . .

Determining a Liberty Interest

In order to answer the question whether the Washington statute violates the Due Process Clause insofar as it prohibits the provision of certain medical assistance to terminally ill, competent adults who wish to hasten their own deaths, we first determine whether there is a liberty interest in choosing the time and manner of one's death—a question sometimes phrased in common parlance as: Is there a right to die? Because we hold that there is, we must then determine whether prohibiting physicians from prescribing life-ending medication for use by terminally ill patients who wish to die violates the patients' due process rights.

The mere recognition of a liberty interest does not mean that a state may not prohibit the exercise of that interest in particular circumstances, nor does it mean that a state may not adopt appropriate regulations governing its exercise. Rather, in cases like the one before us, the courts must apply a balancing test under which we weigh the individual's liberty interests against the relevant state interests in order to determine whether the state's actions are constitutionally permissible. As Chief Justice William Rehnquist, writing for the Court, explained in *Cruzan v. Director, Missouri Dept. of Health*, (1990), the only right-to-die case that the Court has heretofore considered: "[D]etermining that a person has a 'liberty interest' under the Due Process Clause does not end our inquiry; 'whether respondent's constitutional rights have been violated must be determined by balancing his liberty interests against the relevant state interests.'"

> *"We first conclude that there is a constitutionally protected liberty interest in determining the time and manner of one's own death."*

The Court has invoked a balancing test in a number of substantive due process cases, not just in the right-to-die context. For example, as the *Cruzan* Court noted, the Court applied a balancing test in *Youngberg v. Romeo* (1982) and *Mills v. Rogers* (1982), liberty interest cases involving the right to refuse medical treatment. *Youngberg* addressed the rights of patients involuntarily committed to state mental institutions. The Court said: "In determining whether a substantive right protected by the Due Process Clause has been violated, it is necessary to balance the liberty of the individual and the demands of organized society." *Mills* addressed the question of the right of mental patients to refuse treatment with antipsychotic drugs. There, the Court stated explicitly that the "state interests" are "to be balanced against an individual's liberty interests." As the *Cruzan* Court also noted, the use of a balancing test is deeply rooted in our legal traditions. The Court has been applying a balancing test in substantive due process cases at least since 1905, when in *Jacobsen v. Massachusetts*, "the Court balanced an individual's liberty interest in declining an unwanted smallpox vaccine against the State's interest in preventing disease," as stated in *Cruzan*.

> *"In deciding right-to-die cases, we are guided by the [Supreme] Court's approach to the abortion cases."*

As Justice Sandra Day O'Connor explained in her concurring opinion in *Cruzan*, the ultimate question is whether sufficient justification exists for the intrusion by the government into the realm of a person's "liberty, dignity, and freedom." If the balance favors the state, then the given statute—whether it regulates the exercise of a due process liberty interest or prohibits that exercise to some degree—is constitutional. If the balance favors the individual, then the statute—whatever its justifications—violates the individual's due process liberty rights and must be declared unconstitutional, either on its face or as applied. Here, we conclude unhesitatingly that the balance favors the individual's liberty interest. . . .

Abortion and Assisted Suicide

In examining whether a liberty interest exists in determining the time and manner of one's death, we begin with the compelling similarities between right-to-die cases and abortion cases. In the former as in the latter, the relative strength of the competing interests changes as physical, medical, or related circumstances vary. In right-to-die cases the outcome of the balancing test may differ at different points along the life cycle as a person's physical or medical condition deteriorates, just as in abortion cases the permissibility of restrictive state legislation may vary with the progression of the pregnancy. Equally important, both types of cases raise issues of life and death, and both arouse similar religious and moral concerns. Both also present basic questions about an individual's right of choice.

Historical evidence shows that both abortion and assisted suicide were for many years condemned, but that the efforts to prevent people from engaging in the condemned conduct were always at most only partially successful. Even when prohibited, abortions and assisted-suicides flourished in back alleys, in small street-side clinics, and in the privacy of the bedroom. Deprived of the right to medical assistance, many pregnant women and terminally ill adults ultimately took matters into their own hands, often with tragic consequences.

> *"The law does not classify the death of a patient that results from the granting of his wish to decline or discontinue treatment as 'suicide.'"*

Because they present issues of such profound spiritual importance and because they so deeply affect individuals' right to determine their own destiny, the abortion and right-to-die cases have given rise to a highly emotional and divisive debate. In many respects, the legal arguments on both sides are similar, as are the constitutional principles at issue.

In deciding right-to-die cases, we are guided by the Court's approach to the abortion cases. *Planned Parenthood v. Casey* (1992) in particular provides a powerful precedent, for in that case the Court had the opportunity to evaluate its past decisions and to determine whether to adhere to its original judgment. Although *Casey* was influenced by the doctrine of stare decisis, the fundamental message of that case lies in its statements regarding the type of issue that confronts us here: "These matters, involving the most intimate and personal choices a person may make in a lifetime, choices central to personal dignity and autonomy, are central to the liberty protected by the Fourteenth Amendment."

Accurate Terminology

The majority opinion of the three-judge panel that first heard this case [*Compassion in Dying v. State of Washington*] on appeal defined the claimed liberty interest as a "constitutional right to aid in killing oneself." However, the subject we must initially examine is not nearly so limited. Properly analyzed, the first issue to be resolved is whether there is a liberty interest in determining the time and manner of one's death. We do not ask simply whether there is a liberty interest in receiving "aid in killing oneself" because such a narrow interest could not exist in the absence of a broader and more important underlying interest—the right to die. In short, it is the end and not the means that defines the liberty interest. . . .

While some people refer to the liberty interest implicated in right-to-die cases as a liberty interest in committing suicide, we do not describe it that way. We use the broader and more accurate terms, "the right to die," "determining the time and manner of one's death," and "hastening one's death" for an important reason. The liberty interest we examine encompasses a whole range of acts that are generally not considered to constitute "suicide." Included within the liberty interest we examine is, for example, the act of refusing or terminating unwanted medical treatment. A competent adult has a liberty interest in refusing to be connected to a respirator or in being disconnected from one, even if he is

67

terminally ill and cannot live without mechanical assistance. The law does not classify the death of a patient that results from the granting of his wish to decline or discontinue treatment as "suicide." Nor does the law label the acts of those who help the patient carry out that wish, whether by physically disconnecting the respirator or by removing an intravenous tube, as assistance in suicide. Accordingly, we believe that the broader terms—"the right to die," "controlling the time and manner of one's death," and "hastening one's death"— more accurately describe the liberty interest at issue here. Moreover, we have serious doubts that the terms "suicide" and "assisted suicide" are appropriate legal descriptions of the specific conduct at issue here. . . .

Prior Court Decisions

Next we examine previous Court decisions that delineate the boundaries of substantive due process. We believe that a careful examination of these decisions demonstrates that there is a strong liberty interest in determining how and when one's life shall end, and that an explicit recognition of that interest follows naturally, indeed inevitably, from their reasoning.

The essence of the substantive component of the Due Process Clause is to limit the ability of the state to intrude into the most important matters of our lives, at least without substantial justification. In a long line of cases, the Court has carved out certain key moments and decisions in individuals' lives and placed them beyond the general prohibitory authority of the state. . . .

We believe that two relatively recent decisions of the Court, *Planned Parenthood v. Casey* (1992) and *Cruzan v. Director, Missouri Dept. of Health* (1990) are fully persuasive, and leave little doubt as to the proper result.

In *Casey*, the Court surveyed its prior decisions affording "constitutional protection to personal decisions relating to marriage, procreation, contraception, family relationships, child rearing, and education.". . .

Like the decision of whether or not to have an abortion, the decision how and when to die is one of "the most intimate and personal choices a person may make in a lifetime," a choice "central to personal dignity and autonomy." A competent terminally ill adult, having lived nearly the full measure of his life, has a strong liberty interest in choosing a dignified and humane death rather than being reduced at the end of his existence to a childlike state of helplessness, diapered, sedated, incontinent. . . .

> *"A competent terminally ill adult, having lived nearly the full measure of his life, has a strong liberty interest in choosing a dignified and humane death."*

In *Cruzan*, the Court considered whether or not there is a constitutionally protected, due process liberty interest in terminating unwanted medical treatment. The Court said that an affirmative answer followed almost inevitably from its prior decisions holding that patients have a liberty interest in refusing to submit to specific medical procedures. . . .

Determining a State's Interests

Casey and *Cruzan* provide persuasive evidence that the Constitution encompasses a due process liberty interest in controlling the time and manner of one's death—that there is, in short, a constitutionally recognized "right to die." Our conclusion is strongly influenced by, but not limited to, the plight of mentally competent, terminally ill adults. We are influenced as well by the plight of others, such as those whose existence is reduced to a vegetative state or a permanent and irreversible state of unconsciousness.

Our conclusion that there is a liberty interest in determining the time and manner of one's death does not mean that there is a concomitant right to exercise that interest in all circumstances or to do so free from state regulation. To the contrary, we explicitly recognize that some prohibitory and regulatory state action is fully consistent with constitutional principles.

> "*Casey and* **Cruzan** *provide persuasive evidence that the Constitution encompasses a due process liberty interest in controlling the time and manner of one's death.*"

In short, finding a liberty interest constitutes a critical first step toward answering the question before us. The determination that must now be made is whether the state's attempt to curtail the exercise of that interest is constitutionally justified.

To determine whether a state action that impairs a liberty interest violates an individual's substantive due process rights we must identify the factors relevant to the case at hand, assess the state's interests and the individual's liberty interest in light of those factors, and then weigh and balance the competing interests. The relevant factors generally include: 1) the importance of the various state interests, both in general and in the factual context of the case; 2) the manner in which those interests are furthered by the state law or regulation; 3) the importance of the liberty interest, both in itself and in the context in which it is being exercised; 4) the extent to which that interest is burdened by the challenged state action; and 5) the consequences of upholding or overturning the statute or regulation.

We . . . begin by considering the first: the importance of the state's interests. We identify six related state interests involved in the controversy before us: 1) the state's general interest in preserving life; 2) the state's more specific interest in preventing suicide; 3) the state's interest in avoiding the involvement of third parties and in precluding the use of arbitrary, unfair, or undue influence; 4) the state's interest in protecting family members and loved ones; 5) the state's interest in protecting the integrity of the medical profession; and 6) the state's interest in avoiding adverse consequences that might ensue if the statutory provision at issue is declared unconstitutional. . . .

We consider the state's interests in preventing assisted suicide as being different only in degree and not in kind from its interests in prohibiting a number of other medical practices that lead directly to a terminally ill patient's death.

> *"The Constitution and the courts stand as a bulwark between individual freedom and arbitrary and intrusive governmental power."*

Moreover, we do not consider those interests to be significantly greater in the case of assisted suicide than they are in the case of those other medical practices, if indeed they are greater at all. However, even if the difference were one of kind and not degree, our result would be no different. For no matter how much weight we could legitimately afford the state's interest in preventing suicide, that weight, when combined with the weight we give all the other state's interests, is insufficient to outweigh the terminally ill individual's interest in deciding whether to end his agony and suffering by hastening the time of his death with medication prescribed by his physician. The individual's interest in making that vital decision is compelling indeed, for no decision is more painful, delicate, personal, important, or final than the decision how and when one's life shall end. If broad general state policies can be used to deprive a terminally ill individual of the right to make that choice, it is hard to envision where the exercise of arbitrary and intrusive power by the state can be halted. In this case, the state has wide power to regulate, but it may not ban the exercise of the liberty interest, and that is the practical effect of the program before us. Accordingly, . . . we hold that the "or aids" provision of Washington statute RCW 9A.36.060 is unconstitutional as applied to terminally ill competent adults who wish to hasten their deaths with medication prescribed by their physicians. . . .

Due Process Was Violated

We hold that a liberty interest exists in the choice of how and when one dies, and that the provision of the Washington statute banning assisted suicide, as applied to competent, terminally ill adults who wish to hasten their deaths by obtaining medication prescribed by their doctors, violates the Due Process Clause. We would add that those whose services are essential to help the terminally ill patient obtain and take that medication and who act under the supervision or direction of a physician are necessarily covered by our ruling. That includes the pharmacist who fills the prescription; the health care worker who facilitates the process; the family member or loved one who opens the bottle, places the pills in the patient's hand, advises him how many pills to take, and provides the necessary tea, water or other liquids; or the persons who help the patient to his death bed and provide the love and comfort so essential to a peaceful death. We recognize that this decision is a most difficult and controversial one, and that it leaves unresolved a large number of equally troublesome issues that will require resolution in the years ahead. We also recognize that other able and dedicated jurists, construing the Constitution as they believe it must be construed, may disagree not only with the result we reach but with our method of constitutional analysis. Given the nature of the judicial process and the complexity of the task of determining the rights and interests comprehended by the Constitution, good faith disagreements within the judiciary should not surprise or disturb anyone who follows the development of the law. For these reasons, we express our hope that whatever debate may accompany the future exploration of the issues we have touched on today will be conducted in an objective, rational, and constructive manner that will increase, not diminish, respect for the Constitution.

There is one final point we must emphasize. Some argue strongly that decisions regarding matters affecting life or death should not be made by the courts. Essentially, we agree with that proposition. In this case, by permitting the individual to exercise the right to choose we are following the constitutional mandate to take such decisions out of the hands of the government, both state and federal, and to put them where they rightly belong, in the hands of the people. We are allowing individuals to make the decisions that so profoundly affect their very existence—and precluding the state from intruding excessively into that critical realm. The Constitution and the courts stand as a bulwark between individual freedom and arbitrary and intrusive governmental power. Under our constitutional system, neither the state nor the majority of the people in a state can impose its will upon the individual in a matter so highly "central to personal dignity and autonomy," as stated in *Casey*. Those who believe strongly that death must come without physician assistance are free to follow that creed, be they doctors or patients. They are not free, however, to force their views, their religious convictions, or their philosophies on all the other members of a democratic society, and to compel those whose values differ with theirs to die painful, protracted, and agonizing deaths.

Assisted Suicide Is an Individual Freedom

by James Kilpatrick

About the author: *James Kilpatrick is a syndicated columnist.*

At the time the New York suit was filed in 1994, George A. Kingsley was slowly going blind. A victim of AIDS, he was suffering terribly from parasitic infections that had caused lesions on his brain. He knew he was in the terminal phase of his illness. In an affidavit, he said:

"It is my desire that my physician prescribe suitable drugs for me to consume for the purpose of hastening my death . . ."

Profoundly Important Cases

Across the continent, John Doe, a 44-year-old artist in Washington state, signed a similar statement. He too was going blind as a consequence of AIDS. He was in constant intractable pain. He too wanted his physician to help him die.

The laws of New York and Washington make it a crime for physicians to assist in suicide. Are these laws constitutional?

Before the Supreme Court's 1996 term expires in summer 1997, the high court will let us know. The companion cases of *Vacco v. Quill* (New York) and *Washington v. Glucksberg* (Washington) will confront the Court with decisions of the most profound importance. Judge Stephen Reinhardt of the 9th Circuit put it this way:

"This case requires us to confront the most basic of human concerns—the mortality of self and loved ones—and to balance the interest in preserving human life against the desire to die peacefully and with dignity." [On June 26, 1997, the Supreme Court overturned both decisions and ruled that the Constitution does not guarantee a "right to die."]

The moral and ethical questions raised by doctor-assisted suicide are off my beat. The questions of constitutional law are sufficiently engrossing. Both the 2nd Circuit in New York and the 9th Circuit in Washington came to the same conclusion: The criminal statutes violate the Constitution. But the two courts reached that conclusion by different paths.

Two provisions lie at the core of the 14th Amendment. The first decrees that no state may deprive a person of "liberty" without due process of law. The second ordains that no state may deprive any person within its jurisdiction of the equal protection of its Laws.

In the 9th Circuit, Judge Reinhardt relied upon the due process clause. In the 2nd Circuit, Judge Roger J. Miner relied upon equal protection.

The Liberty Interest and Death

Reinhardt began his opinion by describing three petitioners who wanted to die "peacefully and with dignity." In addition to John Doe, the artist, there were Jane Roe, a 69-year-old retired pediatrician, and James Poe, a 69-year-old retired salesman. Dr. Roe was dying of cancer that had metastasized throughout her skeleton. She was incontinent and in constant pain. Poe was dying of emphysema and heart disease.

The three patients, said Reinhardt, have a "liberty interest" in the choice of how and when one dies. The state may not deprive them of that interest without compelling reason. No such reason had been shown. The court acknowledged that many persons may

> *"Judge [Stephen] Reinhardt's due process opinion strikes me as better reasoned than Judge [Roger] Miner's invocation of equal protection."*

disagree, believing that death must come without physician assistance; they are free to follow that creed.

"They are not free, however, to force their views, their religious convictions or their philosophies on all the other members of a democratic society, and to compel those whose values differ with theirs to die painful, protracted and agonizing deaths."

Unequal Treatment

Judge Miner in the 2nd Circuit echoed this view. In addition to Kingsley and William A. Barth, who were dying of AIDS, Jane Doe was party to the suit. A 76-year-old retired physical education instructor, she was dying of a large cancerous tumor that had wrapped around her right carotid artery. Unable to swallow or to speak, she existed through an implanted tube.

The point of Miner's opinion was that under New York law, terminal patients are treated differently. After careful consideration, physicians are free to remove life support systems at the request of a competent patient. They are not free—indeed, they risk criminal prosecution—if they go beyond the passive act of turning off a respirator and actively provide lethal drugs.

The distinction serves no legitimate state purpose, said Judge Miner. It deprives such patients as Kingsley, Barth and Doe of equal protection of the laws.

"What interest can the state possibly have in requiring the prolongation of a life that is all but ended? Surely the state's interest lessens as the potential for life diminishes. And what business is it of the state to require the continuation of agony when the result is imminent and inevitable? The greatly reduced interest of the state in preserving life compels the answer to these questions: None."

Judge Reinhardt's due process opinion strikes me as better reasoned than Judge Miner's invocation of equal protection. Either way, the result accords with the highest principles of individual freedom.

Assisted Suicide Is a Fundamental Constitutional Right

by Ronald A. Lindsay

About the author: *Ronald A. Lindsay is an attorney in Washington, D.C. He prepared an amicus brief for the Supreme Court on behalf of the Council for Secular Humanism, arguing in favor of the right to assisted suicide.*

In October 1996, the Supreme Court announced that it will review decisions by the U.S. Courts of Appeals for the Second and Ninth Circuits that have held that a state's blanket prohibition of assisted suicide for terminally ill patients is inconsistent with the Constitution. (The Second Circuit ruled on a New York statute; the Ninth Circuit ruled on a Washington statute.) The Supreme Court will hear arguments in these critical cases early in 1997, and its rulings will be issued at the end of the Court's term, in late June or early July. Although some commentators have predicted that the current Court is too conservative to uphold even a limited right to assisted suicide, there is a basis for cautious optimism in some recent Court decisions, including the Court's 1992 decision in *Planned Parenthood v. Casey,* which struck down a statute unduly restricting a woman's right to secure an abortion. In that decision, the Court recognized that the Constitution precludes government interference in those matters "involving the most intimate and personal choices a person may make in a lifetime, choices central to personal dignity and autonomy." On the other hand, there is no question that there are three solid votes against recognition of a right to assisted suicide: Chief Justice William Rehnquist, Justice Antonin Scalia, and Justice Clarence Thomas. Thus, if the Court does uphold a right to assisted suicide, it will likely be by a narrow majority. [On June 26, 1997, the Court ruled that the Constitution does not contain a "right to die." However, states are not precluded from passing laws that would establish this right.]

Reprinted from Ronald A. Lindsay, "Assisted Suicide: Will the Supreme Court Respect the Autonomy Rights of Dying Patients?" *Free Inquiry,* Winter 1996/1997, by permission of *Free Inquiry.*

Two Different Rationales

Complicating the picture is the fact that the decisions in the Second Circuit and Ninth Circuit were predicated on different rationales. While the Ninth Circuit concluded that a dying person has a fundamental liberty interest in bringing about his or her death with the assistance of another, the Second Circuit declined to recognize such a liberty interest. Instead, the Second Circuit concluded that New York's prohibition of assisted suicide violates the Equal Protection Clause of the Fourteenth Amendment because New York allows physicians to withdraw life-sustaining medical treatment at the request of a dying patient. Since a physician's withdrawal of life-sustaining treatment brings about a patient's death as surely as the provision of lethal medication, the Second Circuit decided there is no rational basis for distinguishing the two methods of causing a patient's death. Accordingly, if New York allows withdrawal of life-sustaining treatment, it must permit physician-assisted suicide.

Given that there are these two independent rationales for holding prohibitions of assisted suicide to be unconstitutional, it is conceivable that, even if a majority of the Court finds that there is at least a qualified right to assisted suicide, there will be no majority opinion. In other words, there could be three Justices who conclude there is a fundamental liberty interest in assisted suicide and another two Justices who are not persuaded there is such an interest but who believe that it is a

> *"History cannot be the sole guide for determining whether a person has an interest protected by the Constitution."*

violation of the Equal Protection Clause to allow withdrawal of life-sustaining treatment while prohibiting assisted suicide.

The only certainty at this stage is that New York and Washington, and their supporting *amici curiae,* including the Catholic church and the Clinton administration, will trot out the same tired arguments for the constitutionality of bans on assisted suicide that have always been advanced. These arguments fall into two broad categories. One category of argument will be a contemptuous rejection of the claim that there is a fundamental liberty interest in assisted suicide. How can there be such a liberty interest given that in this country's early history most states treated suicide itself as a felony? Another category of argument will be an invocation of the abuses and fatal mistakes that will allegedly follow legalization of assisted suicide. In other words, even if there were a liberty interest in assisted suicide, the state's interest in protecting the lives of those who might be negatively affected by legalization outweighs the interest of those who want to hasten their deaths through assisted suicide. The latter argument is the focus of the brief just filed with the Court by the Solicitor General (i.e., the attorney representing the Clinton administration). In that brief the Solicitor General contends that

The difficulty that physicians have in determining whether requests for assisted suicide come from patients with treatable pain or depression, the vulnerability of terminally ill patients to subtle influences from physicians [and] family members . . . and the continuing possibility that someone can be misdiagnosed as terminally ill all support a state's decision to ban all assisted suicides.

Neither category of argument is persuasive.

A Changing Society

History cannot be the sole guide for determining whether a person has an interest protected by the Constitution. Were that true, we would still have segregated schools and laws against miscegenation, since both practices were prevalent at the time the Fourteenth Amendment was adopted. In a multitude of other cases, the Supreme Court has recognized that the practices that were in place at the time any particular guarantee was enacted into the Constitution did not fix forever the meaning of that provision. The Constitution was not intended to be a static and lifeless document, but rather a document adaptable to changing social circumstances.

There are two principal changes in our social circumstances that indicate why we should not be forever bound by the eighteenth- or nineteenth-century understanding of fundamental liberty interests. First, the criminal prohibitions against suicide were motivated primarily by religious dogmas. In an increasingly secular society, these dogmas should no longer influence public policy. Second, the ways in which people die have changed dramatically. Two hundred, one hundred, and even fifty years ago people were usually carried off swiftly by contagious diseases. Pneumonia, for example, was widely acknowledged as the "old man's friend." However, given the greater control of contagious diseases, persons are now more likely to die through longer lasting— and agonizing—conditions, such as

> *"By denying [a terminally ill] person necessary assistance in dying, we have taken control away from him or her and have totally eliminated autonomy."*

cancer, heart disease, progressive renal failure, etc. These conditions can debilitate a person and inflict horrible pain without immediately bringing about that person's death. Prohibition of assisted suicide under these circumstances is to require a person to live a life he or she no longer finds worthwhile.

Eliminating Autonomy

This last point shows why there is not only a liberty interest in assisted suicide, but a fundamental liberty interest. By preventing a person from obtaining assistance in dying we may literally be forcing that person to endure a limited, painful life that he or she has unambiguously rejected. Many patients with terminal conditions are incapable of bringing about their own deaths effectively.

By denying that person necessary assistance in dying, we have taken control away from him or her and have *totally* eliminated autonomy. A compelled life is not a free life.

With respect to the abuse and mistake arguments, they prove too much. Yes, there is always the risk of a mistaken diagnosis, but not only is this risk minimal, it should be left up to the individual to decide whether this risk should be taken. After all, it is *his* or *her* life. Moreover, if we allowed the risk of a mistaken diagnosis to be dispositive, then we would never allow life-sustaining medical treatment to be withdrawn either. As to the fear that dying persons will be manipulated into requesting assisted suicide, no important life choice is immune from the possibility of such manipulation. How many manipulated marriages, child-bearing decisions, and career choices have there been? The government cannot and should not be our nanny. To argue that these situations are not comparable because a decision for assisted suicide is irreversible overlooks the fact that virtually every proponent of assisted suicide has recognized the need for rigorous procedural safeguards. The possibility of greater harm justifies greater caution; it does not justify a paralyzing fear for the safety of others that can be removed only by eliminating their autonomy. We can only hope the Supreme Court will agree.

Assisted Suicide Is the Ultimate Civil Right

by Barbara Dority

About the author: *Barbara Dority is president of Humanists of Washington and vice president of the Hemlock Society of Washington State, an organization that seeks to legalize physician-assisted suicide.*

In early 1996, right-to-die advocates began to see the results of 25 years of social, political, and legal struggle. Looking back at my July/August 1993 *Humanist* column announcing the formation of Compassion in Dying, I realize the incredible progress which has been made. Serving at the time as the organization's founding president, I wrote of our deliberations, our plans, and our hopes. But none of us could have foreseen the recent landmark events that have resulted from the dedicated efforts of educational organizations, legal advocates, tireless volunteers, generous financial supporters, and courageous individuals within the death-with-dignity movement.

A Victory in Court

A major victory has been achieved with the ruling of the Ninth Circuit Federal Appeals Court striking down Washington State's law against "aiding" a suicide. This challenge by three dying patients and four Washington State doctors, initially sponsored by Compassion in Dying, was reheard *en banc* by 11 appellate court judges for the Ninth Circuit Court in October 1995. On March 6, 1996, by a vote of eight to three, the court held that the law violates the human rights of terminally ill, mentally competent adults who want the option of assisted death.

Federal Appeals Court Judge Stephen Reinhardt, principal author of the majority opinion, declared:

> Those who believe strongly that death must come without physician assistance are free to follow that creed, be they doctors or patients. They are not free, however, to force their views, their religious convictions, or their philosophies on all the other members of a democratic society, and to compel those whose values differ with theirs to die painful, protracted, and agonizing deaths.

Reprinted from Barbara Dority, "'In the Hands of the People': Recent Victories of the Death-with-Dignity Movement," *Humanist*, July/August 1996, by permission of the author.

For someone, like myself, enamored of court rulings on issues bearing upon individual liberties, reading this 100-plus-page document may well prove to be a once-in-a-lifetime experience. There is nary a word too many or too few; no argument against physician-aid-in-dying unexamined or unrefuted; no point unsupported with meticulous care in extensive footnotes; no relevant legal precedent undocumented; no part of the historical framework omitted. In short, this is the most beautifully crafted and eloquent court ruling I've ever read. All of us who have worked for and supported the right to die with dignity in America have ample reason to rejoice in this eloquent declaration of human freedom and autonomy. However, the Washington state attorney general's office is apparently not of the same opinion; it has already announced the state's intention to appeal the case to the U.S. Supreme Court.

Kevorkian's Acquittals

In two separate trials in March 1996 and May 1996 (his second and third, respectively), Dr. Jack Kevorkian was acquitted of charges stemming from his continuing efforts to help the terminally ill or those suffering from acute chronic pain put an end to their agony. Defense attorney Geoffrey Fieger successfully argued in both cases that his client's intent as a physician was to relieve intolerable suffering and that, for the people who requested Kevorkian's assistance, death was the only way to do so.

A measure of the state's willingness to stretch the rules in its efforts to stop Kevorkian was the fact that, after unsuccessfully prosecuting him under a law that was *specifically passed* to convict him, it reached back, in the third trial, to a 200-year-old *unwritten* "common law" prohibition against assisting suicide. This "common law," established centuries ago in Europe, was conveniently "upheld" by a Michigan Supreme Court decision in order to give the state another shot at putting Kevorkian in jail.

> *"I believe that history will remember Jack Kevorkian as the truly great man he is."*

During testimony in his second trial, Kevorkian revealed more of his personal feelings than he has at any previous time:

> My desire always is to aid the suffering human being as I would any suffering entity. When I wince at their suffering, I must do something. Even if I didn't wince, as a physician I must do something. It is never nice to see a human life ended. But when the agony ends, it ameliorates what I feel.

After his acquittal in March, Kevorkian was asked whether the jury's decision made him feel free to continue assisting suicides. Kevorkian responded: "I have always been free to do so and will continue to do so as long as I have my personal liberty." (This was no empty rhetoric, as it turned out: Kevorkian defiantly assisted a suicide while his third trial was still in progress!) Kevorkian went on: "This is the very essence of human autonomy, something that goes way beyond a so-called right, and I am honored as a healer to help any suffering patient whose condition medically warrants it."

Kevorkian also told reporters that assisting suicides for the rest of his life is not his aim: "What I really want is to set up a clinic and a research facility where we can get some good for humanity out of all this. I am a researcher at heart. My only wish is that some other doctors would be brave enough to join me."

> *"This profoundly intimate human-rights issue has finally become so compelling to the American people that the courts have had no choice but to address it."*

Having carefully followed Kevorkian's late-life career and the responses of those who condemn him, I have learned one thing in particular: nothing is more feared or hated by those who hold established power than a genuinely righteous person—a person who knows he or she is right, who doesn't need or seek their approval, and who absolutely refuses to pay homage to their "superior" wisdom and authority. I believe that history will remember Jack Kevorkian as the truly great man he is. Future generations will look back at the appalling suffering of the dying in our time with the same horror we feel when looking back at barbaric "medical treatments" such as bleeding with leeches or inflicting circular burns over the entire bodies of those afflicted with certain "nervous disorders."

Judge Miner's Ruling

On April 2, 1996, in *Quill v. New York*, the federal Court of Appeals for the Second Circuit struck down two state laws prohibiting assisted suicide. Judge Roger J. Miner, writing for the majority, asked:

> What interest can the state possibly have in requiring the prolongation of a life that is all but ended? And what business is it of the state to require the continuation of agony when the result is imminent and inevitable? The answer to these questions: None.

Predictably, New York State authorities have already announced that this decision, too, will be appealed to the Supreme Court.

I'm astonished by the number of national columnists and media pundits who have responded to these events with blatant fear-mongering. They actually seem to believe that we've been forced down this treacherous road by militant federal judges who have imposed these decisions on us quite suddenly without a full national debate and without the consultation of patients or doctors. Many say that the federal court system should not be permitted to issue rulings on such matters. These legal reforms, they say, should be left up to individual state legislatures!

Where have these people been living for the past 25 years? How could they be unaware of the vigorous national—and international—dialogue about this issue during that time? How could they not know that both these suits were brought by patients and doctors? For that matter, how could they have missed three aid-in-dying initiative attempts undertaken by the citizens of California, the 1991 grass-roots campaign for the Death with Dignity Initiative 119 in Washington State (supported by 47 percent of the state's voters), the Death with Dignity Act passed by Oregon voters in 1994, the intense public discussion generated by the media's sensationalistic coverage of Dr. Jack Kevorkian's every move, or the thousands of column inches (especially during the past five years) devoted to every aspect of this issue in newspapers, magazines, books, and prestigious medical journals nationwide?

For anyone who cares to look objectively into the opinions of the American public on this issue, there is evidence of increasing support revealed by numerous credible surveys. To name just two: the latest survey of doctors in Washington State found that over 50 percent supported the option of aid-in-dying for the terminally ill, and one recent public-opinion poll shows that 73 percent of American citizens agree.

The truth is self-evident: this profoundly intimate human-rights issue has finally become so compelling to the American people that the courts have had no choice but to address it. Judge Reinhardt acknowledges as much in the Ninth Circuit Court ruling when he writes:

> In this case, by permitting the individual to exercise the right to choose, we are following the constitutional mandate to take such decisions out of the hands of government and to put them where they rightly belong: in the hands of the people.

No one proposes to force anything upon those who choose not to confront this issue and take responsibility for their fate. But a great many of us have labored for years to secure our human right to make a different choice.

Gaining the Ultimate Right

It remains to be seen whether the Supreme Court will decide to hear either or both of these cases. [On June 26, 1997, the Court ruled that the Constitution does not contain a "right to die." However, states are not precluded from passing laws that would establish this right.] Similar challenges are being brought in other states, which increases the likelihood that the High Court may consolidate and accept them. The current composition of the Court makes some of us extremely nervous about this possibility. It is conceivable that these nine justices could, in fairly short order, overturn 25 years of grass-roots activism and destroy any hope of legal reform well into the foreseeable future. Personally, I believe that the best outcome for us would be for the Supreme Court simply to let these federal court decisions stand without comment. Then the next phase of our work can begin without further delay: the formidable task of helping to craft implementation procedures (with appropriate safeguards) through the legislative process.

Chapter 2

We were in desperate need of the clarity and focus of these federal court decisions and the jury exonerations of Dr. Kevorkian. They have established a solid foundation upon which to build. As Judge Reinhardt wrote:

> The Constitution and the courts stand as a bulwark between individual freedom and arbitrary and intrusive governmental power. Under our constitutional system, neither the state nor the majority of the people in a state can impose its will upon the individual in a matter so highly central to personal dignity and autonomy.

We couldn't ask for a better statement of principle as we continue our work to gain the ultimate civil right: the right to die with dignity, in our own time and on our own terms.

Bans on Assisted Suicide Do Not Violate the Fourteenth Amendment

by William Rehnquist

About the author: *William Rehnquist is the chief justice of the United States Supreme Court.*

Editor's Note: The following viewpoint is excerpted from the U.S. Supreme Court's decision in Washington v. Glucksberg *(1997).*

The question presented in this case is whether Washington's prohibition against "caus[ing]" or "aid[ing]" a suicide offends the Fourteenth Amendment to the United States Constitution. We hold that it does not. . . .

A History of Assisted Suicide Bans

We begin, as we do in all due process cases, by examining our nation's history, legal traditions, and practices. See, e.g., *Planned Parenthood vs. Casey* (1992); *Cruzan vs. Director, Missouri Dept. of Health* (1990); *Moore vs. East Cleveland* (1977) (plurality opinion) (noting importance of "careful 'respect for the teachings of history'"). In almost every state—indeed, in almost every Western democracy—it is a crime to assist a suicide.

The states' assisted suicide bans are not innovations. Rather, they are long-standing expressions of the states' commitment to the protection and preservation of all human life. . . .

Though deeply rooted, the states' assisted suicide bans have in recent years been reexamined and, generally, reaffirmed. Because of advances in medicine and technology, Americans today are increasingly likely to die in institutions, from chronic illnesses.

Public concern and democratic action are therefore sharply focused on how best to protect dignity and independence at the end of life, with the result that

Reprinted from William Rehnquist, decision in *State of Washington v. Glucksberg*, 96-110, June 26, 1997.

there have been many significant changes in state laws and in the attitudes these laws reflect. Many states, for example, now permit "living wills," surrogate health care decisionmaking, and the withdrawal or refusal of life-sustaining medical treatment. At the same time, however, voters and legislators continue for the most part to reaffirm their states' prohibitions on assisting suicide. . . .

Expanding Due Process

The due process clause guarantees more than fair process, and the "liberty" it protects includes more than the absence of physical restraint. The clause also provides heightened protection against government interference with certain fundamental rights and liberty interests. In a long line of cases, we have held that, in addition to the specific freedoms protected by the Bill of Rights, the "liberty" specially protected by the due process clause includes the rights to

marry, to have children, to direct the education and upbringing of one's children, to marital privacy, to use contraception, to bodily integrity, and to abortion. We have also assumed, and strongly suggested, that the due process clause protects the traditional right to refuse unwanted lifesaving medical treatment.

> *"The states' assisted-suicide bans . . . are long-standing expressions of the states' commitment to the protection and preservation of all human life."*

But we "ha[ve] always been reluctant to expand the concept of substantive due process because guideposts for responsible decisionmaking in this unchartered area are scarce and open ended," as stated in *Collins vs. Harker Heights* (1992). By extending constitutional protection to an asserted right or liberty interest, we, to a great extent, place the matter outside the arena of public debate and legislative action. We must therefore "exercise the utmost care whenever we are asked to break new ground in this field," ibid., lest the liberty protected by the due process clause be subtly transformed into the policy preferences of the members of this court. . . .

Is Assisted Suicide a Liberty?

The Washington statute at issue in this case prohibits "aid[ing] another person to attempt suicide," Wash. Rev. Code Sec. 9A.36.060(1) (1994), and, thus, the question before us is whether the "liberty" specially protected by the due process clause includes a right to commit suicide which itself includes a right to assistance in doing so.

We now inquire whether this asserted right has any place in our nation's traditions. Here, as discussed above, we are confronted with a consistent and almost universal tradition that has long rejected the asserted right, and continues explicitly to reject it today, even for terminally ill, mentally competent adults. To hold for respondents, we would have to reverse centuries of legal doctrine and practice, and strike down the considered policy choice of almost every state. See *Jackman vs. Rosenbaum Co.* (1922) ("If a thing has been practiced for two hundred years by common consent, it will need a strong case for the Fourteenth Amendment to affect it"); *Reno vs. Flores* (1993) ("The mere novelty of such a claim is reason enough to doubt that 'substantive due process' sustains it").

"We certainly gave no intimation that the right to refuse unwanted medical treatment could be . . . transmuted into a right to assistance in committing suicide."

Respondents contend, however, that the liberty interest they assert *is* consistent with this Court's substantive due process line of cases, if not with this nation's history and practice. Pointing to *Casey* and *Cruzan*, respondents read our jurisprudence in this area as reflecting a general tradition of "self-sovereignty" and as teaching that the "liberty" protected by the due process clause includes "basic and intimate exercises of personal autonomy"; see *Casey* ("It is a promise of the Constitution that there is a realm of personal liberty which the government may not enter").

According to respondents, our liberty jurisprudence, and the broad, individualistic principles it reflects, protects the "liberty of competent, terminally ill adults to make end-of-life decisions free of undue government interference." The question presented in this case, however, is whether the protections of the due process clause include a right to commit suicide with another's assistance. With this "careful description" of respondents' claim in mind, we turn to *Casey* and *Cruzan*.

Cruzan and Patients' Rights

In *Cruzan,* we considered whether Nancy Beth Cruzan, who had been severely injured in an automobile accident and was in a persistive vegetative state, "ha[d] a right under the United States Constitution which would require the hospital to withdraw life-sustaining treatment" at her parents' request. We began with the observation that "[a]t common law, even the touching of one person by another without consent and without legal justification was a battery." We then discussed the related rule that "informed consent is generally required for medical treatment." After reviewing a long line of relevant state cases, we concluded that "the common law doctrine of informed consent is viewed as generally encompassing the right of a competent individual to refuse medical treatment."

Next, we reviewed our own cases on the subject, and stated that "[t]he principle that a competent person has a constitutionally protected liberty interest in refusing unwanted medical treatment may be inferred from our prior decisions." Therefore, "for purposes of [that] case, we assume[d] that the United States Constitution would grant a competent person a constitutionally protected right to refuse lifesaving hydration and nutrition." We concluded that, notwithstanding this right, the Constitution permitted Missouri to require clear and convincing evidence of an incompetent patient's wishes concerning the withdrawal of life-sustaining treatment.

Respondents contend that in *Cruzan* we "acknowledged that competent, dying persons have the right to direct the removal of life-sustaining medical treatment and thus hasten death," and that "the constitutional principle behind recognizing the patient's liberty to direct the withdrawal of artificial life support applies at least as strongly to the choice to hasten impending death by consuming lethal medication." Similarly, the Court of Appeals concluded that "*Cruzan*, by recognizing a liberty interest that includes the refusal of artificial provision of life-sustaining food and water, necessarily recognize[d] a liberty interest in hastening one's own death."

The right assumed in *Cruzan*, however, was not simply deduced from abstract concepts of personal autonomy. Given the common-law rule that forced medication was a battery, and the long legal tradition protecting the decision to refuse unwanted medical treatment, our assumption was entirely consistent with this nation's history and constitutional traditions. The decision to commit suicide with the assistance of another may be just as personal and profound as the decision to refuse unwanted medical treatment, but it has never enjoyed similar legal protection. Indeed, the two acts are widely and reasonably regarded as quite distinct.

In *Cruzan* itself, we recognized that most states outlawed assisted suicide—and even more do today—and we certainly gave no intimation that the right to refuse unwanted medical treatment could be somehow transmuted into a right to assistance in committing suicide.

Respondents also rely on *Casey*. There, the Court's opinion concluded that "the essential holding of *Roe v. Wade* should be retained and once again reaffirmed." We held, first, that a woman has a right, before her fetus is viable, to an abortion "without undue interference from the state"; second, that states may restrict post-viability abortions so long as exceptions are made to protect a woman's life and health; and third, that the state has legitimate interests throughout a pregnancy in protecting the health of the woman and the life of the unborn child.

In reaching this conclusion, the opinion discussed in some detail this Court's substantive due-process tradition of interpreting the due process clause to protect certain fundamental rights and "personal decisions relating to marriage, procreation, contraception, family relationships, child rearing, and education," and noted that many of those rights and liberties "involv[e] the most intimate and personal choices a person may make in a lifetime."

> *"The asserted 'right' to assistance in committing suicide is not a fundamental liberty interest protected by the due process clause."*

Assisted Suicide

The Court of Appeals, like the District Court, found *Casey* "highly instructive" and "almost prescriptive" for determining "what liberty interest may inhere in a terminally ill person's choice to commit suicide": "Like the decision of whether or not to have an abortion, the decision how and when to die is one of 'the most intimate and personal choices a person may make in a lifetime,' a choice 'central to personal dignity and autonomy.'"

Similarly, respondents emphasize the statement in *Casey* that "At the heart of liberty is the right to define one's own concept of existence, of meaning, of the universe, and of the mystery of human life. Beliefs about these matters could not define the attributes of personhood were they formed under compulsion of the state."

By choosing this language, the Court's opinion in *Casey* described, in a general way and in light of our prior cases, those personal activities and decisions that this Court has identified as so deeply rooted in our history and traditions, or so fundamental to our concept of constitutionally ordered liberty, that they are protected by the Fourteenth Amendment. The opinion moved from the recognition that liberty necessarily includes freedom of conscience and belief about ultimate considerations to the observation that "though the abortion decision may originate within the zone of conscience and belief, it is *more than a philosophic exercise*" (emphasis added).

That many of the rights and liberties protected by the due process clause sound in personal autonomy does not warrant the sweeping conclusion that any and all important, intimate, and personal decisions are so protected, and *Casey* did not suggest otherwise.

The history of the law's treatment of assisted suicide in this country has been and continues to be one of the rejection of nearly all efforts to permit it. That being the case, our decisions lead us to conclude that the asserted "right" to assistance in committing suicide is not a fundamental liberty interest protected by the due process clause.

The Constitution also requires, however, that Washington's assisted suicide ban be rationally related to legitimate government interests. This requirement is unquestionably met here. . . .

We need not weigh exactly the relative strengths of these various interests. They are unquestionably important and legitimate, and Washington's ban on assisted suicide is at least reasonably related to their promotion and protection. We therefore hold that Wash. Rev. Code Sec. 9A.36.060(1) (1994) does not violate the Fourteenth Amendment, either on its face or "as applied to competent, terminally ill adults who wish to hasten their deaths by obtaining medication prescribed by their doctors."

Throughout the nation, Americans are engaged in an earnest and profound debate about the morality, legality, and practicality of physician-assisted suicide. Our holding permits this debate to continue, as it should in a democratic society.

Arguments Supporting a Constitutional Right to Suicide Are Illogical

by Michael M. Uhlmann

About the author: *Michael M. Uhlmann is a Washington attorney and senior fellow at the Ethics and Public Policy Center.*

Editor's Note: On June 26, 1997, the U.S. Supreme Court ruled that the Constitution does not guarantee a "right to die." However, states are not precluded from passing laws that would establish this right.

Critics of *Roe v. Wade* have long contended that the principles used to justify abortion would soon or late be used to justify other forms of medical killing such as voluntary and, eventually, involuntary euthanasia. Slippery slope arguments are often overdone, but the fact remains that virtually every argument for taking a human life in utero can be applied to a human life ex utero, including yours and mine. Is the person "unwanted"? Medically compromised? Unwilling or unable to lead a "meaningful" life? A heavy economic burden? A hindrance to another's health or happiness? Abortion advocates, of course, dismiss the analogy as so much tendentious rabble-rousing, definitely not the sort of thing serious people should take seriously. A woman's "right to choose" bears no relation to euthanasia, and only a fool or a demagogue would argue otherwise.

The Rationale for Assisted Suicide

What that suggests about the U.S. Court of Appeals for the Ninth Circuit, I do not know, but its March 6, 1996, opinion in *Compassion in Dying v. State of Washington* turned precisely on the point that abortion and assisted suicide share a common rationale. That rationale will be found, the court said, in the liberty guarantee of the Due Process Clause of the Fourteenth Amendment ("No State shall . . . deprive any person of life, liberty, or property without due pro-

Reprinted from Michael M. Uhlmann, "The Legal Logic of Euthanasia," *First Things*, June/July 1996, by permission of *First Things* magazine.

cess of law"). Citing abundant Supreme Court precedent, the court pointed out that liberty is an evolving concept whose content cannot be limited by historical understanding, customary usage, or, for that matter, the words of the Constitution itself. Although the specific content of one's "liberty" at any given time may be difficult to assess, we know at least this much: choices central to personal autonomy are also central to liberty under the Fourteenth Amendment. A right of autonomy broad enough to cover a woman's right to kill her offspring, declares the Ninth Circuit, is broad enough to cover (at the very least) a terminally ill person's right to determine the time and manner of death. And thus it is that the American Proposition, which began with the declaration that all men are endowed by their Creator with an unalienable right to life, now means that they are also endowed (by whom it is not clear) with the right to die.

Two weeks after the Ninth Circuit's decision, what had been done with abandon in San Francisco was done more carefully—and perhaps more seductively—in New York City. There, the Second Circuit Court of Appeals handed down its decision in *Quill v. Vacco*, a case brought by three doctors against New York State's ban on assisted suicide. The court struck down the law as applied to terminally ill patients, but refused to follow the Ninth Circuit's reliance upon the Due Process Clause. Instead, Judge Roger Miner ruled that the prohibition violated the Fourteenth Amendment's Equal Protection Clause ("No State shall . . . deny to any person within its jurisdiction the equal protection of the laws").

> *"Virtually every argument for taking a human life in utero can be applied to a human life ex utero, including yours and mine."*

Precisely because it is less abstract and highflown than the Ninth Circuit's embrace of autonomy, the implications of the Second Circuit's opinion may seem less radical. The "softer" language of equal protection, however, cannot mask the fact that precious little room is left for states to assert their traditional interest in protecting human life. In either circuit, the most vulnerable of patients are now at risk.

The Ninth Circuit's case grew out of a complaint filed by four doctors and three terminally ill patients against a Washington State statute making it a crime to knowingly cause or aid an attempted suicide. A federal district court, Judge Barbara Rothstein presiding, noted a long line of Supreme Court cases protecting "personal decisions relating to marriage, procreation, contraception, family relationships, child rearing, and education." She was particularly impressed by the Court's reasoning in *Planned Parenthood v. Casey*, the 1992 case that sustained the result in *Roe v. Wade* while refabricating the entire constitutional argument on which it had rested. *Casey* cashiered Harry Blackmun's right-to-privacy rationale, which had hovered in the constitutional air for nearly two decades without a satisfactory textual landing spot. Henceforth, the right to abort was to be understood as a liberty interest under the Due Process Clause, which included (so the plurality opinion of the Supreme Court said) "the right to define one's own concept of existence and to make the most basic decisions about bodily integrity."

A Mysterious Passage

As a tour de force of semantic gymnastics, *Casey* has few equals in the annals of modern jurisprudence; it is, next to *Roe* itself, perhaps the starkest reminder of the extent to which our Constitution has become, at the hands of the Court, a thing of almost infinite plasticity. Indeed, it was precisely the open-ended and mushy quality of *Casey*'s language that Judge Rothstein found so comforting when she analogized the right to die to the right to abort. She cited as "highly instructive and almost prescriptive" a passage from the *Casey* decision:

> These matters, including the most intimate and personal choices a person may make in a lifetime, choices central to personal dignity and autonomy, are central to the liberty protected by the Fourteenth Amendment. At the heart of liberty is the right to define one's own concept of existence, of meaning, of the universe, and of the mystery of human life. Beliefs about these matters could not define the attributes of personhood were they formed under compulsion of the State.

Critics call this the "Mystery Passage." But Judge Rothstein thought it ideally suited to her purposes, and who could blame her? If indeed choices "central to personal dignity and autonomy" are what lie at the heart of the liberty protected by due process of law, how can it be said that a terminally ill person's decision to end his or her life is any less "intimate and personal" than the decision to have an abortion? Judge Rothstein, believing she was following the implications of High Court logic, became the first federal judge to find the right to die in the Constitution.

Not all of her colleagues agreed. On the first of two appeals to the Ninth Circuit, Judge Rothstein's opinion ran into a three-judge panel headed by the formidable John Noonan, a prolific author and scholar who has spent a lifetime studying common, canon, and natural law. Judge Noonan completely demolished the ruling. Whatever the Court may have intended by its *Casey* language, he said, one simply cannot excise it from context and

> *"Indeed, it was . . . Casey's language that Judge [Barbara] Rothstein found so comforting when she analogized the right to die to the right to abort."*

apply it willy-nilly to facts that were not even remotely at issue in the case. Judge Rothstein conveniently ignored the fact that virtually all states forbade assisted suicide, either by express statute or well-settled common law precedent—which fact the Supreme Court noted without reservation in the one case it has heard dealing, albeit peripherally, with a so-called "right to die." Rothstein further failed to distinguish between suicide and refusing treatment, a dis-

tinction long recognized in medical practice, justified by an extensive and sophisticated literature, and endorsed by every important medical society in
America. She radically underestimated the potential risk that licensed killing
would pose to the poor, the elderly,
and the handicapped, for whom the
Fourteenth Amendment ought to be
particularly solicitous. In short,
Judge Rothstein's invention of a constitutional right to die was dangerous
as a matter of policy and unfounded
as a matter of law. "Unless the fed-
eral judiciary is to be a floating constitutional convention," Noonan added, "a
federal court should not invent a constitutional right unknown in the past and
antithetical to the defense of human life that has been a chief responsibility of
our constitutional government."

> *"Judge Rothstein's invention of a constitutional right to die was dangerous as a matter of policy and unfounded as a matter of law."*

Reinhardt's New Right

There was more to Noonan's opinion, but you get the idea. Unfortunately, the
tale did not end there. Those who are enamored of floating constitutional con-
ventions are also the Energizer Bunnies of constitutional litigation. After re-
grouping, the plaintiffs filed an *en banc* appeal (a motion to have the case reheard by a larger group of judges from the same court). Their motion was
granted and the case reargued before eleven judges (not including the first
three), who voted eight to three to reverse Noonan and reinstate Rothstein's ruling. This time the pen was wielded by Judge Stephen Reinhardt, a sharp-
tongued liberal activist only too happy to discover new rights in the penumbras,
emanations, and hitherto undiscovered corners of the Constitution.

In his 109-page dissertation, Judge Reinhardt seeks to do for assisted suicide
what Harry Blackmun tried (but failed) to do for abortion: fix a place for it in
the Constitution, but in such a way as to obscure its radical implications. To the
legally uninitiated, Reinhardt's conclusion will appear to be the inexorable ful-
fillment of a legal process that began decades, if not centuries, ago and flows
ever so naturally and gradually out of recent Supreme Court precedent. It is a
clever piece of work, designed both to give the newly minted right a plausible
historical pedigree and to demonstrate its similarity and proximity to already
recognized constitutional guarantees. Reinhardt clearly wishes to convey the
impression that he is advancing the law only a tiny millimeter beyond where it
had rested yesterday. He also wants to box the Supreme Court (where this case
will almost certainly end up) with the logic of its own precedent.

Reinhardt's opinion may seduce those who are unwilling to pay close attention. He begins by noting the agonizing nature of the decision before him and
the necessity of prudent caution. No radicals here, just some compassionate
judges trying to do their sworn duty as they wrestle with their consciences and

empathize with the suffering of others. There are no easy answers to such a complicated problem, he says. Clearly, a balance will have to be struck between individual rights and the interest of the state in protecting life. In pondering just where and how to strike that balance, Reinhardt says he is marvelously struck by "the compelling similarities" between this case and the abortion cases: both involve matters of life and death; both arouse similar moral and religious passions; in both, the strength of the state's interest may vary with the circumstance (age of the fetus in one, mental and physical condition of the patient in the other); and both raise fundamental questions about an individual's right of choice. There is one other similarity, he claims: as with abortion before legalization, assisted suicide is widely although secretly practiced.

The message is, if they are going to do it anyway, what possible purpose, other than the further misery of suffering patients, will be served by our continuing to forbid it? (If that sounds familiar, it's because the same argument was made twenty-five years ago in the early stages of the battle over legalized abortion.)

Having analogized assisted suicide to abortion (and thereby segued into a body of law that can be ever so flexibly adopted to his purposes), Judge Reinhardt undertakes an historical exegesis of opinions about the ethics and legality of suicide. About the best that can be said of his effort is that it would be laughable were the subject not so grave. As with Harry Blackmun's bowdlerized history of abortion laws in *Roe v. Wade*, Judge Reinhardt's abridged intellectual history seeks to show that there never was any real consensus on the subject and that much opposition to suicide is based on foolishness or hypocrisy. Legal prohibitions against assisted suicide have no genuine intellectual foundation; they are but the arbitrary moral sentiments of prior eras that make no binding claim upon us. We have no choice but to make our own rules for our own time.

With the stage thus set, Reinhardt returns to the jurisprudence of the abortion cases and concludes that denying a terminally ill patient the right to assisted suicide may work an even greater injustice than "forcing a woman to carry a pregnancy to term." And just in case you miss the point, he then recounts the gruesome details attending the death of an AIDS patient. The example stirs our compassion, as it should, but hardly settles the moral or legal question of assisted suicide in the way Reinhardt obviously thinks it does.

> *"About the best that can be said of [Judge Stephen Reinhardt's] effort is that it would be laughable were the subject not so grave."*

He fashions the final brick in his constitutional edifice by turning to the Supreme Court's opinion in *Cruzan v. Director*, a 1990 case brought by parents who wished to remove the life-sustaining feeding tube from their daughter, a patient in a persistent vegetative state. The Missouri Supreme Court denied permission because there was no "clear and convincing, inherently reliable evidence" that the patient would have wished such a fate for herself. On appeal, the U.S. Supreme Court affirmed the Missouri judgment but drew up far short of recognizing a right of individual patient autonomy. The most that can be said is that the Court's decision presumed for the sake of discussion a competent patient's right to decline food and water, but did so without examining the implications of such a right or its constitutional status.

> *"If **Cruzan** had in fact held what Reinhardt says it held, he would not have had to write a 109-page opinion to justify his own ruling."*

Consider now what Judge Reinhardt does to *Cruzan*: (1) he cites it as if the Supreme Court had already ruled that there was a constitutional guarantee to refuse life-terminating treatment; (2) he notes that the Court expressed no objection per se to the removal of Nancy Cruzan's feeding tube; (3) he thus concludes that the High Court has implicitly recognized a due process right to bring about one's own death. That's the kind of reasoning that used to get you into trouble in legal method courses during the first year of law school for failing to distinguish between the actual holding of a case and the obiter dicta of the judges. If *Cruzan* had in fact held what Reinhardt says it held, he would not have had to write a 109-page opinion to justify his own ruling.

At every turn, Reinhardt gives the appearance of being led to his conclusion by the logic of governing precedent, but upon closer examination his reasoning is little more than ex post facto rationalization of a conclusion already arrived at. Thus, he provides us with a generic history of recent constitutional jurisprudence as it relates to liberty interests under the Fourteenth Amendment, but emphasizes only those features that tend to make the Constitution a servant of autonomous individualism. He serves up a Procrustean history of suicide and the laws against it, but only to suggest the absence of persuasive argument. He craftily recasts the one case decided by the Supreme Court that is even arguably on point. And of course he wraps himself in the logic and rhetoric of the abortion cases, especially *Casey*, because they make of the Constitution an open-ended invitation to enact a postmodernist rights agenda.

The Slippery Slope

Judge Reinhardt does one more thing: he dismisses as improvident, antiquated, or unwarranted all of the traditional arguments asserted by medical professionals, courts, and legislatures against assisted suicide. He is particularly dismissive of arguments making use of the slippery slope, even as he unwittingly makes them credible. Throughout his opinion, Reinhardt is at pains to note that the right he is carving into constitutional stone is carefully circumscribed. Specifically, he says (sometimes) that the right will be limited to mentally competent, terminally ill adults seeking to determine the time and manner of their death. The particular examples he cites reinforce the same impression.

Then a startling passage occurs:

> Our conclusion is strongly influenced by, *but not limited to*, the plight of men-
> tally competent, terminally ill adults. We are influenced as well by the plight
> of others, *such as those whose existence is reduced to a vegetative state or a*
> *permanent and irreversible state of unconsciousness.* (Emphasis added.)

That's the kind of language that could get a person killed. Precisely. Those
two sentences, which may end up being the most important in the opinion, send
a chill up the spine. All the talk about the limited and completely voluntary nature of the right now appear as so much dissembling. Clearly the compassion of
the courts is going to reach far and wide under the new dispensation, even unto
those who cannot speak for themselves because they are "in a vegetative state
or a permanent and irreversible state of unconsciousness."

As amended by the Plight Passage, *Casey* and *Cruzan* taken together now
have the power to erase the line between voluntary and involuntary death. You
will want to choose your doctors carefully, particularly with respect to their attitudes toward suicide and the use of the medical profession in hastening death.
Doctors are not inherently less virtu-
ous than the rest of us, but they are
conspicuously more powerful. No
one knows for sure what the medical
world will be like once the legal
shackles against assisted suicide are
removed, but we can guess. The example of the Netherlands is not reas-

> *"No one knows for sure what*
> *the medical world will be like*
> *once the legal shackles against*
> *assisted suicide are removed,*
> *but we can guess."*

suring. About twenty years ago, the Dutch "reformed" their laws against assisted suicide, and the latest data from Holland now confirm what was once
only a dark suspicion: thousands of patients a year are now being killed without
their consent by doctors.

You may even want to choose your relatives with care. Much common and
statutory law has been erected over the centuries on the possibility that some of
your family may love you less than they love your possessions. Once Reinhardt's Rule gets set in law, you will have to take very special care about who
will be attending to the details of your hospital stay.

Autonomous Individualism

Close students of the Supreme Court will tell you that they could see this
coming: *Compassion in Dying* is only the first of many cases based on claims
of autonomous individualism that the Court invited with its loose and grandiose
Casey language. It is also the logical culmination of a process that began some
decades ago when the Court untethered itself from the text of the Constitution
and began to sit like an omniscient council of elders uniquely empowered to in-
tuit and act upon the aspirations of the people.

Central to this Court-led revolution is the idea that the Constitution is in a state of more or less perpetual evolution, whence it follows that judges need not be bound by the precise words of the document, or by prior precedent, or by settled historical meaning. Once this predicate of a Plastic Constitution has been conceded, it is child's play for Reinhardt and his colleagues to reach the conclusion they do. To them, it is simply irrelevant that no federal judge (prior to Rothstein) had ever before found a right to die in the Due Process Clause, just as it is irrelevant that every state in the union, save one, forbids assisted suicide. What appears to be supremely relevant is that the *Casey* language incorporates

> *"Though the Second Circuit did not follow the Ninth Circuit's metaphysical flight into autonomous individualism, its own decision . . . may in fact be more dangerous."*

the concept of autonomous individualism and places it at the center of the liberty interests said to be guaranteed by the Constitution.

Though the Second Circuit did not follow the Ninth Circuit's metaphysical flight into autonomous individualism, its own decision, based on the Equal Protection Clause, and apparently safer, may in fact be more dangerous. Generally speaking, the Equal Protection Clause requires that similarly situated people must be treated alike. If members of the affected class are treated differently, the state must provide and defend a rational basis for the distinction.

In the case at hand, Judge Miner and his colleagues determined that the relevant class was "all competent persons who are in the final stages of fatal illness and wish to hasten their deaths." Under New York law, patients may legally refuse treatment and authorize the withdrawal of life-support systems, including nutrition, even in those instances where such steps would undoubtedly hasten death. To ban assisted suicide, however, means that some members of the class, i.e., those who wish to hasten their deaths with the help of their physicians, are being treated differently. Because he could not find that the state had demonstrated a legitimate state purpose in making such a distinction, Judge Miner ruled that an unconstitutional discrimination had taken place. In short, New York's distinction between passive and active measures was a distinction without a difference.

The Danger of Miner's Opinion

It is worth noting that Judge Miner's inability to parse that distinction was not shared by the New York State Task Force on Life and the Law, a twenty-four-member commission appointed by Governor Mario Cuomo in 1985 to advise on questions of biomedical ethics. In 1994, the Task Force recommended unanimously *against* the legalization of assisted suicide and said why in an exceptionally thoughtful two-hundred-page report. Few states have ever provided a more cogent explanation for any public policy, and none has ever furnished a more coherent defense of the ban against assisted suicide. If the Task Force Report couldn't pass muster with the Second Circuit, it is virtually impossible to think of a rationale that would.

Be that as it may, Judge Miner's reasoning may be more attractive to the Supreme Court than Judge Reinhardt's aggressive candor, and that is exactly what makes it more dangerous. There is precious little to prevent an expansion of Judge Miner's logic. Given the class interests as he defined them, and given his dismissal of the Task Force Report, what "rational basis" might the state have for restricting the right of assistance to doctors? And what is the "rational basis" for limiting the class to those who are "terminally ill" or to mentally competent adults? It is only a matter of time before non-doctors, non-terminally ill patients, and guardians of incompetent individuals will be arguing that state restrictions violate *their* equal protection rights. And there is little if anything in the Second Circuit's rationale that can stop such a progression.

Perhaps anticipating just such a possibility, Judge Guido Calabresi joined in the court's conclusion while departing from its reasoning. In a lengthy concurrence, he invited New York to enact new laws against assisted suicide. He also implied that to analyze the issue as if it were solely one of class discrimination was a subterfuge that begged important underlying questions. It is a slim reed that Calabresi extends, but he is at least open to the possibility that the state might be able to demonstrate—in a way he thought it had not adequately done—a sufficient rationale for prohibiting doctors from killing.

What will the Supreme Court do with all this? There are both political and legal reasons why it may not want to address this issue at this time, and both cases could be sent back for further adjudication. On the other hand, when the two most important federal circuits in the country have taken on an issue of this gravity, the Court may find itself duty-bound to provide definitive constitutional guidance. In the event, the justices are going to find themselves in a bit of a pickle. Judge Miner's cautious, essentially procedural approach may appear to offer a "safe" way out because it denies that patients have a substantive right to die while permitting them to exercise such a right in fact. On the other hand, if the Justices embrace the substantive approach of Reinhardt and Company, they could put themselves in the middle of a passionate political and moral controversy every bit the equal to the one they generated with *Roe v. Wade*. No matter which way the Court goes, it will risk opening another door to the bottomless pit of constitutional litigation based on claims of individual autonomy, whether it is called by that name or not. In short, unless the Court is prepared to think about this issue with greater care than was evinced by the Ninth and Second Circuits—and there is little in its opinions of late to suggest that it has the moral imagination to do so—the question will be not how far we slide down the slippery slope of legally sanctioned killing, but how fast.

A Constitutional Right to Assisted Suicide Would Threaten Patients' Right to Refuse Treatment

by Wendy K. Mariner

About the author: *Wendy K. Mariner is a professor of health law at Boston University's Schools of Medicine and Public Health. She is a contributing editor for health law and ethics of the* American Journal of Public Health.

The Health Law Department at Boston University's School of Public Health has long championed patients' rights. Department Chair George J. Annas, the Edward Utley Professor of Health Law, wrote the book on *The Rights of Patients*—literally. So it may have surprised some observers to see three of the department's faculty members writing a brief amicus curiae to the United States Supreme Court arguing against a constitutional right to physician-assisted suicide for terminally ill patients. In fact, Professors Annas and Leonard H. Glantz and I did not attack physician-assisted suicide itself. Rather, we and other bioethics professors, for whom the brief was written, warned that the rationale put forth by proponents of physician-assisted suicide, if adopted by the Supreme Court, would destroy important rights that patients have now.

Supreme Court Reversals

On June 26, 1997, the Supreme Court unanimously upheld statutes in New York and Washington making it a crime to assist another person to commit suicide. In 1996, in *Washington v. Glucksberg*, the Ninth Circuit Court of Appeals had decided that the liberty protected by the due process clause of the Fourteenth Amendment to the United States Constitution granted mentally competent terminally ill patients a fundamental right to "hasten death" by having a physician assist them to commit suicide, and that Washington's law against as-

Reprinted from Wendy K. Mariner, "From *Where* to Eternity?" *Bostonia*, Fall 1997, by permission of the author and *Bostonia* magazine.

sisted suicide infringed on that right. The Supreme Court reversed that decision, finding that the Constitution did not contain any such fundamental right.

In *Vacco v. Quill,* also in 1996, the Second Circuit Court of Appeals in New York had not found any constitutional right to physician-assisted suicide, but did hold that the Fourteenth Amendment's equal protection clause entitled mentally competent terminally ill patients to physician-assisted suicide. Again, the Supreme Court reversed, finding no violation of equal protection.

> *"Even if it refused to recognize any constitutional right, the [Supreme Court] should not strike down existing patients' rights to refuse treatment."*

When the federal courts of appeals issued their decisions in 1996, we believed that the Supreme Court would certainly reverse them. The Supreme Court has been loath to recognize new constitutional rights, and it was unlikely to do so in these cases. The real question was how the Supreme Court would reverse the lower courts—what reasons would the court give to justify its decision? If the Supreme Court accepted the arguments of the proponents of physician-assisted suicide and still upheld state laws against it, patients would end up with a much bigger loss of rights than that of physician-assisted suicide alone. It was for this reason that we agreed to submit an amicus brief to the Supreme Court—to explain why, even if it refused to recognize any constitutional right, the court should not strike down existing patients' rights to refuse treatment and to make other important personal medical decisions.

Defining Constitutional Rights

The threshold problem facing the physicians and patients who sought physician-assisted suicide was to define what they wanted in terms of a constitutional right. Constitutional rights are a small subset of the legal rights that Americans enjoy. Most rights have their source in statutes or common law. The Constitution protects only those rights that are deemed to be essential to democratic freedom, such as freedom of speech and the right to vote. Proponents of new constitutional rights face a heavy burden of proving that something is so important that government should almost never interfere. A general right to assistance in suicide was not likely to qualify as that important, especially when laws against assisting someone to commit suicide have been in effect since before the United States became an independent country.

The plaintiffs, therefore, claimed a very limited right: only mentally competent terminally ill patients who were close to death and voluntarily decided to commit suicide should be entitled to a physician's assistance. This assistance was to be limited to a physician's prescribing a lethal dose of drugs. Moreover, the plaintiffs recommended that the exercise of this right be carefully regulated, as by requiring a second opinion on the patient's medical condition and competence, an evaluation of whether the patient's decision was voluntary, and a waiting period before prescribing any drugs that could be used to commit suicide.

These limitations posed significant problems for defining a constitutional right because constitutional rights generally apply to everyone and do not entail preconditions like those proposed. It was difficult to justify limiting the proposed right to one small class of people and one method of assistance. The number of people who might desire assistance in committing suicide is much larger than the terminally ill (a group difficult to identify in any event). The plaintiffs focused on the suffering of terminally ill patients who were in pain, but people who are not terminally ill may also be in unbearable pain, and suffering is not limited to physical pain. If terminally ill patients had a right to assistance in suicide, why shouldn't anyone who suffers enough to want to commit suicide be entitled to assistance? Further, there was no reason why physicians should be the only ones the Constitution permits to provide assistance, or why assistance should be limited to prescribing drugs instead of, for example, a gun. There is no constitutional principle that can distinguish "good" suicides from "bad" ones, and therefore, no constitutional basis to prevent everyone from having a right to assistance in suicide, from the elderly patient dying of cancer to the homeless drug addict to the executive who just lost his job to the lovelorn teenager.

No Right to Assisted Suicide

The Supreme Court took this argument seriously, citing our brief among others, and said: "[I]t turns out that what is couched as a limited right to 'physician-assisted suicide' is likely, in effect, a much broader license, which could prove extremely difficult to police and contain." The court defined the constitutional question before it as "whether the 'liberty' specially protected by the due process clause includes a right to commit suicide which itself includes a right to assistance in doing so." All nine justices answered no to that question.

It should be noted that suicide is not a crime in any state in the country. Although suicide was a crime in the American colonies, it was decriminalized long ago because the penalties inflicted (loss of property) punished only the surviving family; the deceased cannot be punished. Every year more than 30,000 people commit suicide in the United States without any help from anyone. But this does not mean that people have a right to have someone help them commit suicide.

> *"Not only is refusing treatment different from suicide, but it deserves constitutional protection."*

All states have suicide prevention programs to help people who resort to suicide because of depression or other problems that could be remedied. And all states [except Oregon] make assisting suicide illegal.

The Supreme Court recognized the risks of granting a right to assistance in suicide and found that laws making it a crime served several legitimate govern-ment interests, including protecting mentally ill, depressed, and other vulnera-ble people from suicidal impulses, and protecting the elderly, disabled, and poor from abuse, neglect, and mistakes. In upholding the laws as constitutional, the states only needed to show that their laws were rationally related to a legiti-mate state interest. The court concluded, "This requirement is unquestionably met here."

The Second Circuit's Flawed Decision

In the case of *Vacco v. Quill,* the Second Circuit Court of Appeals had con-cluded that New York's law against assisted suicide violated the equal protec-tion clause of the Fourteenth Amendment, which provides that no state shall deny to any person the equal protection of the laws. Like all other states, New York permits everyone to refuse medical treatment, even treatment that could save or prolong life. The Second Circuit had decided that refusing (or ending) lifesaving medical treatment, such as a mechanical ventilator, was the same as committing suicide, and that a physician who withdrew lifesaving medical treatment was, in effect, assisting the patient to commit suicide. Therefore, the Second Circuit had concluded that by prohibiting physician-assisted sui-cide, New York treated terminally ill patients who were not on life-support systems differently from patients who were on life-support systems, because the latter could "hasten death" by refusing treatment, while

> *"People who refuse treatment do not necessarily want to die; rather, they do not want to undergo the burdens of treatment."*

the former could not because they had nothing to refuse. In the Second Circuit's opinion, such different treatment amounted to a violation of the equal protec-tion clause.

My colleagues and I were deeply concerned by the Second Circuit's equating refusing medical treatment with suicide. We feared that if the Supreme Court accepted this notion, it would effectively eliminate the well-established right to refuse treatment. For example, if the proposed right to assisted suicide were limited to terminally ill patients, as the plaintiffs argued, then the right to refuse treatment could also be limited to terminally ill patients, whereas today it is en-joyed by everyone. And if the right to assisted suicide were subjected to exten-sive regulation, the right to refuse treatment could also be encumbered by bur-densome regulations that have no place in personal medical care. Thus, our brief laid out the history and purpose of this right and argued that not only is re-fusing treatment different from suicide, but it deserves constitutional protection.

The Supreme Court's opinion tracked our arguments, although without citing our brief, perhaps because there was ample authority for our position and virtu-ally none for the Second Circuit's. The Supreme Court said, "The distinction between assisting suicide and withdrawing life-sustaining treatment, a distinction widely recognized and endorsed in the medical profession and in our legal traditions, is both important and logical; it is certainly rational."

Refusing Treatment

The right to refuse treatment is based on well-established common law principles of bodily integrity and self-determination that allow all individuals to refuse to permit another person, including a physician, to touch them. The modern formulation is the doctrine of informed consent. Courts that have considered the issue (primarily state courts) have uniformly distinguished between refusing lifesaving treatment and committing suicide. In 1976, in the case of Karen Ann Quinlan, the New Jersey Supreme Court made clear that a competent patient's decision to refuse life-sustaining treatment is not at all the same as a decision to commit suicide, and until the Second Circuit's decision, all other courts had agreed. In the 1990 case of Nancy Cruzan, the U.S. Supreme Court followed this reasoning. It assumed, for purposes of that case, that the Constitution would grant a competent person a right to refuse lifesaving hydration and nutrition, but it never even considered that this could amount to suicide.

When life-sustaining treatment is stopped, a person dies from her underlying disease, not from ending treatment. Suicide, however, requires an external cause of death, such as a lethal dose of a drug. More important, the intentions of both patient and physician differ in suicide and refusing treatment. A person who commits suicide must intend to kill himself, and a physician who assists that person must provide the means for the person to kill himself with the specific intention that that person should die. In contrast, people who refuse treatment do not necessarily want to die; rather, they do not want to undergo the burdens of treatment. Physicians who stop treatment at the patient's request, as they must by law, do not intend to cause the patient's death. Both may accept the risk of death, but as expressed in the principle of double effect, an action intended to achieve a morally permissible goal, such as pain relief or avoidance of a bodily invasion, is legitimate even if it can have undesirable consequences, such as death. For example, most surgical operations carry a risk of death, but this does not mean that a physician who performs the surgery is guilty of murder if the patient dies. Similarly, some drugs needed to relieve pain in terminally ill patients may hasten

> *"The Supreme Court's decisions have ended the quest for a constitutional right to physician-assisted suicide."*

death by slowing bodily functions, but this risk does not transform the intention to relieve pain into an intention to assist a suicide.

Thus, the court held that it was entirely rational for a state to treat refusal of treatment differently from assisting suicide: "*Everyone*, regardless of physical condition, is entitled, if competent, to refuse unwanted lifesaving medical treatment; *no one* is permitted to assist a suicide." (Supreme Court's emphasis.)

The Supreme Court's decisions have ended the quest for a constitutional right to physician-assisted suicide. Those who seek such a right remain free to ask their state legislatures to enact legislation permitting the right they sought for mentally competent terminally ill patients. It should be remembered, however, that Americans have no constitutional right to health care. Before we worry about how best to help people commit suicide, we would do well to make sure that everyone has access to the kind of health care that makes suicide unnecessary.

The Supreme Court's Position on Assisted Suicide Is Valid

by Alexander Morgan Capron

About the author: *Alexander Morgan Capron is a professor of law and medicine at the University of Southern California. He is a coauthor of the series* The Treatise on Health Care Law.

In polls of public opinion, a clear majority of Americans report that they favor making it legal for physicians to prescribe or administer lethal drugs to dying patients who want a quick and painless end to life. Therefore, a lot of people are probably unhappy—or even angry—with the Supreme Court of the United States, which in two unanimous decisions handed down at the end of June [1997] declined to constitutionalize the "right to death with dignity." They shouldn't be.

Reversing judgments from the Second and Ninth Circuits, the Court held that neither the equal protection nor the due process clauses of the Fourteenth Amendment preclude states from making it a crime to aid a suicide, even when such assistance takes the form of a physician prescribing lethal medication to a competent, terminally ill adult who voluntarily requests the physician's help.

The Ruling Aids Reformers

In 1973 the Supreme Court in *Roe v. Wade* declared that the "right of privacy" . . . "is broad enough to encompass a woman's decision whether or not to terminate her pregnancy." The subsequent quarter century of nearly continuous litigation suggests that had the justices announced this June that the Constitution protects a right to assistance in terminating one's life, they would not only have been faced with an endless stream of cases on the topic but also—and worse—might unintentionally have impeded the movement now underway to improve the care of the dying.

At present, reformers are focused on a multipart strategy. They are educating

Reprinted from Alexander Morgan Capron, "Death and the Court," *Hastings Center Report*, September/October 1997, by permission of the author and the *Hastings Center Report*. Notes in the original article have been omitted here.

physicians, nurses, and other health care professionals about how to respond to dying patients' needs, creating new care settings for these patients and improving existing settings, empowering dying patients and their families, and seeking changes in governmental and private policies on payment for appropriate care, on the availability of narcotic drugs for pain control, and the like. Had the Court upheld the constitutional challenges to the bans on assisting suicide, advocates for the dying would have had to shift their efforts to defending the formal legal right they had won. One can only shudder at the prospect that care at the end of life would have become mired in a situation akin to the dichotomized debate about the legal limits of abortion that has resulted in nearly three decades of political acrimony and personal violence, leaving few openings for honest dialogue on the personal and social dilemmas that inhere in any resolution of the choice whether to abort a pregnancy.

> *"The 'right of privacy' does not provide a general basis for protecting personal choices distinct from the liberties protected by the Fourteenth Amendment."*

It is thus ironic that the parties pressing the Supreme Court to recognize a constitutional right to assisted suicide relied heavily upon the *Roe* line of cases, and that the Court, in rejecting this argument, again made clear that the "right of privacy" does not provide a general basis for protecting personal choices distinct from the liberties protected by the Fourteenth Amendment, and that the case law on whether to "bear or beget children" does not establish legal standards broadly applicable to new situations.

Disputing the Liberty Interest

The first of the two assisted suicide cases—and the one that excited the most comment and criticism since being handed down in March 1996 by an *en banc* bench of the U.S. Court of Appeals for the Ninth Circuit—originated in a challenge to the law in Washington State that makes causing or aiding a suicide a felony. Called *Washington v. Glucksberg* by the time it reached the Supreme Court, the case was brought by four physicians who claimed that they would assist dying patients to take their own lives were it not for this statute.

The plaintiffs contended that the statute violated their patients' Fourteenth Amendment "liberty interest," and the district court agreed. In affirming that decision, the circuit court concluded that "the Constitution encompasses a due process liberty interest in controlling the time and manner of one's death . . . in short, a constitutionally recognized 'right to die'" that outweighs the state's interests in preventing suicide by "terminally ill competent adults who wish to hasten their deaths with medication prescribed by their physicians."

In a lengthy opinion for himself and four others, Chief Justice William Rehnquist framed more narrowly the question to be decided: "whether the 'liberty' specially protected by the Due Process Clause includes a right to commit suicide which itself includes a right to assistance in doing so." At the same time, he broadened the claim not merely as a challenge to the statute as applied to a specific group, but to the law's constitutionality on its face.

In throwing out the Washington statute, the trial and appellate courts had both relied heavily on *Planned Parenthood v. Casey,* a 1992 Supreme Court decision that reaffirmed *Roe*'s essential holding. Quoting from *Casey,* Judge Reinhardt had written:

> Like the decision of whether or not to have an abortion, the decision how and when to die is one of "the most intimate and personal choices a person may make in a lifetime," a choice "central to personal dignity and autonomy."

Chief Justice Rehnquist brushed aside this reliance on *Casey* as summarily as a philosophy professor might a sophomore's failure in basic logic. That many due process rights "sound in personal autonomy" does not warrant the converse conclusion, that all intimate choices about one's life qualify as protected rights.

Determining Fundamental Rights

Instead, the Court applied the test usually used to determine whether a previously unrecognized right is among those so deeply rooted in history and tradition as to be ranked as fundamental, as implicit in the concept of "ordered liberty." The Court found a "consistent and almost universal tradition" rejecting a right to commit suicide that even predated common law courts in England and continued in state court decisions and legislation from the beginning of the Republic. Though attempting suicide has lately been decriminalized, the state's interest in preventing it—including through penalizing those who aid the attempt—has not wavered.

Nor did the Court read its prior substantive due process cases as supporting a general tradition of "self-sovereignty," as the plaintiffs put it. While the lower courts had relied on *Casey*'s standard that the government may not "unduly burden" personal liberty, Chief Justice Rehnquist showed that this test could not be employed in order to answer the very question whether a right is fundamental. Instead of a broad statement of the issue at stake, he repeatedly insisted on a more precise formulation, namely whether the due process clause protects "a right to commit suicide with another's assistance."

> *"Though attempting suicide has lately been decriminalized, the state's interest in preventing it . . . has not wavered."*

Besides *Casey,* the lower courts had relied on the landmark 1990 *Cruzan v. Director, Missouri Dept. of Health* decision, in which the Court had assumed that the due process clause protects the traditional right to refuse unwanted lifesaving medical treatment. Whereas the court of appeals had opined that *Cruzan* "necessarily recognize[d] a liberty interest in hastening one's own death," Chief Justice Rehnquist reiterated that the case simply reflected a long legal tradition of protecting people from un-wanted interference with their person, and he pointed out that *Cruzan* itself had recognized (with apparent approval) that most states explicitly prohibit assisted suicide.

> *"The Court's resolution leaves open several significant issues."*

Having found that the asserted right is not a fundamental liberty in-terest protected by the Fourteenth Amendment, the only remaining question was whether the assisted-suicide ban is rationally related to legitimate state interests. Needless to say, the Court had no trouble answering in the affirmative since such interests as pre-serving human life and protecting the medical profession's integrity are clearly served by a ban on aiding suicide. Still, the Court's resolution leaves open sev-eral significant issues.

Quality of Life

First, the court of appeals had held that the weight of Washington's interest in protecting life depended on the "medical condition and the wishes of the person whose life is at stake." The Court rejected this conclusion, stating that *Cruzan* had made clear that it is proper for a state to decline to make "quality of life" judgments, even for persons near death. Yet the quality of life issue is not so easy to escape.

As Justice John Paul Stevens notes in his concurring opinion, the common law right to refuse treatment is not absolute and individuals' interest in auton-omy must in "most cases . . . give way to the State's interest in preserving hu-man life." Yet the *Cruzan* majority did not reject withdrawing life-support from Nancy Cruzan, provided that her desire not to be treated was proven convinc-ingly. Thus, in Justice Stevens' view, *Cruzan* establishes that "individuals who no longer have the option of deciding whether to live or die because they are al-ready on the threshold of death have a constitutionally protected interest that may outweigh the State's interest in preserving life at all costs."

Justice Stevens uses this reading of *Cruzan* to support his conclusion that the case rests on more than just the common law right and encompasses a liberty interest in "avoiding intolerable pain and the indignity of living one's final days incapacitated and in agony." But his reading also underlines that some judg-ment about "quality of life" may well be an inescapable feature of any scheme to regulate actions that lead to death, by separating those that the state may (or ought to) prevent from those that it ought to tolerate (or perhaps encourage).

A second state interest discussed in *Glucksberg*—protecting vulnerable groups from abuse, neglect, and mistakes—is of particular salience because it is the interest at issue in *Lee v. Oregon,* the challenge to that state's 1994 ballot measure legalizing physician assistance in the suicides of terminally ill patients. [On October 14, 1997, the Supreme Court rejected the final appeals of those who had blocked the Oregon initiative.] Although the issue in *Glucksberg* was merely whether the protection of vulnerable persons (such as disabled or terminally ill patients) from negative stereotyping and societal indifference is a legitimate state interest that supports Washington State's ban on assisted suicide, the majority opinion takes the risks to vulnerable patients so seriously that it seems likely that these justices would scrutinize any statute allowing assisted suicide to see whether its safeguards were adequate to prevent discriminatory acts that would put this group of patients at unreasonable risk of dying involuntarily.

Equal Protection

Although equal protection arguments had not been addressed by the Ninth Circuit, they were clearly presented in the other assisted-suicide case, the Second Circuit's decision overturning the New York statute that makes it a crime to aid another to commit or attempt suicide. The plaintiffs in that case were also physicians who were willing to prescribe lethal medication for "mentally competent, terminally ill patients" to take their own lives. They claimed that New York violated the equal protection clause because it permits a competent patient to refuse life-sustaining treatment but not to obtain physician-assisted suicide, which is "essentially the same thing."

The question at issue here can seem like the lawyer's equivalent of a Mobius strip. If one looks at the law on its face, it draws no distinctions: everyone is permitted to refuse medical treatment (even if it is life-sustaining), and no one is permitted to assist a suicide (even of a dying patient). Yet this simply reframes the issue: is this classification of people constitutional, or should terminally ill patients be regarded as the relevant group and the distinction be between those who can hasten death by having their physicians cease life-sustaining treatment and those who may not hasten death by having their physicians prescribe a lethal drug?

To break out of this loop, the Supreme Court decided to take on the question whether forgoing life-support is, as the Second Circuit opined, "nothing more or less than assisted suicide." Although it claimed not to agree with the Ninth Circuit on the question of whether assisted suicide was a fundamental right, the Second Circuit's decision that New York's law violated the equal protection clause seemed to slip into assuming that the law's treatment of the two groups of dying patients—those on life-support and those not—was subject to the sort of strict judicial scrutiny that alleged violations of fundamental rights receive. Not so, declared the chief justice. Since the Court concluded in *Glucksberg* that the asserted right was not fundamental, a court need only determine whether the

> *"Does the state have some reason to conclude that assisted suicide creates risks to important interests . . . that are not equally undermined by forgoing life-support?"*

distinction between the two groups of patients bears a rational relationship to some legitimate end. In other words, does the state have some reason to conclude that assisted suicide creates risks to important interests (already catalogued in *Glucksberg*) that are not equally undermined by forgoing life-support?

Ethical Distinctions

The Court's answer to this question is not entirely satisfactory. It first cites the medical profession's endorsement of the distinction between assisting suicide and withdrawing treatment. While this view is now a well-accepted precept, it was not always so, and its formal endorsement by the AMA's Council on Ethical and Judicial Affairs is less than two decades old. And just as physicians once resisted withdrawing care on the grounds that doing so would be equivalent to homicide or suicide, many physicians today individually agree with the Second Circuit that the equivalence of the two should now make both legally as well as ethically acceptable.

Turning to legal traditions, the Court asserts that the "distinction comports with fundamental principles of causation and intent." Many judicial decisions and some statutes do indeed assert that when patients refuse life-support, their deaths result from an underlying pathological condition (such as the inability to breathe or to swallow), and not from anyone's act.

> *"Were a person without authority to turn off a life-supporting respirator, we would have no problem saying that the person had caused the patient's death."*

Yet as every ethics committee member knows, this view of causation is much too simple, for every event has many causes; a conclusion about causation simply reflects a judgment about the right place to assign responsibility. Were a person without authority to turn off a life-supporting respirator, we would have no problem in saying that the person had caused the patient's death. Conversely, when we say that physicians are not liable for homicide for following a patient's directions to disconnect a respirator, it is not because their act was causally unrelated to the patient's death but because they have not acted wrongfully since they had no duty (and, indeed, no right) to continue this treatment against the patient's wishes.

The Patient's Intent

The second legal principle on which the Court relies, intent, also does not map precisely with a sharp distinction between killing and letting die. In the polar cases the difference is clear: a patient may refuse life-sustaining treatment yet not want to die, while a doctor who assists suicide must, in words the chief justice quotes from congressional testimony by Leon Kass, "necessarily and indubitably intend primarily that the patient be made dead." But in many cases, the intent of a patient forgoing treatment (and perhaps even more frequently of a surrogate decision-maker) is to allow death to occur, to end an existence that no longer benefits the patient.

Intent is both an essential part of the criminal law and a concept that is easier to articulate than to use. Like the much disputed "doctrine of double effect," intent allows us to reach differing moral assessments of two acts with similar effects: acting to achieve a prohibited result and acting to achieve a licit aim that may also produce a prohibited result.

> *"The decisions in both assisted-suicide cases are as important for medicine as any ever delivered by the Court."*

Since the only legal issue facing the Court was whether New York had a rational basis for permitting treatment refusals while outlawing suicide assistance, there was really no need to try and explain its conclusion as a formal working out of legal principles. It would have been more straightforward simply to assert that treatment refusal is both more integral to long-standing rules (such as protection of a person from unconsented interference) and less likely to represent a wrongful taking of life than is assisted suicide, and hence that a state may reasonably treat the two differently in criminal law.

The Future of Assisted Suicide

What further challenges may lie ahead regarding legal regulation of the end of life? Several justices appear ready to entertain a test of any undue legal restrictions on pain control. For example, Justice Stephen Breyer thinks that a "right to die with dignity" might be a protected liberty, though he joined Justice Sandra Day O'Connor in concluding that the present cases did not present an occasion to decide whether the right is fundamental, since the statutes in question do not preclude "the avoidance of severe physical pain (connected with death)" that "would have to comprise an essential part of any successful claim" that the right had been violated.

The decisions in both assisted-suicide cases are as important for medicine as any ever delivered by the Court. While *Glucksberg* seems the more foundational, *Vacco* could have been more momentous, for had it gone the other way, the effects would have been harder to contain. Just as the right of privacy was found to encompass a woman's abortion decision, advocates for a broadened "right to die" would have pressed for constitutional protection of expanded categories of controlled dying had *Glucksberg* been differently decided.

But had the Court announced that equal protection requires assisted suicide to be treated the same as forgoing treatment, the expansion would have been faster. If physician-assisted suicide at the request of terminally ill, competent patients is constitutionally indistinguishable from forgoing life-support, how could it be different from family-assisted suicide, physician-performed euthanasia, or the use of such means on patients who are no longer competent (but who had executed an advance directive) or were never competent (but who are seen as suffering)?

The Court wants to avoid dealing with the series of future cases in which these subsequent expansions of the "right to die" would be fought out, but the justices clearly know that the issues of managing death have not disappeared forever from their docket. Though no generalized right exists such that any assisted-suicide statute is invalid on its face, legal barriers that prevented a dying patient from receiving treatment necessary to relieve pain—even at the risk of hastening death—might state a cognizable constitutional claim. Justice Stevens clearly reaches this conclusion, and Justice O'Connor's concurring opinion hints at it, though she also suggests that the state's interests in protecting vulnerable patients could still be "sufficiently weighty" to justify the prohibition on assisting a suicide.

Justice Souter's Opinion

In a lengthy and scholarly opinion, Justice David Souter seeks to establish the views of the late Justice John Marshall Harlan as the correct theory of substantive due process, namely whether the law sets up an "arbitrary imposition" or "purposeless restraint." Were this to be the reigning standard, the legal regulation of care at the end of life could become a prime topic for litigation, since this field is noteworthy for the extent to which legislators must deal with "clashing principles" in the process of crafting policy, thus providing fertile ground for judges whose due process mandate would in Souter's

> *"The chief justice and others observe that people . . . are grappling seriously with how to provide appropriate care at the end of life."*

terms be to engage in detailed review of such regulation and "to supplant the balance already struck between the contenders only when it falls outside the realm of the reasonable." To avoid having to review every claim in detail, Justice Souter takes refuge in a requirement that the right at issue be fundamental. Yet after presenting potent reasons for finding "no stronger claim" than for a dying patient to have a physician's counsel and assistance in ending life, Justice Souter delivers an anticlimax: he refrains from finding the right "fundamental" because the state's interests are "sufficiently serious" to outweigh the (unevaluated) right.

In the end, Justice Souter's idiosyncratic approach brings him to the same resolution as the rest of the Court. He concludes that the judiciary lacks the ability to resolve the factual controversy over whether adequate regulations could be devised to ensure that assisted suicide does not imperil especially vulnerable patients or expand beyond the bounds now contemplated. This is a task better suited to the legislature, though he does not think the courts need wait forever if other policymakers drag their feet. Striking a more hopeful note, the chief justice and others observe that people across the country and in state legislatures are grappling seriously with how to provide appropriate care at the end of life, including whether to prohibit assisted suicide. However imperfect this process is sure to be, it will be better for being free to consider a wide range of alternatives, which would not have been the case had the Supreme Court ruled otherwise than it did on 26 June.

Chapter 3

Should Physician-Assisted Suicide Be Legalized?

Chapter Preface

Assisted suicide advocates believe that physicians should have the legal right to provide their patients with aid in dying. Their efforts to legalize physician-assisted suicide have sparked a great deal of controversy in recent years. One area of debate concerns how legalizing physician-assisted suicide could affect patients' willingness to trust their doctors.

Opponents of assisted suicide maintain that legalizing the practice would create distrust in patients, particularly the elderly and disabled, who would fear that their doctors might pressure them into choosing assisted suicide over more expensive and possibly unsuccessful treatments. This sense of distrust is expressed by columnist Nat Hentoff, who writes, "If euthanasia becomes legal in this country, will future generations of American physicians feel no qualms about disposing of the unworthy?"

Supporters of assisted suicide claim that legalization would not reduce patients' trust because regulations would prevent doctors from making arbitrary decisions about if and when to assist with a suicide. According to supporters, laws would set consistent guidelines and ensure that all competent, terminally ill patients have control over their dying process. Stephen Jamison, a former regional director of the Hemlock Society, a group that seeks to legalize physician-assisted suicide, maintains, "If assisted dying were legally available as an extraordinary option under strict rules, and patients knew that if they were suffering their issues of pain and dignity would be addressed, then public fear of the dying process might lessen and trust in physicians might consequently increase."

Oregon is the only state that currently permits physician-assisted suicide, but interest in the topic is not limited to that state. The authors in this chapter consider whether laws allowing physician-assisted suicide are needed and whether those laws could cause more harm than good.

Legalized Physician-Assisted Suicide Would Improve Treatment of the Terminally Ill

by Stephen Jamison

About the author: *Stephen Jamison directs Life and Death Consultations, a bioethics education program, and facilitates workshops on life and death decision making. He is a former regional director for the Hemlock Society U.S.A., a group that seeks to legalize physician-assisted suicide.*

In my presentations the same general questions are asked again and again, regardless of the setting and the audience. I offer those questions here and provide some of the responses that I have often given. Most of these questions require each of us to draw our own conclusions. As a result I have no "answers," only comments. . . .

Flaws in Current System

Would legalized aid in dying be better than the current practice?

The drawbacks of the current practice are obvious. Patients who are suffering are at the mercy of physicians who may not be willing to take risks, and these physicians either refuse to help or often respond in professionally "safe" ways by providing commonly prescribed—but less-than-adequate—means to die. In either case, the unintended result can be unwanted involvement by significant others who, without access to proper drugs are forced to go to great extremes to ensure a loved one's last request to die. This is usually done without counseling and full assessment and discussion of alternatives, and can seriously magnify the loss felt by survivors while increasing the legal risks. Assisted death in its current form doesn't provide the safeguards that legislation could require. To protect themselves legally, physicians often avoid talking in-depth with patients or patients' significant others about the decision to die and may fail to seek consulting medical opinions or request evaluations by mental-health professionals. The current system, therefore, does nothing to ensure that all other options are explored, that those requesting this action have the opportunity to receive counseling, that those who are assisted qualify for it, and those most in need have the option of receiving it.

> *"[The physician-patient] relationship can only improve if assisted death is seen as an extraordinary act that requires extensive dialogue."*

Would legalization damage the physician-patient relationship?

Evidence suggests that such relationships are currently not always positive. In fact, opponents of legal assisted death point to these problems to explain away public demand for legal change, and argue that the answer is more compassionate care, not assisted death. They further argue that some physicians may find it easier to help patients die than to respond to their therapeutic needs, pointing to research that shows that physicians are seldom comfortable, intimate, and competent in the management of terminal suffering, and that they frequently fail to respond to the needs of dying patients, but instead often feel an antipathy toward the dying that may arise from their own anxieties about death and feelings of failure about their inability to cure these patients. As a result, physicians may emotionally withdraw from the dying and minimize and undertreat their pain.

This relationship can only improve if assisted death is seen as an extraordinary act that requires extensive dialogue, and is legalized with guidelines, safeguards, and a model of clinical practice that opens up this currently private relationship to professional input and scrutiny. It must increase—rather than decrease—the accountability of physicians for (1) meeting the needs of dying patients; (2) communicating with patients and their significant others about their end-of-life concerns; and (3) addressing issues of relentless pain, suffering, and possible depression.

Abuse Is Unlikely

Would legalization undermine public trust in physicians?

Some opponents believe that physician aid-in-dying would undermine public trust in medicine's dedication to preserving the life and health of patients, and that physicians may be more reluctant to invest their energy and time serving patients whom they believe would benefit more from a quick and easy death. In rebuttal, I would argue that one of the reasons behind the public demand for legal change in assisted dying is both patients' desire for more control and the *existing* lack of trust in the ability of physicians to relieve their suffering. If assisted dying were legally available as an extraordinary option under strict rules, and patients knew that if they were suffering their issues of pain and dignity would be addressed, then public fear of the dying process might lessen and trust in physicians might consequently increase.

Wouldn't legalized assisted dying lead to abuse?

Just the opposite. Legal change with strict controls would reduce the current problems of inappropriate aid-in-dying by physicians and significant others, and ensure quality of care for the dying. It could do so by opening up the decision process and requiring documentation and supporting evidence in the case of each death, and also including strong clinical guidelines for physicians to use in determining when to assist a patient to die and criminal penalties for any violation. . . .

How might the rights of patients to an assisted death be ensured?

Since both the request and provision of aid-in-dying must be voluntary, a list of physicians could be maintained by local patients' rights groups, the patients' rights advocate in the area, or even by hospital or hospice social workers. Beyond this, I foresee this role being taken over by nonprofit organizations like Seattle's Compassion in Dying, or local Hemlock Society chapters or similar organizations that could provide referrals to physicians and counselors willing to work with patients who potentially qualify to receive aid. These groups would *not* provide aid-in-dying but would ensure that patients could be placed in contact with physicians who are not morally opposed to assisted dying "under every circumstance." In this way, a patient could begin the qualifying process, but would not be guaranteed assistance. Such a physician would still be

> *"I do not favor assisted-suicide specialists or 'underground' physician-aid-in-dying."*

required to follow strict clinical guidelines, such as seeking a consulting opinion from a specialist in the patient's disease and working with an ethics committee. I do not favor assisted-suicide specialists or "underground" physician-aid-in-dying. Instead, I believe that the person best able to determine the validity of a patient's request is the patient's own physician, who has provided care over time. This assumes, however, that this physician is adequately trained in pain control and palliative care. As this is seldom the case, I would argue that the consulting physician should have these credentials or hospice experience.

The Economic Factor

How would the disadvantaged be protected?

I would argue that assisted death be considered as an extraordinary act, and that the involvement of hospital social workers, counselors, and hospice could do much to eliminate this threat of abuse. Legal provision should also be made to restrain physicians or anyone else from proposing it as an option to patients. While opponents claim that legalizing assisted dying should not even be considered until we have universal health care, this denies the fact that (1) many patients are currently suffering; (2) plans for universal coverage have been proposed without solution since the early 1970s; (3) both "passive" and active euthanasia in the form of withdrawal or withholding of life-sustaining treatment and "double effect" are widespread and occur without similar concern; and (4) assisted dying is widely practiced without any present controls or guidelines. Any legislation allowing for assisted dying should also require private and public insurers to guarantee payment for other possible options such as hospice and in-home nursing care as well as for end-of-life counseling for the patient and significant others. In the absence of this possibility, other approaches might include tying legislation to increased public funding for community-based residential and home hospice programs or even the drastic act of prohibiting private or public insurers from paying any associated costs of assisted death except for counseling services.

The assumption here is that these populations, for economic reasons, would feel the psychological pressure to choose death over the high cost of end-of-life medical care. This economic argument hasn't been borne out in studies of other behaviors, such as the relationship between income and family size, and it most certainly hasn't yet been shown to exist in end-of-life decision making. It's not as if people would be faced with only the choice of relentless suffering or assisted death. And it's not as if economics is the only factor individuals and families take into consideration in making decisions. Nevertheless, rationing of health care, futility of care, and health care costs are issues that are only now being addressed, and the debate will continue for several years. I envision that assisted death and termination of care will unavoidably be at the center of these issues.

Surrogacy Standards

What about surrogate decision making?

I have serious problems with surrogate authority to make *any* termination-of-care or assisted-death decisions without written intent for those no longer competent. Current laws in most states allow withdrawal or withholding of treatment from such patients, in the absence of knowledge of prior intention, at the request of legal surrogates. This implies a current willingness to "allow" patients to die in ways that are *not* voluntary. This can especially be seen in neonatal futility cases involving infants with severe life-threatening abnormalities, which place hospitals—even Catholic hospitals— and physicians in conflict with surrogates desiring continued care for their family members. I am troubled by the entire panorama of this practice and believe that standards need to be established for all futility and end-of-

> *"It's not as if people would be faced with only the choice of relentless suffering or assisted death."*

care cases. Moreover, consistency in all surrogacy decisions is necessary whether we're talking about "only allowing"—or actively helping—a patient to die. To place assisted dying in a special category in terms of surrogacy ignores the fact that "allowing to die" and "helping to die" have the same result.

One way out of this dilemma is to err on the side of caution, with assisted-dying legislation excluding the possibility for surrogate decisions—without prior documented indication of desire—until *all* surrogate end-of-life decisions can be resolved in a consistent manner by a special commission. Furthermore, I believe that all such surrogate decisions, regardless of prior documented indication of desire, need to be subject to automatic review by hospital ethics committees. All of this may seem a step backward given current practices in terms of "allowing to die" but, as I've said, perhaps these current practices need to be revisited.

> *"The current call for legalizing physician-assisted dying is rooted in the concept of freedom of choice for the individual."*

Wouldn't legalized assisted dying lead to involuntary euthanasia?

Much of the opposition to legalized assisted dying is based on the fear that voluntary requests for aid-in-dying would soon move to these surrogate decisions and then to involuntary euthanasia of incompetent patients whom physicians or others felt no longer had any quality of life. As I described earlier, the surrogacy argument seems to bear some weight as court decisions from Quinlan to Cruzan have upheld the request of surrogates to withhold or withdraw life-sustaining treatments when these patients made their attitudes known prior to loss of competence. This is the basis of current "living will" provisions. In essence, the courts might eventually see no difference between "allowing to die" and easing suffering by "helping to die" more quickly. In terms of moving to nonvoluntary euthanasia, opponents of assisted death point to both the Netherlands and Nazi Germany as examples to be avoided. These arguments, however, ignore the facts.

In the Netherlands qualified patients can request and receive either lethal prescriptions or direct euthanasia (lethal injections). Government studies have found that one thousand patients a year are "euthanized" without such a request. What is lost in this argument is that the Dutch make no distinction between passive and active euthanasia, and that many of these "life-terminating acts without explicit request" (LAWER) result from withholding or withdrawing life-sustaining treatment—a practice that is widespread in America. Moreover, many other deaths involved prior discussions between patients and physicians. These LAWER cases have come to public attention only because the Dutch have created a system that allows qualified patients to request and receive assistance, and requires physicians to report them. Also ignored is the fact that nonvoluntary euthanasia is quite common in American hospitals but goes unreported as it's often sheltered under the wider umbrella of "double effect," even though in some cases it's obvious that the intention of massive pain relief has indeed been to end life, not just pain. Furthermore, in my own research I uncovered instances of physicians also providing family or partners with lethal medications to be used for one who was dying, but who was no longer competent due to AIDS dementia or end-of-life sedation in cancer cases. Although these are all anecdotal reports, they suggest that the slippery slope already exists. Legal controls can do much to make this slope explicit and bring abuses to light.

Opponents of assisted death, who cite the abuses in official programs for euthanasia in Nazi Germany, seem to forget that these were designed from above with the intention from the very beginning of gradually creating a system of genocide rooted in the concept of racial purity. This was *never* voluntary or based on freedom of choice. The true slippery slope in Nazi Germany was the loss of civil liberty and freedoms. By contrast, the current call for legalizing physician-assisted dying is rooted in the concept of freedom of choice for the individual. Totally restricting choice and enforcing a public health model that protects individuals from harming themselves—even in the case of terminal illness—is more dangerous to civil liberty than an approach that provides guarantees of freedom under strict guidelines.

The Ethics of Assisted Suicide

Will legalization mean that physicians will have a duty to assist patients to die?

Some ethicists have argued that what will begin as a right of patients to request aid-in-dying from their physicians under specified conditions will soon become a duty of the physicians. I would counter this by saying that autonomy works for both patients and doctors, and that physicians should never be required to provide such assistance, just as they are not now required to perform other surgical procedures they are morally opposed to, such as abortions. The right to receive, and therefore to perform, abortions has not resulted in such a medical "duty." Very few physicians currently perform abortions, and special clinics and family-planning centers have had to be established to fill this need without, I should add, the strict controls and counseling requirements that I'd recommend in cases of assisted death. . . .

Does assisted dying violate medical tradition?

There is no such thing as a linear medical "tradition" that has been handed down over thousands of years. Each new generation of physicians has reinterpreted this ethos for themselves, influenced by social conditions and technological changes. These shifts especially can be seen in the treatment of the dying. For example, Hippocrates, in *The Arts,* wrote that the physician was to "refuse to treat" those who are overwhelmed by their diseases, realizing that in such cases medicine is powerless. In ancient medicine and until the time of Bacon and Newton, the care of the dying and the hopelessly ill was not considered to be part of a physician's obligation. Indeed, to do so was felt to be immoral. Similarly, physicians who believed a case was hopeless routinely suggested suicide, and often supplied the lethal drugs with which to accomplish it.

Earlier in this century, the ethos of medicine moved swiftly in the direction of prolonging life as a result of advances in medical technology. This technological ability to keep patients alive, even against their will or when they're in persistent vegetative states, has led to numerous court cases and legislation over the past twenty years on behalf of patients' rights. In addition, these legal actions have been followed in the past few years by reversals in hospital policies of just a decade ago regarding the use of cardiopulmonary resuscitation. As a result, do-not-resuscitate (DNR) orders by physicians are becoming commonplace. And though physicians cannot legally "help patients to die," they can— and frequently do—"allow patients to die," even mentally incompetent patients, by withholding and withdrawing life-sustaining treatments, including artificial nutrition and hydration. These various changes clearly show that the ethos of medicine is not something that has remained the same even during the past fifty years. Now the question to be asked is whether the ethos will change further to recognize that more harm may be done by favoring a slow and agonizing death for a patient than by following a patient's desire to alleviate suffering quickly and gently with assistance from a physician.

How is assisted death compatible with biomedical ethics?

The four principles of biomedical ethics include beneficence, nonmaleficence, autonomy, and justice. Beneficence can be understood as the opportunity for a patient to be released from suffering. Nonmaleficence, to do no harm, can be interpreted as doing less harm by not prolonging unnecessary suffering. Autonomy can be seen by respecting the rights, desires, individuality, and personhood of the patient, with final authority for all decisions resting with this person. And justice can reside in equality of care for all terminally ill with availability for both hospice care and aid-in-dying.

Safeguards Can Prevent the Abuse of Physician-Assisted Suicide

by Sherwin Nuland

About the author: *Sherwin Nuland is a Yale University surgery professor and the author of* How We Die.

Not long ago, a leading U.S. medical school held a conference on the subject of death. The most hotly debated topic was the role of physicians when life nears an end. Late on the morning of the first day, as arguments moved back and forth, an audience member made a stunning declaration.

A Doctor's Declaration

In the unemotional manner he might use to describe a clinical report, a respected oncologist who had treated thousands of late-stage cancer patients announced that he had kept count of the patients who had asked him to help them die. "There were 127 men and women, and I saw to it that 25 of them got their wish."

Later, as the audience members filed out for lunch, some were overheard praising the oncologist for what they called his courage in helping his patients, as well as his courage in declaring it publicly. Others were scathingly critical, saying the doctor had disgraced the medical profession by murdering 25 patients—then having the gall to speak about it.

My response was simple but direct: This oncologist was known to me as a nurturing physician of high ethics. If this skilled, thoughtful colleague had followed such a course of action, it is within my own moral code to accept it. And yet there remains a troubling uncertainty in any easy acceptance of my colleague's actions—and even of my own, on the far fewer occasions when I have done exactly as he has. The oncologist and I, as well as the thousands upon thousands of other doctors who quietly have helped patients die, have done it

Reprinted from Sherwin Nuland, "The Debate over Dying," *USA Weekend*, February 3–5, 1995, by permission of the author.

within the sanctity of the privileged doctor-patient partnership. We have done it for people we know well, whose desperation for the relief only death can bring seemed entirely appropriate.

What troubles me is the very privateness of that decision. Usually, there are plenty of undiscussed issues when only a doctor and patient know such an irrevocable step is to be taken. Some doctors feel personal morality and a long empathetic relationship are sufficient bulwark against error. I no longer believe that, although I remain

> *"Sometimes helping someone die is an act of mercy."*

committed to the concept of euthanasia. Other doctors—thankfully very few—feel it is proper to provide means for any suffering patient to die, even if the patient was previously unknown to the provider. Those doctors (I refer here to such as Jack Kevorkian) seem to lack the clinical, and perhaps even the moral, judgment to fully comprehend the implications of what they are doing.

A Need for Safeguards

Some of these issues have been addressed by legislation. In the Netherlands, the Dutch Medical Association and the government have set guidelines under which euthanasia is permissible. Oregon voters passed the so-called Death With Dignity Act, permitting physicians to prescribe lethal drugs for terminally ill patients. As in the Netherlands, consultation with another doctor is required.

In neither case, in my view, are there proper safeguards against abuse, including inadvertent abuse by well-intentioned physicians, patients and families. Not surprisingly, a U.S. District Court judge has issued a temporary restraining order against the Oregon measure until its constitutionality can be determined. There is far more to a legislative decision to end life that Oregonians seem to have considered. [In October 1997, the U.S. Supreme Court upheld the Death With Dignity Act. In November 1997, Oregon voters rejected a measure that would have repealed the law.]

Three terms are commonly used in this debate: "Active euthanasia" is taking a specific action to end a patient's life, such as injecting a lethal drug. "Passive euthanasia" is withholding life support, such as feeding tubes for the comatose. In "assisted suicide," a patient is provided the means to take his or her own life. Writing a lethal prescription, as the Oregon measure would allow, is an example.

It is over active euthanasia and assisted suicide that the battle rages. Some opponents felt either practice undermines respect for, and ultimately the value of, life. Some fear doctors will use active euthanasia or assisted suicide as an "easy way out" instead of vigorously seeking other ways to relieve suffering. Others fear widespread use would lead to laxness in other areas of medical ethics and lessen faith in the medical profession. Most difficult to argue against are objections based on personal morality. As much as we would like to think otherwise, euthanasia is killing. There is no way to avoid that grim reality.

But killing and murder are different. Sometimes helping someone die is an act of mercy. Let me describe the situation of a patient I know well.

One Man's Torment

A patient I'll call "Henry Clarke" was a man in his 70s who had reached the terminal stages of leukemia after a battle of several years. His spleen had grown huge and overactive, compromising his immune system. It had become impossible to follow the last-ditch course of near-experimental chemotherapy. Understanding the great risk, Clarke agreed to surgery to remove the spleen, in the hope he might then undergo drug treatment.

Despite antibiotics and meticulous surgery, however, Clarke developed an abdominal abscess. It was necessary to operate again to drain it. A week later, the problem recurred. Again Clarke had surgery; again the abscess returned. As the physicians and consultants were coming to the conclusion that controlling the infections would be impossible, Clarke began to go in and out of unconsciousness. It was clear that he might go on for weeks racked by pain.

Clarke's wife and family could not bear watching the torment and loss of dignity of a man who often had told them he wanted to die peacefully when all hope was gone. There seemed to be no solution until Clarke's physician brother-in law took the surgeon aside and suggested active euthanasia. The surgeon felt his duty was clear: He injected a lethal dose of morphine into Clarke's intravenous tubing.

> *"Any attempt to set clear, universally acceptable criteria for euthanasia certainly will have many opponents."*

If asked, the surgeon would say his decision was based on his idea of a physician's primary obligation. There are physicians who believe their most basic obligation is to fight disease and prolong life; there are physicians who believe their most basic obligation is to relieve suffering. Clarke's surgeon was one of the latter. He would point out that there are situations—fortunately rare—in which the two obligations are inconsistent with each other, when disease no longer can be fought and both patient and doctor are left with only suffering. In the surgeon's view, if determined efforts to relieve the patient's pain fail, the physician should, if asked, end the suffering as humanely as possible. I am in complete agreement with this view.

But even in a situation as apparently clear as Clarke's, there are problems. Here again I am not untroubled by my support of the surgeon's decision. I worry about the "slippery slope": Once we permit active euthanasia, where will it take us? Will the rigid criteria loosen? Will we end up turning a blind eye to things that in the present debate we might consider morally questionable?

An example less clear than Clarke's is that of an elderly diabetic woman whose gangrenous left leg was amputated below the knee two years ago. The stump became infected, requiring a higher amputation, at mid-thigh. The woman, nearly blind and in almost constant pain from arthritis, recently has been told her right leg must be amputated at the calf. This amputation, too, might fail. She wants to die. And yet she has no disease that can be called terminal.

It would be a rare physician indeed who would consider helping this woman die. But to her, life is not worth living. Where on the slippery slope is this woman, and at what point would assenting to her wish be justified?

A Possible Solution

Any attempt to set clear, universally acceptable criteria for euthanasia certainly will have many opponents. Nevertheless, the growing complexity of medicine and the intense involvement in the debate by so much of our citizenry demands some solution. I propose a series of steps that I believe are responsive to the many criticisms of euthanasia:

• A request by a patient or family member to end life must be defensible. Patients who ask for death must be challenged to be certain that they have examined all the alternatives, and that they are not in a state of depression treatable by psychotherapy or antidepressant drugs. Commonly, an outlook of unreasoning despair is transformed into a realistic appraisal of what can be faced.

• If after a reasonable challenge the doctor is convinced that a request for death is appropriate, another specialist in treating the patient's disease should be consulted. Any other physician who has special skills in relieving the patient's distress, especially experts in the field of palliative care (comfort care), also should be consulted. For many patients, spiritual counseling is a necessity.

• If after these consultations it is generally agreed that the patient's suffering cannot be relieved, one final step should be taken. I suggest a final step because the decision to end one's life does not occur in a vacuum. Even if my life has ceased to have meaning for me, it still has meaning for others—particularly for those who love me, but also for society. I take issue with those who say, "It's my life; I can do what I want with it." Each of us is responsible to the community of which we are a part.

The decision to end a life reflects on the moral standards of all humankind. I believe such a decision, once affirmed by the process just described, should be presented to a group of people representing society's collective wisdom. For want of a better term, I will call such a group a "council of sages." In every community and institution, we know who such people are. They are

> *"The decision to end a life reflects on the moral standards of all humankind."*

those whom we admire for their thoughtfulness, restraint, sensitivity and ability to command respect. Among them might be educators, civic leaders, philosophers, members of the clergy, lawyers or lay people. A series of consultations and the convening of a council of sages could be carried out in a matter of days.

This is about compassion for our fellow humans who suffer. This is about doctors' role in society and obligation to relieve the agonies that too often destroy the peace we seek in the final days of life. In my experience, most people who ask for death do so because of symptoms or a state of mind that can be relieved by proper attention and consultation. When the symptoms lessen, these people no longer want to die. Not only that, but the mere knowledge that euthanasia is available prevents patients from requesting it prematurely.

Without question, the number of requests for death that will be granted will be very small—far smaller that the number secretly granted today, and far, far smaller than Kevorkian has ever imagined.

Legalizing Physician-Assisted Suicide Would Not Threaten the Disabled

by Karen Hwang

About the author: *Karen Hwang, a spinal cord injury survivor since 1988, is working toward a Ph.D. in counseling psychology at Rutgers University and is a research assistant at the Kessler Institute of Rehabilitation in West Orange, New Jersey.*

Assisted suicide is again in the news, and it's not likely ever to go away until we accept it. That's a pretty sweeping statement. People sometimes ask me how, as a person with a disability, I can be such an ardent supporter of Dr. Kevorkian and the legalization of assisted suicide. Don't I care about discrimination against the disabled?

Aren't I helping to contribute to the public myth that a life of illness or disability is a fate worse than death? Do I want to be a party to the government and the health care industry's efforts to sweep us under the carpet? After all, to cite the spokesperson for the group blocking Oregon's Measure 16 [an initiative legalizing physician-assisted suicide that passed in November 1994], we're so "scattered and isolated" that we're sitting ducks for "the well-oiled right-to-die PR machine that says Oregon's law bolsters the right to self-determination." So it's all for our own good, see? [In October 1997, the U.S. Supreme Court upheld Measure 16. In November 1997, Oregon voters rejected a measure to repeal the law.]

Now, wait a minute. I was under the impression that we were a buyer-beware culture, sufficiently media-literate to be reasonably skeptical of everything we hear from television commercials or political campaigns.

So it is regrettable that certain "advocates" insist on treating us as if we were too naive or ignorant to make rational choices regarding our own lives.

As novelist Tom Robbins once wrote, there are many ways to victimize people. One way is to convince them that they are victims. A more empowering solution can be achieved by treating people with disabilities not as children who need to be protected from the twin evils of the government and the health care industry, but as intelligent and active participants in the political and medical decisions affecting their lives on all levels. Given this framework, the push for legalizing assisted suicide for the terminally ill (and even, I might add, for medically stable people facing extended life spans under intolerable conditions) need not be seen as inconsistent with the interests of disability rights.

Ethical Issues

Before I continue, let me clarify that I will be using the terms "assisted suicide" and "euthanasia" interchangeably. To further dispose of red herrings, let me also specify that I refer only to decisions made by competent, conscious adults. Situations where this is not the case constitute a separate set of ethical problems.

Of the various religious and existential objections to assisted suicide I will also say little, mainly because people with disabilities comprise such a wide and diverse spectrum of religious and philosophical positions that each argument really needs to be addressed on its own terms. My own feeling about this is that, if we are not allowed the right to define the terms by which we want to live (or perhaps not to live), then we lose an essential quality of what defines us as human. The "value" of life should not be cheapened by extending it past the point where it is no longer treasured or desired (nor do I

> *"The push for legalizing assisted suicide for the terminally ill . . . need not be seen as inconsistent with the interests of disability rights."*

hold any stock with the alleged "redemptive value of human suffering"; anyone who engages in suffering for its own sake seriously needs to think about taking up a hobby). Of course, psychological evaluations are and should be necessary to weed out the "merely" depressed, but it is undoubtedly wishful thinking to assume that everyone seeking assisted suicide is suffering from an impairment in judgment of one form or another. If a person can demonstrate a rational appraisal of his situation, then why should a request to seek voluntary euthanasia not be accorded the same respect as a request to seek medical treatment? From this perspective, the choice must be that of the person living the life: It is equally abhorrent for another to force one to live, as to force one to die.

Answering Arguments

One major argument the disabled groups make against euthanasia is that every time a Dr. Kevorkian aids a sick or disabled patient in committing suicide, it sends a larger message to society that a life of disease or disability is a fate worse than death. Although the concern has merit, their position serves only to perpetuate a vicious cycle. The reason individuals take suicide requests public is precisely because the practice is thus far illegal; therefore, in order to mitigate the legal and social repercussions of their actions, they become compelled to use the mass media to garner as much public sympathy for their position as possible.

If, on the other hand, the practice of assisted suicide were legalized, individual decisions could then remain private between patient and doctor, because the stigma and fear of legal reprisal would be eliminated. If we allow the few who choose to die the right to do so quietly (and legally), we can then concentrate on shifting public attention back toward addressing the needs of the many more who choose to live.

The other major argument used by disability advocates against legalizing assisted suicide is the "slippery slope" argument, wherein the legalization of voluntary euthanasia will somehow lead to some dystopian scenario in which large numbers of the old and frail are herded off into mass extermination, as was the case in Nazi Germany. This vision, however, is equally unfounded.

An Option, Not a Requirement

We live in a society that, unlike Nazi Germany, supports a multiplicity of views, endorses freedom of speech and press, and places a high value on individual autonomy. Arguments based on pure "utilitarianism" have never had the strength in themselves to affect a broad social policy. Even with the legal option of assisted suicide, people will still find stronger reasons—ethical, religious or personal—not to pursue this option.

If anyone has any doubts about this argument, consider the case of legalized abortion. Whatever one's personal opinion on abortion, there is absolutely no evidence to suggest that the 1973 *Roe v. Wade* decision has coerced large numbers of women—even those who are underage, indigent and without health insurance—into terminating their pregnancies. The majority of Americans support legal, well-regulated abortion for those who want it, just as the majority of Oregonians supported Measure 16. In addition, the truth is that everybody in health care and government knows that euthanasia is already being carried out. There is an enormous gray area that easily allows this to happen. For instance, many pain relief treatments also have the effect of shortening life. The higher the amount of pain, the higher the dosage of morphine necessary, and the more toxic the effects. A while back the practice was called "snowing" the patient, by giving enough morphine to shut down respiration. There would be less of an opportunity for abuse if this practice were legalized.

All other things being equal, it is even possible that the legalization of assisted suicide may actually enhance a person's quality of life. Recent accounts of patients in Holland show that the availability of euthanasia prolongs life by reassuring people that an end to suffering will be there when needed. This is closely related to a psychological concept called "locus of control." The principle seems self-evident: The more control we feel we have, the better we feel about ourselves. Of course, our society would be sorely lacking if this were the only issue in which we were allowed a free choice. Voluntary euthanasia should be seen as only one of a wide range of options within a person's control.

We shouldn't have to accept unquestionably whatever decisions—of any sort—other people want to make for us, based simply on the claim that it's for our own good.

There should be safeguards, but ultimately the decision should be the consumer's. Buyer, beware.

Arguments Against Legalizing Physician-Assisted Suicide Are Unconvincing

by Barbara Dority

About the author: *Barbara Dority was the founding president of Compassion in Dying, an organization that provides information on hospice care, pain management, and assisted suicide to patients who are near the end of their life. She is also vice president and newsletter editor of the Hemlock Society of Washington State, a group that seeks to legalize physician-assisted suicide.*

It seems that many generally supportive people have begun to express grave reservations and questions and to reveal serious misconceptions about the legalization of physician-assisted suicide. After over a decade of direct involvement in the right-to-die movement, I feel partly responsible for the movement's failure to adequately inform and educate those most inclined to support right-to-die efforts.

No Moral Distinction

Perhaps the most significant source of confusion for these individuals is the effort to make a moral distinction between withdrawal of life support systems (everything from ventilators to nutrition and hydration) and physician aid in dying, as proposed by the right-to-die movement.

Under current law, a clear moral distinction has been assumed. One group of actions taken to bring about the death of a dying patient (withdrawal of life support, referred to by some as *passive euthanasia*) has been specifically upheld by the courts as a legal right of a patient to request and a legal act for a doctor to perform. A second, admittedly different, group of actions taken to bring about the death of a dying patient (physician-assisted death, referred to by some as

Reprinted from Barbara Dority, "The Ultimate Liberty," *Humanist*, July/August 1997, by permission of the author.

active euthanasia) is specifically prohibited by laws in most states banning "mercy killing" and is condemned by the American Medical Association. Although it is not a crime to be present when a person takes his or her life, it is a crime to take direct action intentionally designed to help facilitate death—no matter how justifiable and compassionate the circumstances may be.

Supporters of physician-assisted suicide maintain, however, that, despite the fact that both groups of actions clearly involve the performance of different procedures by doctors, both remain essentially equivalent morally. Motivated by the same compassion, they both initiate active steps that will lead to the patient's death. Yet, only by instituting new laws permitting and regulating physician assistance can the law be brought into alignment with this moral reality.

> *"For some dying patients experiencing extreme suffering, a lethal prescription is the only way to end an extended and agonizing death."*

The Need for Right-to-Die Laws

As proposed by right-to-die advocates, physician aid in dying is the direct prescription of lethal drugs intended to cause the death of terminally ill patients who request them and who meet specific criteria. During the 1990s, laws have been proposed in several states to legalize and regulate this practice. Essentially, these proposals would eliminate current laws banning assisted suicide and create procedures, protocols, and safeguards to regulate its careful application to certain qualified, terminally ill people.

Reality dictates the necessity of such laws because, for some dying patients experiencing extreme suffering, a lethal prescription is the only way to end an extended and agonizing death. Consider the terrible dilemma created when so-called passive measures fail to bring about the hoped-for death. Are we to stand helplessly by while a patient whose suicide we legally agreed to assist continues to suffer and deteriorate—perhaps even more so than before? Or do we have a moral imperative, perhaps even a legal responsibility, to not only alleviate the further suffering we have brought about but to take action to fulfill our original agreement?

Thanks to the educational efforts of the right-to-die movement regarding the plight of patients like these, national polls continue to show that growing numbers of Americans support regulated physician-assisted death for qualified terminally ill patients. . . . The movement's extraordinary educational strides were also reflected in the passage of Oregon's Measure 16 and the narrow loss of Initiative 119 in Washington State (both would legalize physician-assisted suicide). But in spite of these high levels of public support, elected officials nationwide remain opposed to this form of aid for the terminally ill. [The Oregon measure withstood a repeal effort in 1997.]

Chapter 3

The Role of Courts

Another argument offered is that the issue of death with dignity doesn't belong in the courts at all and shouldn't have been taken there by the Quinlans back in 1975. [Karen Ann Quinlan fell into an irreversible coma in 1975. Her parents won the right to remove her from a respirator in a landmark 1976 New Jersey Supreme Court decision.] The argument goes that we are wrong-headed in trying to change the law; that the law is somehow (or ought to be) irrelevant; and that the problem can and should be solved discreetly by "families, friends, physicians, churches, and communities."

I sincerely hope I'm correct in assuming that this objection is also the result of inadequate or erroneous information, for only a historical misinterpretation of both the right-to-die movement and the intended function of the judiciary in our constitutional system could lead to such a conclusion. Clearly, lack of legal immunity and actual legal prohibitions were in the past, and still are, the single most significant barrier in the path of physician-assisted suicide for the terminally ill. Nevertheless, some adamantly maintain that both litigation and legislation remove the issue from the realm of compassion and concern for the dying and into some sort of coldly detached alternate reality. This is a puzzling stance, since it is just such highly charged issues involving fundamental human rights—from abortion to desegregation—that we have always relied upon our courts to interpret and clarify. Indeed, this is the central function for which the courts—the Supreme Court, in particular—are intended. . . .

Still, some lament that the process has been stolen from family, church, and community and stripped of its "humane informality." But leaving the dying process "informal" has, to date, resulted in the rights of the dying being denied, ignored, and overridden in a random and arbitrary fashion by virtually everyone involved. So, yes, it is entirely accurate that we seek to wrest the individual's right of self-determination in dying away from family, church, and community, as well as from the state and the medical profession, and put it directly in the hands of the dying person—the only place it belongs.

How else can we aspire to the goal of death with dignity for all who seek its solace? The *Quinlan* ruling marked the first time a legal right to facilitate death by withdrawing life support was declared in any court. Although only applicable under narrowly defined circumstances, it still represents the first step in the necessary legal process employed for decades by democracies to establish and codify human rights.

> *"It is now our responsibility to complete the necessary legal process to secure for all Americans the ultimate civil right of self-determination in dying."*

The *Quinlan* decision did not, however, remedy the needless and cruel suffering of most dying patients. Since that first ruling, the situation has become many times worse, as a growing number of the terminally ill have fallen victim to ever more sophisticated medical technology. It is now our responsibility to complete the necessary legal process to secure for all Americans the ultimate civil right of self-determination in dying.

Medical Inconsistencies

Those, however, who maintain that there is some "better" way to secure physician aid in dying for terminally ill Americans in great suffering must bear the burden of formulating and presenting that alternative. Similarly, those who insist that we don't need a legal right to die or that the problem is being adequately managed by the medical profession must prove that a significant number of doctors are now providing this benefit. They aren't, of course, because it is currently illegal for doctors to prescribe or administer lethal doses of drugs.

Isn't it self-evident, therefore, that, in order to grant the wishes of dying patients for help to end their suffering, we have to change the fact that doing so is against the law? How can we ask doctors—in consultation with "families, clerics, and communities"—to commit a serious crime for which they risk losing their licenses and possibly being arrested and going to prison? The legal issues must be confronted and a legal right to request physician aid in dying for the terminally ill secured.

> *"Shall we curtail our available choices . . . because we fear possible abuses?"*

Even if a large percentage of doctors were already providing aid in dying, the question of whether they should continue to do so covertly, free from any legal oversight or protocols, would still demand an answer. Those who cringe at the highly public nature of Dr. Jack Kevorkian's activities should give special consideration to this question.

They should also give consideration to the reason why many of us who essentially support Kevorkian are nonetheless uneasy with his inconsistent criteria and minimal safeguards. The thought of thousands of individual doctors applying an equal number of different subjective criteria to their practice of aid in dying should be profoundly unsettling to anyone. Midge Levy, president of the Hemlock Society of Washington State, summed it up in a letter to the *Seattle Times:*

> We look forward to the legalization of physician assistance for qualified patients who meet all the criteria, complete with reporting requirements to eliminate the possibility of abuse. Without laws governing the practice, we will continue to deal with the equivalent of back-alley abortion in the right-to-die movement.

In this regard, our experience regarding doctors' reliability when it comes to honoring living wills is anything but reassuring. Refusal of heroic measures and requests for withdrawal of life support are being blatantly ignored, sometimes even in the face of living wills and the instructions of the patient's designated durable power of attorney for health care. Our worst fears were confirmed in a recent study reported in the *Journal of the American Geriatrics Society*, conducted by doctors Joan Teno and Joanne Lynn at the George Washington University Center to Improve Care for the Dying and by their colleagues at seven other medical centers. This study of 4,804 terminally ill patients found that only 688, a mere 14 percent, had prepared written directives regarding what medical care they wanted or did not want, or had designated a durable power of attorney for health care. Of those, only twenty-two—or 0.5 percent—were as detailed as they should have been in their directives. Worse yet, nearly half of those were later contravened.

> *"We have no reason to believe that granting the terminally ill the right to voluntary, assisted suicide would somehow lead to coerced deaths."*

An earlier ten-year study, published in 1996 in the *Journal of the American Medical Association*, revealed that over 50 percent of patients ended up in a "highly undesirable state"—in other words, being kept alive despite their wishes. Even more troubling, researchers found that, despite several attempts by families to communicate the patients' wishes, doctors still ignored them and put patients in intensive care units under highly dehumanizing conditions. . . .

Exaggerated Fears

Those in the right-to-die movement agree that as much as possible needs to be done to ensure that no one is coerced into requesting physician-assisted death. This is why all proposed aid-in-dying laws make it a crime for anyone to engage in such coercion.

Of course, no law can ultimately guarantee that coercion will never occur. Likewise, there is no guarantee that all forms of coercion have been eliminated from a host of other life decisions and situations. We can't know for sure what family members' motives may be in any number of already-legal health care and other decisions in which they participate. But shall we curtail our available choices because we don't believe people can always make them for the right reasons or because we fear possible abuses? Or should we continue to expand our individual choices and freedoms while doing our best to prevent inappropriate and coercive influences and to educate all people in critical decision making?

Bishop John Shelby Spong, Episcopal priest and president of Churchman Associates, addressed this issue in 1996 in his statement to a House subcommittee hearing testimony about proposed aid-in-dying legislation:

> I suppose it will be quite impossible for all malfeasance to be eliminated from this area of life. Malfeasance has not been eliminated completely from any other area of human activity. I do suggest, however, that this is only an excuse, and a poor one at that, when we assume that the same human brilliance

that has produced the miracle of modern medicine cannot also solve the problem of prohibiting improper decisions while still allowing individuals the choice of how they want to live out their final days.

The truth is, however, we have no reason to believe that granting the terminally ill the right to voluntary, assisted suicide would somehow lead to coerced deaths. Back when living wills were controversial, opponents made the same dire prediction, insisting that allowing people to refuse "heroic measures" would lead to the virtual collapse of the medical infrastructure as we know it and turn doctors into Nazis. Nothing of the kind has happened.

Recent claims that involuntary deaths have occurred in the Netherlands (where assisted suicide, although not officially legal, is regulated and not prosecuted) are much exaggerated and distorted. Furthermore, the situation in the Netherlands is not comparable to ours in several important aspects. Perhaps the most significant difference is that the Dutch enjoy national health care. To name a few others, the Dutch guidelines require that doctors determine when their patients' suffering has become "unbearable" and do not require that patients be able to request assistance several times before and at the time of death. In any event, due to the rigorous safeguards built into recent proposals in the United States, abuses would be extremely difficult to perpetrate.

In fact, abuses are far more likely to occur within the present unregulated, covert, and occasional practice of assisted suicide. There is no accountability for such deaths, no procedures, no safeguards, and no reporting requirements. How much safer and more empowered all those involved would be if laws such as Oregon's Measure 16 were in place nationwide.

Women and Physician-Assisted Suicide

Still, there is the concern some feminists raise that many more women than men reportedly choose physician-assisted suicide, and that so many of Kevorkian's patients are women. The fear is that, in our society, women are especially vulnerable to the gender-biased pressures of duty and the expectation that they should put the needs and desires of others ahead of their own.

To answer this, it is important to first ask how possible it is to reliably determine anything about requests for physician-assisted suicide. In the present state of the law, few records are kept. Doctors performing illegal acts can hardly write "physician-assisted suicide" on death certificates.

"Physician-assisted death for the terminally ill has nothing to do with the disabled."

If, however, such a sexual disparity were someday verified, it isn't automatically clear how this data should be interpreted. Other highly significant factors could also contribute to a disproportionate number of terminally ill women seeking assisted suicide. For example, there is the fact that women currently live longer, tending to die more slowly from longer-term conditions than do men, and the fact that women tend to feel freer to seek any sort of medical care, to acknowledge pain and suffering, and to classify it as unendurable. By contrast, men who are trained from an early age to be stalwart about pain and sickness, to not show weakness, and to "tough it out" may be less inclined to seek a relief that they, in fact, desire.

> *"Why should we delay establishing a legal right to die for terminally ill patients . . . because we don't yet have a right to adequate health care?"*

Again, we must acknowledge that we cannot guarantee that no one will ever seek physician-assisted suicide in response to unfair social, cultural, family, or other pressures, even those rooted in gender bias. Many aspects of our lives are influenced in some way by enforced gender roles—which are no less despicable than any other sort of bias. So it is just as important to confront and challenge gender bias as it is to work against all other bigotries. . . .

The Disabled and the Poor

Another source of opposition to physician aid in dying comes from some advocates for America's 49 million citizens with disabilities who are rightly concerned about society's tendency to negatively regard the disabled and to devalue their lives. These advocates fear that this attitude will effectively induce many disabled people to seek (or will encourage their families to induce them to seek) an earlier death through assisted suicide.

But the simple truth is that physician-assisted death for the terminally ill has nothing to do with the disabled. Disabled people are not terminally ill. Aid in dying would be available only upon repeated request and only to terminally ill individuals for whom death is imminent. I have encountered the convoluted assertion that to say aid in dying has nothing to do with disabled people is to deny that terminally ill people are disabled. But this is an irrelevant statement devoid of any logical significance. The relevant fact is that the vast majority of disabled people are not terminally ill. A person must be terminally ill to request physician aid in dying, period. . . .

We also hear that no dying person should have to think about the financial aspects of her or his final medical care. Certainly some—perhaps many—may not choose to think about it, but those for whom this issue is of great importance should not be discouraged from doing so. Families should be willing to discuss the question openly when terminally ill relatives express economic concerns. After all, isn't it only natural for the terminally ill to consider the possibility of leaving their families in poverty should they decide to prolong their final dying process? What a tragic legacy to leave to one's family. Not wanting to be remembered in this way is a perfectly valid choice.

Clearly, the problem of how to deal with the allocation of extraordinarily expensive medical treatment is a profound one. We in the right-to-die movement do not claim to have the answer. But we do know that this problem has little to do with voluntary physician-assisted suicide for those whose imminent death the medical profession can do nothing to prevent.

The economics of health care have always been, are now, and always will be profoundly problematic. It is a travesty that some 37 million Americans have no health insurance. But even under the best national health care program we can ever hope to achieve, the economics of death will not go away. So long as we live in a capitalistic system, the rich will always be able to purchase the best medical experts and the best treatment. Why should we delay establishing a legal right to die for terminally ill patients for whom death is inevitably imminent because we don't yet have a right to adequate health care? . . .

Ending Suffering

Still, some otherwise supportive people think that, if adequate palliative care were used, the pain of all terminal illnesses could be controlled and that antidepressant drugs could relieve the depression which results from a dying person's awareness of increasing deterioration and powerlessness. Using these methods, many believe that hospices can facilitate serene and painless death—and we most certainly need better pain management, more palliative care (including more hospices), and a long-avoided acknowledgment of the inevitability of death. These things would alleviate the suffering of many.

But these reforms alone will not stop the needless suffering of all dying patients. The pain of some is intractable and cannot be controlled even in a hospice setting. There are also other sources of suffering: severe physical deterioration and dependency; decline of mental capacities; inability to interact with others; and loss of personal privacy, dignity, and identity, to name a few. Hospice workers are truly compassionate people, and they provide an essential and invaluable service. But these facilities do not provide lethal amounts of drugs to those who desperately want to end their suffering.

That's why we still need the right to ask our doctors to end our lives when our pain or deterioration has become unbearable. Physician-assisted death is the only possible solution for those patients experiencing unrelievable pain or unbearable deterioration who plead with us as fellow human beings to help them die.

> *"Surely our intrinsic right of self-determination must include the next breath we draw."*

We in the right-to-die movement are determined to put an end to the anguish being unjustly inflicted upon the dying and their loved ones. The obscenity of the state denying its citizens the ultimate human and civil right to own and control their own lives and bodies is intolerable. Surely our intrinsic right of self-determination must include the next breath we draw.

We are not arguing for a limitlessly broad right to die. We seek to secure the right of mentally competent, terminally ill individuals to choose a death with dignity and without needless suffering. To quote again from Bishop Spong's House subcommittee testimony:

> I believe that we live in a country which endows its citizens with certain inalienable rights. Among those rights, newly given, is a peculiar gift of this modern world: the right to participate in the management of our own deaths. . . . The legal right to die with dignity is an essential modern freedom from which mature human beings dare not shrink. . . . Assisted suicide must never be a requirement, but it should always be a legal and moral option.

Support for Legalized Physician-Assisted Suicide Is Based on Mistaken Notions

by Ezekiel Emanuel

About the author: *Ezekiel Emanuel is an associate professor at Harvard Medical School. He is also the author of* The Ends of Human Life: Medical Ethics in a Liberal Polity.

In 1996 the Second and Ninth Circuit Courts of Appeals handed down momentous decisions striking down state laws in New York and Washington that forbid physician-assisted suicide. Although the Second and Ninth Circuit Court cases focus on physician-assisted suicide, and although there are important differences between physician-assisted suicide and voluntary euthanasia, the legal reasoning that would justify physician-assisted suicide would almost certainly extend to voluntary euthanasia. The intensity of the debate on both issues will grow during the wait for rulings in 1997 by the Supreme Court, which has accepted the two circuit-court cases for review. [On June 26, 1997, the Supreme Court ruled that the Constitution does not guarantee a "right to die." However, states are not prevented from passing laws that would establish this right.]

In physician-assisted suicide a doctor supplies a death-causing means, such as barbiturates, but the patient performs the act that brings about death. In voluntary euthanasia the physician performs the death-causing act after determining that the patient indeed wishes to end his or her life. . . .

Mistaken Assumptions

In formulating their decisions the circuit-court judges made a number of assumptions about the actual or likely circumstances surrounding cases of death by active intervention. Their judgments are based on misreadings of history, mis-

Reprinted from Ezekiel Emanuel, "Whose Right to Die?" *Atlantic Monthly*, March 1997, by permission of the author.

interpretations of survey data, mistaken reasoning, and simple misinformation.

Myth No. 1: It is primarily advances in biomedical technology—especially life-sustaining technology—that have created unprecedented public interest in physician-assisted suicide and voluntary euthanasia. . . .

Physician-assisted suicide and euthanasia have been profound ethical issues confronting doctors since the birth of Western medicine, more than 2,000 years ago. All the arguments made today to justify—or condemn—the two practices were articulated before any modern biomedical technology existed. The ancient Hippocratic Oath enjoins physicians to "neither give a deadly drug to anybody if asked for it, nor make a suggestion to this effect." The oath was written at a time when physicians commonly provided euthanasia and assisted suicide for ailments ranging from foot infections and gallstones to cancer and senility. Indeed, the Hippocratic Oath represented the *minority* view in a debate within the ancient Greek medical community over the ethics of euthanasia.

Even in America legalized euthanasia, rather than being a new issue, has been publicly debated and rejected—a fact the courts failed to mention. Modern interest in euthanasia in the United States began in 1870, when a commentator, Samuel Williams, proposed to the Birmingham Speculative Club that euthanasia be permitted "in all cases of hopeless and painful illness" to bring about "a quick and painless death." The word "painless" is important: the idea of euthanasia began gaining ground in modern times not because of new technologies for agonizingly prolonging life but because of the discovery of new drugs, such as morphine and various anesthetics for the relief of pain, that could also painlessly induce death. . . . The debate culminated in 1906, after the Ohio legislature took up "An Act Concerning Administration of Drugs etc. to Mortally Injured and Diseased Persons"—a bill to legalize euthanasia. The merits of the act were debated for months and were covered extensively in the pages of the *New York Times*, which vigorously opposed legalization, and in medical journals. The Ohio legislature overwhelmingly rejected the bill, effectively ending that chapter of the euthanasia debate. . . .

Rather than creating a perceived need for physician-assisted suicide and euthanasia, advances in life-sustaining technology should help to

> *"Physician-assisted suicide and euthanasia have been profound ethical issues confronting doctors since the birth of Western medicine."*

obviate them. Patients who are being kept alive by technology and want to end their lives already have a recognized constitutional right to stop any and all medical interventions, from respirators to antibiotics. They do not need physician-assisted suicide or euthanasia.

Myth No. 2: Legalizing physician-assisted suicide and euthanasia is widely endorsed. . . .

Yes, polls show that a majority of Americans support physician-assisted suicide and euthanasia—indeed, have supported legalizing them for almost twenty-five years. But the support is neither strong nor deep. Careful analysis of the polling data suggests that there is a "rule of thirds": a third of Americans support legalization under a wide variety of circumstances; a third oppose it under any circumstances; and a third support it in a few cases but oppose it in most circumstances.

Americans tend to endorse the use of physician-assisted suicide and euthanasia when the question is abstract and hypothetical. . . .

> *"Americans tend to endorse the use of physician-assisted suicide and euthanasia when the question is abstract and hypothetical."*

Other, more carefully designed questions can elicit majority support for physician-assisted suicide and euthanasia, but only when patients are described as terminally ill *and* experiencing unremitting physical pain. Support dwindles when the public is asked about physician-assisted suicide and euthanasia in virtually any other situation. . . . The most accurate characterization of the survey data is that a significant majority of Americans oppose physician-assisted suicide and euthanasia *except* in the limited case of a terminally ill patient with uncontrollable pain.

Why Is Assisted Suicide Requested?

Myth No. 3: It is terminally ill patients with uncontrollable pain who are most likely to be interested in physician-assisted suicide or euthanasia. . . .

The empirical studies of physician-assisted suicide and euthanasia in the Netherlands (where the practices have long been accepted), the United States, and elsewhere indicate that pain plays a minor role in motivating requests for the procedures. A 1996 update of the comprehensive and rigorous 1991 Remmelink Report on euthanasia practices in the Netherlands revealed that in only 32 percent of all cases did pain play any role in requests for euthanasia; indeed, pain was the sole reason for requesting euthanasia in no cases. A study of patients in nursing homes in the Netherlands revealed that pain was among the reasons for requesting physician-assisted suicide or euthanasia in only 29 percent of cases and was the main reason in only 11 percent. A study of physicians in Washington State who admitted to having received requests for physician-assisted suicide or euthanasia revealed that severe pain played a role in only about a third of the requests. A study of HIV-infected patients in New York found that interest in physician-assisted suicide was not associated with patients' experiencing pain or with pain-related limitations on function. My own study of cancer patients, conducted in Boston, reveals that those with pain are more likely than others to oppose physician-assisted suicide and euthanasia. These patients are also more likely to say that they would ask to change doctors if their attending physician indicated that he or she had performed physician-assisted suicide or euthanasia. No study has ever shown that pain plays a major role in motivating patient requests for physician-assisted suicide or euthanasia.

What does motivate requests? According to studies, depression and general psychological distress. . . .

These studies highlight an important conflict between people's actual attitudes and likely medical practice. Many Americans say they would support physician-assisted suicide or euthanasia for patients in pain; they oppose the practices for patients who worry about being a burden, about life's being meaningless, about hopelessness. But patients with depression and psychological distress are most likely to request death; patients in pain are less likely to request it.

Euthanasia in the Netherlands

Myth No. 4: The experience with euthanasia in the Netherlands shows that permitting physician-assisted suicide and euthanasia will not eventually get out of hand.. . . .

The slippery slope feared by opponents and supporters alike is the route from physician-assisted suicide or euthanasia for terminally ill but competent adults to euthanasia for patients who cannot give consent: the unconscious, the demented, the mentally ill, and children. Because the Netherlands is the one developed democracy that has experience with sanctioned euthanasia, advocates and adversaries alike invoke it to defend their points of view. What does the Dutch experience actually show?

Contemporary Dutch policy regarding voluntary euthanasia had its origins in 1973, with the case of a physician, Geertruida Postma, who injected a deaf, partially paralyzed seventy-eight-year-old woman with morphine, ending her life. The patient happened to be Postma's mother. Postma was convicted of murder but given a suspended sentence of one week in jail and one year on probation, a sentence that effectively exonerated her. A subsequent case in 1981 resulted in an agreement between Dutch prosecutors and the Royal Dutch Medical Society, under the terms of which physicians who participated in physician-assisted suicide or euthanasia would not be prosecuted for murder if they adhered to certain guidelines. The main guidelines, parts of which have been incorporated into proposals for outright legalization in other countries, are that 1) the patient must make an informed, free, and explicit request for physician-assisted suicide or euthanasia, and the request must be repeated over time; 2) the patient must be experiencing unbearable suffering—physical or psychological—that cannot be relieved by any intervention except physician-assisted suicide or euthanasia; 3) the attending physician must have a consultation with a second, independent physician to confirm that the case is

> *"No study has ever shown that pain plays a major role in motivating patient requests for physician-assisted suicide or euthanasia."*

appropriate for physician-assisted suicide or euthanasia; and 4) the physician must report the facts of the case to the coroner, as part of a notification procedure developed to permit investigation and to ensure that the guidelines have been followed.

It is important to recognize that despite a widespread perception to the contrary, euthanasia has not been legalized under the Dutch penal code—it remains a crime, albeit one that will not be prosecuted if performed in accordance with the guidelines. Several recent efforts in the Netherlands to overtly legalize physician-assisted suicide and euthanasia have been defeated, primarily because of opposition from Dutch religious authorities. The Dutch rules differ from what U.S. proposals (such as those embodied in a 1994 Oregon measure on physician-assisted suicide) would require in the following respects: they do not stipulate that a patient must be terminally ill, and they do not require that a patient be experiencing *physical* pain or suffering—a patient can be experiencing psychological suffering only.

> *"Providing euthanasia to newborns (upon parental request) is not voluntary euthanasia and does constitute a kind of 'mercy killing.'"*

Not until 1990, a decade after the Dutch rules were promulgated, was the comprehensive and reliable empirical study done of physician-assisted suicide and euthanasia in the Netherlands which resulted in the Remmelink Report. The recent update of this report reveals that of about 9,700 requests for physician-assisted suicide or euthanasia made each year in the Netherlands, about 3,600 are acceded to, accounting for 2.7 percent of all deaths in the Netherlands (2.3 percent from euthanasia, 0.4 percent from physician-assisted suicide). Nearly 80 percent of patients who undergo physician-assisted suicide or euthanasia have cancer, with just 4 percent having neurological conditions such as Lou Gehrig's disease or multiple sclerosis. The report revealed that 53 percent of the Dutch physicians interviewed had participated in physician-assisted suicide or euthanasia at some point in their career; 29 percent had participated within the previous two years. Only 12 percent of the Dutch doctors categorically refused to participate in physician-assisted suicide or euthanasia, most likely for religious reasons.

Problems with the Practice

The 1996 data show small increases in the numbers of requests for physician-assisted suicide and euthanasia since 1990, but the overall changes are undramatic. The new research does indicate, however, that problems identified by the Remmelink Report have by no means been eliminated.

First, the update found that beyond the roughly 3,600 cases of physician-assisted suicide and euthanasia reported in a given year, there are about 1,000 instances of nonvoluntary euthanasia. Most frequently, patients who were no longer competent were given euthanasia even though they could not have freely, explicitly, and repeatedly requested it. Before becoming unconscious or mentally incompetent about half these patients did discuss or express a wish for euthanasia; nevertheless, they were unable to reaffirm their wishes when the euthanasia was performed. Similarly, a study of nursing-home patients found that in only 41 percent of physician-assisted suicide and euthanasia cases did doctors adhere to all the guidelines. Although most of the violations were minor (usually deviations in the notification procedure), in 15 percent of cases the patient did not initiate the request for physician-assisted suicide or euthanasia; in 15 percent there was no consultation with a second physician; in 7 percent no more than one day elapsed between the first request and the actual physician-assisted suicide or euthanasia, violating the guideline calling for repeated requests; and in 9 percent interventions other than physician-assisted suicide or euthanasia could have been tried to relieve the patient's suffering.

Second, euthanasia of newborns has been acknowledged. The reported cases have involved babies suffering from well-recognized fatal or severely disabling defects, though the babies were not in fact dying. Precisely how many cases have occurred is not known. One estimate is that ten to fifteen such cases occur each year. Whether ethically justified or not, providing euthanasia to newborns (upon parental request) is not voluntary euthanasia and does constitute a kind of "mercy killing."

The Netherlands studies fail to demonstrate that permitting physician-assisted suicide and euthanasia will not lead to the nonvoluntary euthanasia of children, the demented, the mentally ill, the old, and others. . . .

Third, the Boudewijn Chabot case raises a warning flag. Chabot, a psychiatrist, participated in the suicide of a depressed fifty-year-old woman in 1991. Her first son had committed suicide a few years earlier. Then her father had died. Under the stress her marriage dissolved. In May of 1991 her second son died of cancer, and less than three months later the woman reached Chabot through the Dutch Voluntary Euthanasia Society, seeking someone to help her end her life. She refused antidepressants and additional psychotherapy. She was never seen by another physician in consultation. When Chabot discussed the case with seven colleagues, at least two suggested that he not assist in the suicide. The Dutch Supreme Court ultimately opted not to penalize Chabot, reaffirming the permissibility of providing assisted suicide and euthanasia on grounds of mental suffering alone.

> *"If the law-abiding Dutch violate their own euthanasia safeguards, what can we expect of Americans?"*

The Amsterdam Medical Disciplinary College did reprimand him, however. . . .

Many in favor of legalization urge caution in applying the experience of the Netherlands to the United States, citing the many significant geographic, cultural, and political differences between the countries. The differences suggest, though, that the kinds of departures from agreed-upon procedures that have occurred in the Netherlands are likely to be even more commonplace in America. Whatever the emerging cultural, ethnic, and religious diversity of the Netherlands, it pales in comparison to the raucous diversity of the United States. And the Dutch have relative income equality, whereas income inequality in the United States is among the greatest in the developed world. Such diversity and inequality make it harder to share norms and to enforce them. The Dutch are also a law-abiding people who view government social supports, interventions, and regulations as legitimate. America is a land founded on opposition to government, where candidates for office campaign against government legitimacy. If the law-abiding Dutch violate their own euthanasia safeguards, what can we expect of Americans?

In the Netherlands physician-assisted suicide and euthanasia are provided in the context of universal and comprehensive health care. The United States has yet to provide such coverage, and leaves tens of millions effectively without health care. Paul van der Maas, the professor of public health who conducted the two Netherlands studies, has said that in the absence of health-care coverage he would be loath to permit euthanasia in the Netherlands, fearing that pressure might be brought to bear on patients and doctors to save money rather than to help patients.

> *"Broad legalization of physician-assisted suicide and euthanasia would have the paradoxical effect of making patients seem to be responsible for their own suffering."*

What, then, should be U.S. policy regarding physician-assisted suicide and euthanasia? Magazine and television stories about patients who want to end their suffering by means of physician-assisted suicide or euthanasia help to reinforce the seemingly inherent link between pain and such interventions. As an oncologist I have often personally cared for patients who suffer despite all available treatment. Only the callous and insensitive would deny that in such cases physician-assisted suicide or euthanasia can offer obvious benefits—can end a life that is worse than death.

But these cases distort the picture. The question is not about whether intervention is right for this or that particular patient. In any given case it may be the ethical thing to do, whatever the law says—and should be done. The question confronting the United States is one of policy: Should we broadly legalize physician-assisted suicide and euthanasia? We must not be swayed by a few—or even a few thousand—wrenching cases in which such intervention seems unequivocally right.

The Benefits and the Dangers

Most of the patients interested in physician-assisted suicide or euthanasia will not be suffering horrific pain. As noted, depression, hopelessness, and psychological distress are the primary factors motivating the great majority. Should their wishes be granted? Our usual approach to people who try to end their lives for reasons of depression and psychological distress is psychiatric intervention—not giving them a syringe and life-ending drugs.

Legalizing physician-assisted suicide and euthanasia, some argue, would not benefit only those who eventually made use of these procedures; it would also provide "psychological comfort" or "reassurance" to millions of other Americans, who would know that if they were dying and things got really bad, they could end their lives. However, the one study we have—the Boston study mentioned previously—shows that for every cancer patient who is likely to be reassured by a discussion of physician-assisted suicide or euthanasia, another patient finds that such a discussion would decrease his or her trust in the care being provided.

> *"Once legalized, physician-assisted suicide and euthanasia would become routine."*

Whatever the benefits of legalized physician-assisted suicide and euthanasia, they must be measured against the dangers of legalization. In considering dangers we must consider more than potential violations of safeguards, although the Dutch experience indicates that the danger is real. (It is hardly surprising that, according to surveys, those who are most opposed to physician-assisted suicide and euthanasia include those most likely to experience abuse and coercion: the old, the less well off, and minorities.) For instance, how would legalization affect our society's already tenuous commitment to providing quality health care for the millions of people who die every year? . . .

Social and Economic Considerations

Broad legalization of physician-assisted suicide and euthanasia would have the paradoxical effect of making patients seem to be responsible for their own suffering. Rather than being seen primarily as the victims of pain and suffering caused by disease, patients would be seen as having the power to end their suffering by agreeing to an injection or taking some pills; refusing would mean that living through the pain was the patient's decision, the patient's responsibility. Placing the blame on the patient would reduce the motivation of caregivers to provide the extra care that might be required, and would ease guilt if the care fell short. Such an easy, thoughtless shift of responsibility is probably what makes most hospice workers so deeply opposed to physician-assisted suicide and euthanasia.

There is one final matter to consider: the possibility that euthanasia not only would be performed on incompetent patients in violation of the rules—as an abuse of the safeguards—but would become the rule in the context of demographic and budgetary pressures on Social Security and Medicare as the Baby Boom generation begins to retire, around 2010.

Once legalized, physician-assisted suicide and euthanasia would become routine. Over time doctors would become comfortable giving injections to end life and Americans would become comfortable having euthanasia as an option. . . .

Advocates of physician-assisted suicide and euthanasia urge legalization for reasons of compassion, but there is no guarantee that the reasons offered in 1997 would remain the justification even a few years ahead, under different social and economic circumstances. The confluence of ethical arguments, medical practice, demographic and budgetary pressures, and a social ethos that views the old and sick as burdens would seem capable of overwhelming any barriers against euthanasia for incompetent patients.

The Correct Policy

The proper policy, in my view, should be to affirm the status of physician-assisted suicide and euthanasia as *illegal*. . . .

By establishing a social policy that keeps physician-assisted suicide and euthanasia illegal but recognizes exceptions, we would adopt the correct moral view: the onus of proving that everything had been tried and that the motivation and rationale were convincing would rest on those who wanted to end a life.

Legalized Physician-Assisted Suicide Would Lead to Abuses

by Stephen Chapman

About the author: *Stephen Chapman is a syndicated columnist.*

In Michigan, Dr. Jack Kevorkian continues to defy the law by helping people kill themselves.

In the Netherlands, things are different. Here, doctors have government permission to assist patients who want to commit suicide—and to euthanize those who are unable to do it themselves.

Institutionalized Abuse

By sanctioning and regulating such practices, the Dutch might be expected to avoid the sort of dangers represented by renegade doctors like Kevorkian. Instead, they have ingeniously managed to institutionalize abuses on a mass scale. Allowing patients to choose their own end may sound fine in principle, but it's been a ghastly mess in practice.

Proposals to allow "aid-in-dying," as it is coyly referred to by its supporters, have already made headway among Americans. In 1994, Oregon voters approved a measure to legalize physician-assisted suicide, and the issue has arisen in several other states. Before embracing the concept, we should ponder how it might actually work.

For that, there is no better place to look than the Netherlands, which maintains a formal ban on euthanasia but furnishes physicians with instructions on how to perform it so as to avoid prosecution. For all intents and purposes, it is legal here for doctors who follow these rules—and, for that matter, those who don't.

The Dutch take pride in their realism and aversion to hypocrisy. By letting doctors accelerate the process of departing this world, they say, they are merely

Reprinted from Stephen Chapman, "The Dutch Show Where 'Aid-in-Dying' Leads," *Conservative Chronicle*, November 29, 1995, by permission of Creators Syndicate.

bringing out into the open a custom that elsewhere is practiced covertly. Doctors have to file a detailed report whenever they bring about someone's demise, giving the public a check on misbehavior.

Unreported Deaths

Even here, though, many of them prefer to operate in the dark. A confidential survey of physicians done in 1991 found there were about 2,300 cases a year in which doctors euthanized patients at their request. But the number of cases reported to the authorities has never come close to that figure. In 1994, only about 1,420 cases were reported. The government admits that hundreds of "mercy killings" take place each year outside the law.

The 1991 survey unearthed a yet more disturbing fact. A doctor is supposed to give a patient a lethal potion only if the patient requests it. But physicians admitted killing about 1,000 patients without their consent.

Did this revelation evoke condemnation and stricter regulation? Not at all. Jacob Visser, a spokesman on medical ethics at the Dutch health ministry, excuses the involuntary deaths. "It saves the patient that last bitter end," he says. In most of the cases, he notes, the doctor consulted the family, and in most of those instances the family consented.

> *"Euthanasia continues to spread beyond rational patients who personally choose it to unconscious or incompetent people whose wishes are not known."*

But that's not how it is supposed to work. The regulations forbid euthanasia unless the patient has made a "voluntary and durable" request based on "full information." Doctors often ignore the most fundamental protection in the law—and the government approves.

Guidelines Are Ignored

Euthanasia continues to spread beyond rational patients who personally choose it to unconscious or incompetent people whose wishes are not known. In 1995, a doctor put to death a fatally handicapped infant at the request of her parents, and a Dutch court ruled he was justified in doing so.

The practice is also not limited to terminally ill patients who are suffering unbearable pain—two more conditions set down in the guidelines. In a survey of patients who asked for euthanasia, only 5 percent cited pain as the main reason they wanted to die.

In 1994, a psychiatrist was acquitted after assisting in the suicide of a physically healthy 50-year-old woman who was distraught over the death of her two sons and the collapse of her marriage. He had not even had her see another doctor (much less another psychiatrist), as the guidelines mandate. But the Royal Dutch Medical Society refused to suspend his license.

Chapter 3

It's hard to see what good the regulations do. Despite widespread violations, few doctors have been prosecuted, fewer still have been convicted and none has ever gone to jail. The guidelines are clear, firm and wholly ineffectual.

Do we want a society in which comatose patients are killed without their consent, handicapped babies are given lethal injections and healthy but unhappy adults can get suicide potions from helpful physicians? If not, we should refuse to take the first step of legalizing assisted suicide. As the Dutch have shown, that is a step onto a slippery slope, leading into a deep abyss.

Legalizing Physician-Assisted Suicide Would Harm Society

by Wesley J. Smith

About the author: *Wesley J. Smith is a consumer advocate and an attorney for the International Anti-Euthanasia Task Force. He is the author of* Forced Exit: The Slippery Slope from Assisted Suicide to Legalized Murder.

One October day in 1991, 58-year-old Marjorie Wantz, and 43-year-old Sherry Miller, kept their rendezvous with death when they met an unemployed pathologist named Jack Kevorkian at a rustic cabin near Detroit. Kevorkian was then still relatively unknown, although more than a year before, he had made headlines after hooking up Janet Adkins, who had early-stage Alzheimer's disease, to a suicide machine that killed her by way of intravenously administered poison. (Adkins died a good ten years prior to when her disease could have been expected to end her life—a time during which it is possible that new treatments for Alzheimer's might have been discovered.) Now, it was Wantz and Miller who wanted to die.

Two Deaths

Neither Miller nor Wantz was terminally ill. Miller was disabled by multiple sclerosis. Wantz complained of severe pelvic pain, but her autopsy would show that she had no organic disease. Not coincidentally, Wantz suffered from a depressive disorder, had been treated in mental hospitals, and according to an article in the *Detroit News,* had been using a sleep aid called Halcion in higher-than-recommended doses. It would never be determined whether or not Kevorkian knew or cared that a potential side-effect of Halcion abuse can be suicidal impulse.

Kevorkian hooked Wantz up to his suicide gadget, and she was soon no more. But he couldn't find a vein in Miller's emaciated arms. Always a tinkerer, he im-

Reprinted from Wesley J. Smith, "Demanding Death-On-Demand," *Heterodoxy,* May/June 1996, by permission of the author and *Heterodoxy* magazine.

provised, rushing out to obtain nails, a canister of carbon monoxide and a face mask, then he jerry-built another suicide machine. Soon, Miller was dead too.

On May 10, 1996, a jury acquitted Kevorkian of the crime of assisting the suicides of Wantz and Miller, despite it being undisputed that he did just that. (He has not been tried in the Adkins case.) [Kevorkian was charged with first-degree murder in Adkins's death, but those charges were dropped.]

Much has been made about the jury's acceptance of Kevorkian's specious claim that he did not intend

> *"We have already fallen far down euthanasia's slippery slope before the practice has even been legalized."*

for the women to die, but merely wanted to alleviate suffering. Yet, in all of the commentary, perhaps the most important point has been missed: the statement by jury members that they did not care a whit that neither Miller nor Wantz were terminally ill. This uncontroverted fact, a defining difference between this case and Kevorkian's other two trials for assisting suicides, simply did not matter to them. . . .

Not Limited to the Terminally Ill

The media usually describes the effort to legalize assisted suicide and euthanasia as being limited to people who are terminally ill. It most definitely isn't. As the shrug of the shoulders by the jury—and the nation—over the Wantz and Miller deaths demonstrates, we have already fallen far down euthanasia's slippery slope before the practice has even been legalized.

Actually, "Right-to-Die" is a misnomer for the euthanasia movement, which should properly be named "Death-on-Demand." If this seems an exaggeration, look beyond the Kevorkian verdict to the George Delury case. George Delury, a former editor of the *World Almanac,* served six months in a New York jail (he actually did four), for attempted second-degree manslaughter. That was the result of a plea bargain. What he really did was pressure his multiple sclerosis-disabled wife, Myrna Lebov, into killing herself, and helped her do it on July 4, 1995.

As soon as the news broke about the assisted suicide, and despite the fact that Myrna Lebov was not terminally ill, many in the death-on-demand movement rushed to Delury's support. The Hemlock Society created a legal defense fund for him. William Batt, chairman of the New York chapter of the organization, expressed confidence, without knowing the facts, that Myrna had not been coerced. Clearly, he opined, most people would want to die if they were in her condition.

Most newspapers, including the *New York Times,* accepted at face value (as they usually do in cases of assisted suicide) Delury's claim that he was merely a compassionate husband only doing what his totally debilitated and suffering wife desperately wanted. But then, the *Forward,* a Jewish weekly, reported that all was not as it seemed. For example, contrary to Delury's claim that his wife's life was merely "biological" when she died, it turned out that Myrna had been able to swim twenty-eight laps with the help of a therapist only a week before her suicide. Her sister, Beverly Sloane, described Myrna as engaged in life, albeit struggling against depression caused in part by an emotionally unsupportive husband. The *Forward* also discovered that Delury had convinced Myrna to accept a buy-out of her monthly disability insurance payments by accepting a check for $50,000, which he then proceeded to cash against her express wishes.

Delury's Diary

Whatever was left of Delury's claim of being motivated by selfless altruism was destroyed when the New York District Attorney's office released the contents of his diary. The diary revealed that Myrna did not have an unwavering and long-time stated desire to die. Her moods waxed and waned, one day suicidal, the next day wanting to engage in life. Moreover, the diary demonstrates that it was Delury, not Myrna, who had the relentless suicide agenda.

Delury admits that he encouraged his wife to kill herself, or, as he put it, "to decide to quit." He researched her anti-depressant medication to see if it could kill her, and when she took less than the prescribed amount, which in and of itself could cause depression, he used the surplus to mix the toxic brew that caused her death. He also helped destroy her will to live by making her feel worthless and a burden on him. For example, on March

> *"Nearly every person experiencing a serious malady . . . would be entitled to euthanasia under the 'hopeless illness' category."*

28,1995, Delury wrote in his diary of his plans to tell Myrna: "I have work to do, people to see, places to travel. But no one asks about my needs. I have fallen prey to the tyranny of a victim. You are sucking my life out of me like a vampire and nobody cares. In fact, it would appear that I am about to be cast in the role of villain because I no longer believe in you."

In short, as one police official put it, George Delury didn't help Myrna Lebov die; he put her out of *his* misery.

And how is this man, a man who emotionally abandoned his non-terminally ill, disabled wife, a man who did nothing to seek treatment for her intermittent suicidal inclinations, a man who literally helped push her into an early grave, being treated? The slap-on-the-wrist jail sentence notwithstanding, Delury has become the new hero of the euthanasia movement. He has purportedly signed a book deal; he has already been a featured speaker in front of the American Psychiatric Association where he appears to have been warmly received, and he was lauded by Charles Grodin as a "remarkable figure" who should "not be going to jail" when Delury was a guest on Grodin's CNBC talk show.

Which brings us back to Death-on-Demand versus the Right to Die. In response to Myrna Lebov's death, the *New York Times* editorialized that the Delury matter, "strengthens the case for allowing qualified medical professionals to assist *desperately ill patients* with no hope of recovery to die with dignity." (My emphasis.) The term "desperately ill" is carefully chosen. It implies terminal illness but actually means something quite different. Indeed, the term is used interchangeably in euthanasia advocacy for the more popular "hopelessly ill." According to euthanasia advocates, not only terminally ill but also hopelessly ill people should have a legal right to receive help in committing what proponents call "rational suicide."

Defining Illness

So, who are the "hopelessly ill"? Tens of millions of people among us qualify. One common definition was published in the summer 1995 issue of the journal, *Suicide and Life Threatening Behavior,* based on a survey of psychiatrists who support the concept of rational suicide. According to this definition, hopeless conditions "include but are not necessarily limited to, terminal illnesses, maladies causing severe physical and/or psychological pain, physically or mentally debilitating and/or deteriorating conditions, circumstances where quality of life is no longer acceptable to the individual." In other words, nearly every person experiencing a serious malady, from arthritis, diabetes, and chronic migraine headaches, to paraplegia caused by polio, chronic depression, schizophrenia, HIV, and Alzheimers disease—you name it—would be entitled to euthanasia under the "hopeless illness" category. This is Death-on-Demand.

To help understand the radical devolution in medical ethics now under way in America, we need only look to the Netherlands, historically one of the world's most enlightened nations, which has already blazed this particular trail before us. Euthanasia has never been legalized in the Netherlands, but it will not be prosecuted if Dutch doctors who kill their patients follow so-called protective guidelines. Among these guidelines are the need for the request for death to be made repeatedly, that the request be the patient's and only the patient's, the necessity of a second medical opinion, and the presence of "suffering" that cannot be otherwise alleviated except by death.

Dutch euthanasia began in 1973 when a court refused to meaningfully punish a doctor who had euthanized her aged mother. The court ruled that even though the doctor violated the law, she should not be held accountable because Dutch doctors had achieved consensus about euthanasia, believing it to be ethical and appropriate in a limited number of cases. That being so, the court reasoned, the law should follow the medical consensus, rather than the statute which criminalized euthanasia.

> *"It has gotten to a point in the Netherlands that you don't even have to be physically ill to obtain doctor-hastened death."*

In theory, the hastened death of Dutch patients is supposed to be a rare event, only to be used in the most intractable cases. In actual practice, however, death-causing "medical" practices have expanded almost geometrically, demonstrat-ing empirically the severe incline of the slippery slope. Thus, today, in Holland, you need not be terminally ill to be killed by your doctor. If you can convince your doctor that your suffering is irremediable, you can experience Death-on-Demand. For example, cases have been documented of an asymptomatic HIV positive man being killed (so much for "living" with AIDS) and a woman who had anorexia. There is even one unconfirmed report of a dancer being euthanized because she developed arthritis in her feet and could no longer perform.

> *"The actual practice of euthanasia, once legitimized, is soon virtually uncontrolled."*

It has gotten to a point in the Netherlands that you don't even have to be physically ill to obtain doctor-hastened death. A few years ago, one Dr. Boudewijn Chabot, a psychiatrist, was trolling a Dutch euthanasia society, looking for patients. From that contact, he began treating a woman whose two children had died over the course of several years (one by suicide), and whose marriage had recently dissolved. The woman was deeply depressed and suici-dal. After only five weeks of "treatment," Dr. Chabot assisted in her suicide.

Chabot was charged with the crime of assisted suicide. This is less serious than it sounds. Unlike in the United States, Dutch trials are not based on the ad-versary system. Thus, prosecutors sometimes file cases not to punish wrongdo-ers, but rather to establish a precedent permitting a specific activity. This is the method by which euthanasia practices have expanded in the Netherlands over the years, as was the intent behind the Chabot prosecution.

Both prosecutor and defendant got what they were looking for. The Dutch Supreme Court blessed a lower court ruling that while Dr. Chabot had commit-ted the crime, he should not be punished for his actions. The basis of the ruling was that the law cannot distinguish between suffering caused by physical ill-ness and that caused by mental anguish. Thus, the "guidelines" now permit doctors in the Netherlands to kill patients who are depressed.

Thanks to two other "prosecutions," euthanasia has formally entered the pedi-atric ward. Recently a Dutch trial court refused to punish a doctor who killed a baby born with spina bifida and hydrocephaly. The doctor testified that he killed the child (with her parents' permission) because of the infant's poor prog-nosis and because the baby screamed in pain when touched. Yet, to show the self-justifying, circular thinking involved in medicalized killing, the child was in agony because she was not given medical treatment to correct her medical problems! Moreover, this particular case merely formalizes the already existing consensus among Dutch pediatricians permitting infanticide of dying or dis-abled babies. Once the Dutch Supreme Court approves the lower court's deci-

sion, as it undoubtedly will, the legal precedent will be established allowing babies to be killed based on quality-of-life considerations, even though they cannot ask to be killed.

Despite the guidelines proscribing euthanasia unless specifically requested by
the patient, Dutch doctors also engage in involuntary euthanasia. According to a
1991 Dutch Government-sponsored study (the Remmelink Report), more than
one thousand people were euthanized involuntarily in 1990. (If the same pro-
portionate number were involuntarily euthanized in the U.S., sixteen thousand
per year would be killed without request or consent.) This illustrates a key point
usually ignored by euthanasia proponents: Guidelines are mere window dress-
ing to alleviate public fears. The actual practice of euthanasia, once legitimized,
is soon virtually uncontrolled.

The Courts' Views

Is this really the future we want in the United States? Apparently so, at least
according to Judge Stephen Reinhardt and seven other judges in the Ninth Circuit Court of Appeals, who have ruled that Washington State's law against assisted suicide is unconstitutional. The decision, *Compassion in Dying v. Washington,* formally creates, out of whole cloth, a new "right to die" as a fundamental liberty interest.

> *"Legalized euthanasia would be especially profitable for the for-profit health-care-financing industry."*

The way down the slippery slope can actually be seen in the decision itself. The court formally ruled that a mentally competent, terminally ill
patient has a constitutional right to doctor-assisted suicide. But the court's ac-
tual language goes much farther than that, opening the door to Death-on-Demand. For example, the court opined that the right to be killed should extend to
the disabled, ruling that "seriously impaired individuals, along with non-im-
paired individuals, will be the beneficiaries of the liberty interest asserted here."

Death decisions based on money were also approved, Judge Reinhardt being
"reluctant to say" that people who want to die, should not "take the economic
welfare of their families and loved ones into consideration."

Nor, are the incompetent safe, under the ruling. The court specifically stated
in footnote 120 that "the decision of a duly appointed surrogate to hasten death
is for all legal purposes the decision of the patient himself."

(The Second Circuit Court of Appeals in New York has also ruled that assisted suicide is a constitutional right for dying people. That ruling was based
on the equal protection clause of the 14th Amendment. Both the Ninth and Second Circuit rulings are currently stayed. It is likely that both cases will end up
in the United States Supreme Court, especially since the Michigan Supreme
Court ruled that laws prohibiting assisted suicide are constitutional.) [On June
26, 1997, the U.S. Supreme Court ruled that the Constitution does not grant

Americans the "right to die." However, states are not precluded from passing laws that would establish this right.]

Money Matters

What is driving this rush off the ethical cliff? Looking at the big picture, one realizes that euthanasia is a symptom, not a cause—just one more manifestation of the breakdown of community and of our mutual interconnectedness, the consequences of which can be seen all around us. We have no doubt that the disintegration of family cohesiveness is part of this syndrome, along with the growing nihilism among young people leading to a rise in suicides, drug use, and other destructive behaviors. Why is it that we don't recognize that the growing urge to write off sick and dying people as having lives so meaningless and unimportant that their killing can be countenanced is part of this cheapening and coarsening of life?

The desire to free-up social space and to get rid of the unseemly (dressed up, of course, in the language of social uplift) is one reason for the euthanasia juggernaut. A less visible, but perhaps more influential, force is money. Think of the money government and nonprofit organizations won't have to spend if ill, disabled, and elderly people can be killed rather than receive long-term care. Moreover, legalized euthanasia would be especially profitable for the for-profit health-care-financing industry. Unlike fee-for-service medicine, with HMOs a penny saved is a penny earned. Just imagine the money that can be saved by not treating AIDS patients, or cancer patients, or people with physical disabilities, because they have chosen or been coerced into choosing an early exit.

Bluntly stated, if euthanasia is legalized, Wall Street investors who invest in for-profit HMOs will be dancing in the streets. Surely it is no coincidence then, that the ethics regarding end-of-life care have changed just as the money imperative has changed. When health care profits were made on a fee-for-service basis, the prevailing medical ethic was to keep patients alive at all cost, or at least until the insurance ran out. Now that managed care is supplanting fee-for-service, we suddenly hear much talk about "good death" and "death with dignity." It is thus no surprise that health care foundations are among the primary financiers of the many bioethics think tanks and other "researchers" who promote assisted suicide within the medical community and/or propagandize medical professionals with so-called "Right-to-Die" seminars. Once doctors accept the premise, everyone else will go along.

> *"If embraced as social policy, Kevorkianism will destroy the ethic which has proclaimed the sanctity of life for the last two thousand years."*

What gets lost in all of this is that there are humane, compassionate, and dignified alternatives to killing suffering people, such as hospice-care, pain control, treatment for depression, and other care opportunities. The tragedy is that these underutilized and underfunded programs—which can make all the difference in the lives of suffering people, changing a desire to die into a drive to live—receive short shrift in a media increasingly driven by ratings, sensationalism, superficiality and violence.

A Look into the Future

So, where do we go from here? If the recent court rulings and acquittals of Kevorkian are any indication, the nation seems to be heading toward legalizing "medical" practices that will permit doctors to kill patients. This may be one of those trends in our increasingly individualistic and "rights"-driven society that will be hard to stop. But the implications of this path ought at least to be made clear. If embraced as social policy, Kevorkianism will destroy the ethic which has proclaimed the sanctity of life for the last two thousand years, and with it our traditional Western understanding that all human beings are to be considered of equal inherent worth, whose lives are equally deserving of protection by the state. It will also radically change killing from the rare event which cannot be undertaken by private individuals at all except under extraordinary circumstances (i.e., self-defense), nor by the state except when based on the conduct of the condemned person and, then, only after due process of law.

Where this radical change in the nation's foundational ethic will ultimately take us is anybody's guess. However, our old friend, Jack Kevorkian, gives a clue. On page 214 of his book, *Prescription: Medicide*, Kevorkian made it clear that easing suffering is not his primary goal in assisting suicides. Rather, he states: "[W]hat I find most satisfying is the prospect of making possible the performance of invaluable experiments or other beneficial medical acts under conditions that this first unpleasant step [assisted suicide] can help establish." In other words, Kevorkian's ultimate goal is to use living human beings as guinea pigs in "medical" experiments, as part of their death process.

Although barely reported in the media, under cross-examination in two trials, Kevorkian was forced to concede his goal of establishing the right for doctors, and even nondoctors, to experiment on living patients who have chosen to have their deaths hastened. Illustrating the collapse of critical thinking in this country, and the progressive decay of American culture, even this macabre admission did not affect the juries who acquitted him, or the public's seeming approval of Kevorkian's ends and means.

If we don't return to our senses, if through passivity or judicial tyranny, we permit euthanasia to become just another "medical treatment," big trouble will lie ahead. As we grow desensitized to medicalized killing, the hastened deaths of ill and suffering people will eventually become banal, just as killing brain-damaged people by withdrawing their food and fluids already has. What seems a slippery slope will then be revealed as an ethical abyss that may have no bottom.

Legalized Physician-Assisted Suicide Would Damage the Physician-Patient Relationship

by Jon Fuller

About the author: *Jon Fuller is the assistant director of the Clinical AIDS Program at Boston Medical Center and an assistant clinical professor of medicine at Boston University School of Medicine.*

The contemporary physician-assisted suicide movement has been propelled by the fear that unless a suicide "escape hatch" becomes available, one's dying could become a painful, alienating experience characterized by inappropriate use of technology, even against one's expressed wishes.

The Dying Are Treated Poorly

Unfortunately, an avalanche of data suggests that these fears are well founded. For example, despite the five-year, $25 million SUPPORT [Study to Understand Prognoses and Preferences for Outcomes and Risks of Treatments] study designed to identify and correct problems associated with end-of-life care, post-intervention observations showed little improvement in physician skills regarding the use of do-not-resuscitate orders, intensive care units, pain relief or hospital resources. Among the more than 4,000 patients who died in the post-intervention phase, 10 percent received more care than they wanted and 40 percent had severe pain most of the time. In early June 1997 the Institute of Medicine became the latest professional organization to castigate physicians for what it described as "preventable pain and stress at the end of life." In the words of their report: "The experience is so poorly managed by doctors and other health workers, as well as insurers, that many people see death as a degrading, painful episode that leads to talk of assisted suicide."

Reprinted from Jon Fuller, "Physician-Assisted Suicide: An Unnecessary Crisis," *America*, July 19, 1997, by permission of the author.

We should not be facing this crisis. If patients trusted that their physicians would appropriately treat pain and anxiety as they approached death, there would be no need to look to suicide as a means of escape, and this angry and anxious backlash would not have developed. But even if we agree that the fundamental solution to this problem is to provide more competent terminal care, debate is likely to continue, even though the U.S. Supreme Court on June 26, 1997, unanimously rejected two Federal circuit court opinions that proposed to grant constitutional status to a right to commit suicide for terminally ill patients.

> *"Granting [the power to perform physician-assisted suicide] to physicians would sully our subconscious image of the healer."*

For the sake of this discussion, I will not treat the more general question of whether suicide could ever be moral. My own belief is that the conditions of our stewardship do not give us control over our own life and death. Here, however, I am not defending that belief but addressing the question at hand, which is whether it is appropriate for society to allow physicians to use their knowledge and power to assist patients who voluntarily request help in taking their lives.

Two Arguments Against Physician-Assisted Suicide

I will argue that even if society believes that in certain circumstances a terminal patient may take his or her own life, physician-assisted suicide should not be permitted for two reasons: First, such a practice could be highly vulnerable to abuse and to conflicts of interest on the part of physicians, thereby causing harm to individual patients. The second, intertwined reason is that granting this power to physicians would sully our subconscious image of the healer, which is the basis of the doctor-patient relationship, and thus threaten the capacity of the community to heal itself. While these arguments might be viewed by some as consequentialist in nature, they are rather based on a virtue ethics analysis that is focused on the question of who we are becoming (as individuals and as a society) as a result of our decisions and actions.

If previous experience is any guide, it is unlikely that regulatory oversight will provide a robust limit on the exercise of a power to assist patients in committing suicide, even if the law requires certain procedures, such as confirmation by a physician's colleagues of a patient's terminal status and desire for death. This supposition is based on the experience in the Netherlands of a gradual loosening of legal compliance in cases of voluntary and involuntary euthanasia and on the observation that despite legislation enacted precisely to curb his activities, Jack Kevorkian, M.D., has never been convicted. If it were to become even more risk-free than it is at present for physicians to assist in suicide, it is not so difficult to imagine that some patients would seek out doctors known to have very low thresholds for complying with such requests. After all, if the basis of a legal right to suicide lies in autonomy, one does not have to be non-depressed—or even provide a good reason—in order to exercise that right.

A second area of concern regards conflicts of interest on the part of physicians. Here I think of two principal sources of conflict: workload and finances. With respect to the former, caring for dying patients can be quite labor-intensive and emotionally draining. It is not difficult to imagine that the stress of providing this care might influence decisions regarding assisted suicide, as was most dramatically documented in the landmark anonymous article published in the *Journal of the American Medical Association* in 1988 entitled "It's Over Debbie." In that report, a physician in

> *"If I as a physician have something to gain . . . then the request to assist with suicide will not be viewed impartially."*

training, who describes himself as having come to detest middle-of-the-night phone calls because of how bad they make him feel the next day, gets just such a call to see a 20-year-old woman dying of ovarian cancer. He describes his passage from the on-call room to see her: "I trudged along, bumping sleepily against walls and corners . . . not believing I was up again." He comes upon a wasted figure who hasn't eaten or slept in two days and who is starving for air, evidence of a gross failure to provide even basic palliative care. After she says her only words to him, "Let's get this over with," he returns with an intravenous injection of 20 milligrams of morphine, which kills her within five minutes.

When Debbie died his life became easier. Clearly, he was not free of bias in deciding whether to respond to her request. I can attest to the level of stress that a night on call can bring with it and to the negative psychological reactions that such stress can engender. In fact, the deep resentment toward patients that can develop in young physicians as a result of long hours and unrelenting workloads is a major argument in favor of modifying the structure of graduate medical education. But I can also attest that in my 14 years as a physician, despite the short tempers and regressive behavior I have sometimes seen under such stressed circumstances, I have never doubted that the physicians involved were acting in the best interests of their patients despite the personal cost. If suicide became an option that one could offer patients in the middle of the night, it is not clear how an unbiased approach to that option would be possible, especially by an exhausted, irritable physician.

Financial Conflicts

A second potential conflict of interest is financial. Seven- , eight- and nine-figure salaries for the C.E.O.s of health maintenance organizations [H.M.O.] make it clear that managed care is about making profit by cutting cost, and in this sense it has radically reconfigured the psychology of health care delivery. "Covered lives," that is, the members enrolled in a plan, are becoming commodities that are competed for, much like a company might try to submit the lowest bid to win a construction contract.

Physicians are increasingly the hired agents of this invisible third party, which may be in the relationship with a patient not primarily for the individual's welfare, but rather to make a profit—which is achieved in part by limiting services. In the worst-case scenario, a physician whose contract with an H.M.O. includes sharing in the financial risk for the cost of delivering care will have a blatant conflict of interest, making it personally attractive to accede to the wish of a depressed patient to end life. As Woody Allen once observed, "Death is a great way to save money."

If I as a physician have something to gain—less work, more sleep, less risk to my financial status—then the request to assist with suicide will not be viewed impartially. In this regard, Dr. Shimon Glick reminds us in the *American Journal of Medicine* of the Jewish Halakhic tradition's insistence that it is permissible in grave circumstances to pray for a suffering patient's demise, as long as one is not directly involved in the care of the patient and thereby vulnerable to having a conflict of interest. This position appears to be consistent with the Hippocratic Oath itself, for after pledging to use one's skills for the patient's benefit, the oath specifically notes that the physician will give no deadly medicine, even if asked. While it has been argued that for some individuals being able to commit suicide would be a benefit, Hippocrates is quite explicit that it is a benefit that cannot be conferred by the physician.

The Physician-Patient Relationship

While my first argument relates to harm to individual patients through abuse of power or through conflicts of interest, my second has to do with potential damage done to the common good. If you will allow me to use Jungian imagery to make what I believe is a very concrete point, I would argue that adding the capacity for actively taking life to the armamentarium of physicians would radically mar the archetype of the physician-healer that is carried in the collective unconscious.

Patients give physicians wide access to intimate knowledge—comparable to the trust given to priests and psychotherapists—and there is no comparison to be made to the dropping of physical barriers that occurs in the relationship. Such unparalleled trust and access is granted on the premise that the patient's self-interest is always the physician's priority, and that no advantage will be taken of the pa-

> *"I believe that it is the power of the doctor-patient relationship as much as anything else that is the source of healing."*

tient's vulnerable position. This is why acting on a romantic impulse in such a relationship must be taboo, lest the personal disinterest of the physician be compromised or doubted.

Society also grants physicians permission to "let go" of life precisely because the physician is theoretically best positioned, given the wishes of the particular individual, to know when and how it might be appropriate to withdraw various levels of support. Society even allows physicians indirectly to hasten death through the appropriate use of medications that alleviate pain and anxiety. In these life and death decisions, we consciously and unconsciously trust that our loved ones are receiving care that has their best interests at heart.

> *"The power we give to physicians is a manifestation of the healing that we desire for ourselves."*

In contrast, participation in the active taking of life, even if only by prescribing medications that a patient will self-administer, crosses a threshold and threatens the trust in beneficence that is the root of the physician-patient relationship. Our collective unconscious must already contend with living memories of the abuse of the physician's power, most notoriously in the Nazi medical experiments and in the Tuskegee project. [The project was a government study in which treatment was withheld from a group of African American men who had syphilis.]

A Distrust of Doctors

I work in an inner-city AIDS clinic, where the majority of patients are members of minority communities. There are also a significant number of immigrants who are unfamiliar with and mistrustful of the Western medical system. Tuskegee is quite prominent in the minds of many of them, as are conspiracy theories that H.I.V. was created by the U.S. Government as a way to wage war on blacks—a position that is not contradicted by the increasingly disproportionate burden of AIDS that is borne by minority communities. Not a few believe that AZT is a poison being distributed as part of a related conspiracy.

Whatever one might make of the historical foundation for these viewpoints, they nevertheless have captured the imaginations of many and account for some of the distrust and suspicion that I encounter, and perhaps for some of the delay that is observed in seeking care until long after learning that one is H.I.V.-positive. If the exercise of power by the physician were now legally extended to assisting patients in taking their lives, I can imagine that this would quite reasonably raise even more serious doubts in the minds of many who are already ambivalent about engaging the health care system. In this regard, Dr. Kathleen Foley has commented in the *New England Journal of Medicine* that liberalized assisted suicide legislation in northern Australia has led to an increased distrust of the medical system on the part of aboriginal peoples in the region. [Australia's national parliament has repealed the Northern Territory legislation.]

My chief concern is that this communal loss of confidence in the physician's disinterest will not just damage an individual relationship. I believe that it is the power of the doctor-patient relationship as much as anything else that is the source of healing; it is the relationship, the commitment of one to another for the sake of the other, that elicits a power for self-care and integration in the client. Just as the confessional seal must be absolute lest anyone have doubts about approaching the sacrament, so must the public image of the physician not include the power for taking life lest patients have the slightest fear that their provider might not always be acting in their interest. If this relationship that supports self-integration is compromised, so is its power, and this would weaken one of society's most important healing resources.

Reducing Anxiety

In the best-case scenario, the physician is viewed by society as a professional who is familiar and comfortable with the ways of nature and with the rhythms and stages of human life, who recognizes the waxing and waning of biological processes, who knows when the tide has changed and it is time to take a different tack, who has the skills and tools to ease the transition to death and to maximize comfort both for the patient and for her family and loved ones. Helping patients and family members to understand the provision of adequate analgesia and the possibility of withdrawing support as ways of gently succumbing to the power of nature maintains an ethic of dignity and a relationship with the natural order of the universe. If in such circumstances a patient or family member had to contend with anxiety about the physician's personal approach to suicide, or if the family became concerned that the physician might gain personally if a surreptitious request for suicide on the part of the patient were to be honored, this could add an enormous layer of doubt and anxiety about the physician's true intentions and loyalties at a time that is already emotionally freighted: "Is he giving that much pain medicine because it is really necessary, because Mother has asked him to kill her or because he's trying to end her life to save money?"

I am not dealing here with whether suicide in the face of extreme suffering can or cannot be morally justified, a question Prof. Margaret Farley of Yale University has explored. I am proposing rather that, even if justifiable, this should not become the province of medical care. If society decides that the option of assisted suicide should be made available on some basis to terminally ill patients, there is no reason why this could not be provided by an agency created for the purpose. After all, taking one's life is not usually a technically difficult end to accomplish, as the Heaven's Gate tragedy demonstrated.

I would like to believe that my arguments are not simply a self-serving attempt to maintain the public relations image of a profession that has created the very problem we are addressing. My position, I hope, is more concerned with the impact that such a policy change would have on the community's power to heal itself; for ultimately the healer archetype does not belong to the profession, but to the community. It is an expression of our desire for health, for integration, for life. The power we give to physicians is a manifestation of the healing that we desire for ourselves, and "going to the doctor" is an implicit enactment of a desire to be well, to be whole. If we add to the physician's power the capacity to take life, is this not a reflection of communal ambivalence about healing and wholeness versus despair and withdrawal? We must be careful not to let our communal archetype become two-headed, lest we impair our desire and capacity for maintaining health and life.

Chapter 4

How Would Assisted Suicide Affect Individuals' Rights?

CURRENT CONTROVERSIES

Chapter Preface

A 1994 Dutch television show depicted the last few months in the life of Cees van Wendel, a man who had amyotrophic lateral sclerosis (ALS)—a terminal illness. Van Wendel had chosen assisted suicide, which is permitted in the Netherlands if certain rules are followed. What was not clear from the program was how free his decision to commit suicide was. In the footage, his wife, Antoinette, does not allow him to speak in private with his doctor, Wilfred van Oijen; she is not shown touching her husband; and she discourages van Oijen from comforting the sobbing man. It was not clearly evident whether van Wendel chose death because he wished to die or because he was influenced by his wife's actions.

Supporters say that legalized assisted suicide would respect the rights of individuals. They argue that if the practice were legalized, safeguards would be devised to ensure that no American would be coerced into an assisted death. In testimony before a House subcommittee hearing on proposed assisted suicide legislation, Bishop John Shelby Spong asserted, "Assisted suicide must never be a requirement, but it should always be a legal and moral option."

However, opponents cite the Dutch program and similar examples as indications that assisted suicide, if widely legalized in the United States, will become not a choice but an obligation thrust upon the dying by their families, friends, and society. These critics maintain that the elderly, the disabled, and the uninsured may all be encouraged to choose assisted suicide rather than drain their families' financial resources and patience. As Catholic ethicist Sidney Callahan writes, "If suicide were culturally validated, an ill person would have to justify his or her decision to keep on living."

Many writers have grappled with the question of whether dying people can truly determine their future without being influenced (intentionally or not) by outside forces. In the following chapter, the authors consider whether individual rights are threatened or protected by assisted suicide.

Assisted Suicide Would Threaten the Nonfatally Ill

by David Morrison

About the author: *David Morrison is a researcher and writer for Human Life International, a pro-life organization that conducts research on topics such as euthanasia, population, and abortion. He is also the editor of* PRI Review, *a bimonthly publication that covers worldwide population and development issues.*

Everyone, with the exception of the people who killed her, agrees the only serious things from which Judith Curren suffered were depression and a series of physical symptoms associated with having to carry 269 pounds on a 5′ 1″ frame. Yet for Jack Kevorkian, Michigan's first self-appointed "obitiatrist," this was enough.

Kevorkian joined Judith's husband, Franklin Curren, and a member of the newly formed Physicians for Mercy in killing Judith on 16 August 1996. The mother of two girls, age 10 and 7, was 42 years old.

But of all Kevorkian's victims, Judith Curren may be recognized as the most important because it is her life, suffering and murder which might, finally, awaken the popular mind to what is really at stake in Kevorkian's grisly carnival.

A Troubled Marriage

Although accounts conflict, the bulk of media reports indicate the Currens shared a discordant and turbulent marriage. During the course of almost five years, the couple lived in Winchester, a posh suburb north of Boston. Police were called to their home at least eight times after receiving complaints of domestic abuse. Officers reported Franklin Curren, a psychiatrist, had an "arrogant demeanor" during the course of these calls, an attitude they found puzzling and which "troubled" them.

Police records also show that Judith Curren spoke repeatedly about her need to obtain a court restraining order against her husband, but each time she had "lost her resolve." Finally, in 1993, she filed an affidavit in Woburn District Court alleging that over a two-day period Franklin Curren had broken into their

Reprinted, with permission, from David Morrison, "Killing Us Softly: Kevorkian's Widening Web of Death Snares the Nonfatally Ill," *Human Life International Reports*, October 1996.

home, destroyed property and threatened her.

She further alleged, in a sworn statement, that during her 1988 pregnancy Franklin Curren "punched" her and "fractured several ribs." On 26 July 1996, police arrested Curren for abusing his wife, and he spent the weekend in jail. The court ordered him to undergo counseling and scheduled a follow-up hearing for 7 October 1996. But then his wife died some seven weeks prior to this date.

Issues of Abuse

Police have questioned Curren about Judith's death, but he has denied all intentions to murder and has said that the couple's fights were caused by his refusal to entertain her "death wish," although he finally appears to have enthusiastically approved the killing.

"You have to understand what seems like a horror to us was welcomed by her as the ultimate peace," Curren told reporters after Judith's murder. "It was what she wanted."

Judith Curren's murder at the hands of, among others, an allegedly abusive husband, brings into the open the issues of power, control, expectation and desperation which lurk beneath every case of patient-killing but which the advocates of death and a compliant media either smooth over or fail to discern.

Judith had been one of Franklin Curren's patients before their marriage, a circumstance not formally disapproved by the American Psychiatric Association but at least considered ethically complicated because of the potential for abuse.

Dangerous Drug Use

After they married, Franklin continued to prescribe medication for his wife, and one of the two complaints against his medical practice concern "improper" prescriptions for Judith. At the time of her murder his wife was taking four moderately strong medications, including Xanax, Percocet, Tylenol 4 and Nifedipine.

Two of these, Percocet and Tylenol 4, list dysphoria or depression among their adverse conditions, with Tylenol 4 carrying a particular warning when taken with Xanax. Xanax itself causes obesity in 27 percent of the people who take it.

> *"Judith Curren's murder . . . brings into the open the issues of power, control, expectation and desperation which lurk beneath every case of patient-killing."*

There are no known records of any search for alternative medications for Judith. Nor is it known whether her husband ever formally questioned her continuing medication over a long time. Franklin declared later that although he was not "the primary decision maker" in his wife's case, if "he felt something was wrong" he would "tell the doctors."

No one has yet asked why, as her husband, he apparently found nothing wrong with his obese and depressed wife continuing to take drugs documented to make their users sadder and fatter. Or why, if these measures had not been taken, two medical doctors joined her husband in killing her "to relieve her suffering."

Judith Curren suffered a mixture of drugs, obesity, pain and abuse in her life. Absent any apparent substantial effort to relieve these, is it any wonder that Judith began to crave death, if only to escape a situation in which she was refused help from those most expected to care for her?

People Are Not Autonomous

The question of who controls such "voluntary" decisions is of crucial importance, if not in the moral sphere then at least in the realm of public policy.

In the Netherlands, the one country in the world to have administratively allowed patient-killing, Judith Curren's death would not have been unusual. According to a survey conducted by the Dutch government, families listed the "inability to take it anymore" as the third most common reason for killing a "loved one" without the relative's consent.

God did not create human beings, as John Donne knew, to be autonomous, self-supporting units but to be part of a larger social fabric. In the end we are only as strong as our social links and when those links grow brittle, or overstrained, we need the protection of a strong life ethic to prevent our sacrifice on the altar of convenience or even "mercy."

> *"God did not create human beings . . . to be autonomous, self-supporting units but to be part of a larger social fabric."*

Judith's death also brought further into public view an organization of other physicians which has been formed and sworn to assist Kevorkian in his ghoulish crusade. The Physicians for Mercy first announced its existence in late 1995 at a press conference in which its members professed the intention to begin working as "obitiatrists," physicians who will specialize in killing their patients. They even announced the promulgation of a new set of "guidelines" for the procedure.

Judith Curren had one of these doctors present for her murder and no one has asked how her case fit the Physicians for Mercy's guidelines—whether, for example, she had signed "a written statement that she wanted to die" or whether it was witnessed by people with no "financial interest" in her death. She certainly did not seem to fit the criteria of having an "incurable condition" subject to "medically uncontrollable pain" and yet the "merciful physician" helped kill her anyway.

A Frightened Public

Judith Curren's murder presents the saddest and most savage of all Kevorkian's killings so far, but it is still not the most widely known. Since Judith's death on 16 August 1996, Kevorkian has murdered five more people (at this writing), all weak, depressed and abandoned by the men and women pledged to care most for them.

But there are signs that Judith's death, like each of these others, is failing to motivate an increasingly cynical and frightened public. Richard Thompson, the prosecutor in Oakland County, the public official who pursued Jack Kevorkian through two recent murder trials, lost his bid for re-election in the 1996 Republican primary by a surprisingly wide margin.

Both trials ended with Kevorkian being found innocent and Thompson read his loss as a sign of voters' displeasure that he even tried. "Did I do something politically wrong?" Thompson asked rhetorically at a post-election press conference. "Yes, I prosecuted Jack Kevorkian."

Although other public officials questioned whether voters were criticizing Thompson's attempts or his methods, it seems clear that Jack Kevorkian is not exaggerating when he steps before cameras and claims the public's good will. Whether based upon a misunderstanding of their rights as patients or perhaps an awareness of their familial fragility, a significant number of people fear extended suffering more than they fear Jack Kevorkian.

It is this confusion and fear which dominates the current political landscape on this issue. And in a sad way, Kevorkian's "success," in and of itself, feeds his progress. Dr. Stanton Elias, who works to assist patients with multiple sclerosis (MS) at Detroit's Henry Ford Hospital, has reported the morale of other people with MS has fallen every time Kevorkian kills another one.

"It was extremely demoralizing for [multiple sclerosis patients]" Elias said of one MS patient's death. "They were questioning if others devalue [their] value as human beings."

Assisted Suicide Would Threaten the Rights of the Disabled

by Evan J. Kemp Jr.

About the author: *Evan J. Kemp Jr. was chair of the Equal Employment Opportunity Commission during President George Bush's administration. He is senior partner of Evan Kemp Associates, Inc., a health and mobility company owned and operated by disabled people.*

On Jan. 8, 1997, the Supreme Court heard oral arguments in *Washington v. Glucksberg* and *Vacco v. Quill*. At issue is the question of whether or not "terminally ill" individuals have an inherent "right to die." And, if so, should a licensed physician be granted the legal right to assist in the "suicide" of a patient? [On June 26, 1997, the U.S. Supreme Court ruled that the Constitution does not guarantee a "right to die." However, states are not precluded from passing laws that would establish this right.]

As the case was argued inside the Court, thousands kept vigil outside the Court. I was among them.

Rationing Health Care

You might ask, "Why would a conservative Republican who served as the chair of the U.S. Equal Employment Opportunity Commission in the Bush administration join Clinton Democrats, representatives of the Catholic Church, Orthodox Jews, civil rights advocates, and a large congregation of disabled and elderly people in a noisy street demonstration?"

The answer is simple: I do not believe that doctors should kill their patients.

At the outset, I must acknowledge that the right-to-die proponents have a certain undeniable logic to their argument. I agree with the proposition that every individual has a right to control his or her life. Unfortunately, this logic does not take into account the institutional ramifications of physician-assisted sui-

Reprinted from Evan J. Kemp Jr., "Could You Please Die Now?" *Washington Post National Weekly Edition*, January 13, 1997, p. 23, by permission of the author.

cide and thus misses a much more basic point. In this age of soaring health care costs, I believe the right-to-die option inevitably will be transformed into a means of rationing health care.

As a matter of fact, we've already taken our first few steps down this exceedingly steep and slippery slope. At present, a patient checking into a hospital is routinely given the option of signing a "do not resuscitate" order (DNR), requesting that "heroic measures," such as cardiopulmonary resuscitation, not be taken should such measures be required to keep the person alive.

DNR consent is supposed to be voluntary. In practice, however, that has not always been the case. Some disabled people report instances in which hospitals have pressured patients—most notably, people with disabilities, the uninsured, and the severely ill—to sign DNR orders.

In some cases, the DNR is not explained clearly. The patient, or the patient's family or other representative, is not adequately informed of the nature of the order—especially the fact that it is supposed to be voluntary. The DNR is often included with other routine administrative papers to be signed. This cannot be construed as "informed consent."

Battles with Hospitals

Joe Ehman, a news reporter in Rochester, N.Y., who uses a wheelchair, told me he was "literally hounded by social workers" to sign a DNR when he was hospitalized in 1995 for back surgery. "A few hours after surgery, still delirious from the anesthesia and from postsurgical morphine and demerol, I had to hear from yet another social worker who wanted to force-feed me a DNR. I mustered my strength and screamed, 'I'm 30 years old. I don't want to die!'"

Maria Matzik, a woman in her thirties who lives and works in Dayton, Ohio, says she had a frightening battle with nurses during a 1993 hospital stay. "They kept asking me to sign a DNR order," she told me. "When I wouldn't sign it, they said it didn't matter anyway. Because I use a ventilator, they told me nothing would be done if I had a cardiac arrest." Matzik escaped that fate, but others have not.

Marjorie Nighbert, a 76-year-old Florida woman, was hospitalized in 1996 after a stroke. Before her hospital admission, she signed an advance directive that no "heroic measures" should be employed to save her life. On the basis of that directive and at

> *"In this age of soaring health care costs, I believe the right-to-die option inevitably will be transformed into a means of rationing health care."*

the request of her family, the hospital denied Nighbert's requests for food and water, according to reports in the *Northwest Florida Daily News.* A hurriedly convened hospital ethics committee ruled that she was "not medically competent to ask for such a treatment." Until her death more than 10 days later, Nighbert was restrained in her bed to prevent her from raiding other patients' food trays.

Chapter 4

The Economics of Assisted Suicide

The larger point is that, in evaluating the right-to-die movement, one should not overlook the fundamental importance of money. In the *Washington v. Glucksberg* decision, federal judge Stephen Reinhardt tried to put the best possible face on the economic pressures involved in life and death decisions: ". . . in a society in which the costs of protracted health care can be so exorbitant, we are reluctant to say that it is improper for competent, terminally ill adults to take the economic welfare of their families and loved ones into consideration."

When it comes to spending money on health care, however, "families and loved ones" often are not in a position to call the shots. Insurance companies, hospitals, nursing homes and HMOs are—and they would prefer that the dirty little secret of money be kept out of the public debate about assisted suicide. After all, it's much easier for them to justify their actions on the basis of humanitarian principle than financial self-interest. Once physician-assisted suicide is given the sanction of law, our health care institutions are likely to devise contractual mechanisms that make sure members of targeted groups die as efficiently as possible.

All of this will be justified by the holy grail of the right-to-die movement: "choice." But the laws of economics virtually guarantee that, in practice, those who "choose" assisted suicide will disproportionately come from the lower end of the socioeconomic ladder: people without health insurance, as well as from people who are said to possess a low "quality of life"—i.e., people with disabilities.

> *"As a disabled person, I am especially sensitive to the 'quality of life' rationale that is frequently introduced in the debate."*

As former Surgeon General C. Everett Koop declared at a Washington, D.C., press conference in November 1996, "Toleration of doctor-assisted suicide can lead to acceptance of involuntary euthanasia."

As a disabled person, I am especially sensitive to the "quality of life" rationale that is frequently introduced in the debate. For the past 47 years, I have lived with a progressive neuromuscular disease that first began to manifest itself when I was 12. My disease, Kugelburg Weylander Syndrome, has no known cure, and I have no hope for "recovery."

Upon diagnosis, my parents were informed by the physicians treating me that I would die within two years. Later, another group of physicians was certain that I would live only to the age of 18. Yet here I am at age 59, continuing to have an extraordinarily high quality of life.

And my case is by no means unique. The majority of families I have encountered in my lifetime, and who have been close enough to share details of their extended family life, have had at least one member who defied the medical establishment by living a far longer and more productive life than expected. Should we permit the medical establishment to assist these individuals with disabilities to die before their time at the hands of their physicians? I don't think so.

The Costs of Death

If physician-assisted suicide is decriminalized, the next question to arise will be how to pay for the service. If the suicide services, dubbed "obitiatry" by Dr. Jack Kevorkian, become billable, those services could dovetail all too well with our nation's current drive to cut health care costs. Health maintenance organizations may view the cost of obitiatry as especially cost-effective in that the practice will require neither referrals to specialists nor repeat visits to physicians' offices.

In managed-care parlance, the portion of the premium dollar spent on medical care is called the "medical-loss ratio." Insurance companies and health maintenance organizations could cut that ratio by providing assisted suicide rather than bypass surgeries and the like. After all, many people are cheaper dead than alive.

The American Medical Association has twice affirmed its opposition to physician-assisted suicide and recently filed an amicus brief with the Supreme Court. The AMA wishes for physicians to maintain their role as healers, and not to become potential killers, even for reasons of mercy.

The experience of Nazi Germany is relevant here, not because the advocates of assisted suicide are incipient fascists (they're not) but because of the historical fact that the Holocaust had its beginnings in the systematic elimination of Germans with disabilities. As Hugh Gregory Gallagher noted in his 1990 book, *By Trust Betrayed: Physicians, Patients and the License to Kill in the Third Reich*, Adolf Hitler's order of September 1939 called for physicians to assist in the killings of citizens with illnesses and disabilities. Nazi propagandists, led by a small number of physicians, said that such citizens were "useless eaters" and "life unworthy of life." Today American health planners, while driven by a very different ideology, also speak a dehumanizing language about "health care consumers" and the dubious "quality of life" of our citizens with illnesses and disabilities.

From where I sit, it is undeniably clear that giving physician-assisted suicide the sanction of law will have unintended consequences which vastly outweigh any benefits that might accrue. As Koop puts it, "Society must not allow doctors to be killers as well as healers."

Assisted Suicide Would Create an Inhumane Society

by Rand Richards Cooper

About the author: *Rand Richards Cooper is a fiction writer who has taught at Amherst College in Amherst, Massachusetts, and at Emerson College in Boston, Massachusetts.*

I'm looking for an argument with Jack Kevorkian; or rather, for one against him. Life for Kevorkian lately has come laden with satisfying vindications. Weary prosecutors, having failed to convince three Michigan juries that Kevorkian's eagerness in assisting suicide is a crime, now seem ready to toss in their cards and go home. Once dubbed "Dr. Death" by medical school classmates for his unseemly obsession with terminal illness, the ex-pathologist stands redeemed and embraced as a pioneering American hero. "Jack's doing something that is right," says his lawyer, Geoffrey Fieger. "Everyone instinctively understands that—that's why we're winning."

Jack Kevorkian's Logic

Whatever you may feel about Kevorkian personally—and I admit to finding him an unlikely standard-bearer, with his smug and aggressive looniness, for a human dignity movement—you have to admire how deftly he has taken the pulse of the nation's moral reasoning. Kevorkian has put our agonized ambivalence about life-prolonging medical technologies into the rights-based framework of our political discourse, producing a case for assisted suicide that seems unassailable. Its logic goes like this: If I am afflicted, say, with inoperable cancer, and if after discussions with loved ones I decide I would rather die now, in dignity, than a year from now, why shouldn't I have this right? How does my exercising it conceivably impair the rights of any other person?

It doesn't, say the juries who keep acquitting Kevorkian; that's why the gov-

Reprinted from Rand Richards Cooper, "The Dignity of Helplessness: What Sort of Society Would Euthanasia Create?" *Commonweal*, October 25, 1996, by permission of *Commonweal* magazine.

ernment should butt out. Whose death is it, anyway?

As a means of sparing loved ones suffering, assisted suicide expresses our most compassionate urges and motives. Nevertheless, I believe the notion of a "right" to die provides far too narrow a framework for discussing the widespread institutionalization of the practice. Talk about rights resonates deeply with Americans. It is our strongest political instinct; our melody and our beat. Other societies stress sacrifice or obedience, glory or passion or style or work, but we always come back to rights. And therein lies the rub. The appeal of rights is so compelling that it leaves scant room for realities and interests not easily expressed as rights. And with assisted suicide that means leaving out way too much.

Do the Elderly Have Autonomy?

Consider the predicament of the elderly. Kevorkian pledges himself to "the absolute autonomy of the individual," and insists that practitioners of "obitiatry" (as he proposes calling the new medical specialty) would administer only to those who truly *want* to die. But what exactly is the "absolute autonomy" of an elderly, ailing person convinced he or she is a burden to everyone? I remember how my grandmother, who died a few years ago at ninety-seven, used to lament being a "burden" on the rest of us. "I don't know why I'm still alive," she'd say, sighing. She didn't really mean it; but there's no doubt in my mind that the obitiatric option, had it existed, would have added an extra tinge of guilt to her last couple of years—particularly after she entered a nursing home whose costs began to eat up the savings she and my grandfather had accumulated over decades of thrift. Do we want to do that to our elderly and infirm? How will we prevent the creep toward an increased sense of burdensomeness that the very availability of assisted suicide is likely to cause?

Next, what about creeping changes in the rest of us? In a society in which assisted suicide is a ready option, how will we view those who don't choose it? I'm imagining Ben Jonson's grim sixteenth-century farce, *Volpone*, updated for our time, a circle of heirs crowding round the bedside, impatient for the obitioner. But I'm also thinking about something far subtler, that gradual habituation of mind Alexis de Tocqueville called the "slow action of society upon itself." Much as we like to imagine otherwise, the truth is that our inventions and our beliefs are implacably dynamic. The things we make turn around and remake us; and just as the Pill helped transform our ideas about

> *"How will we prevent the creep toward an increased sense of burdensomeness that the very availability of assisted suicide is likely to cause?"*

sexual freedom, so will the obitioner change the way we regard aging. How often in the assisted-suicide future will someone look at an elderly person and think, consciously or semiconsciously, "Gee, guess it's about time, huh?"

And do we want that?

Such questions find scant place in a discussion that focuses solely on the "autonomous" individual and his "right" to die. That's why I want to take Kevorkianism out of the discussion of individual rights and put it into a discussion of something I'll call, for want of a better phrase, the texture of civic life. By this I mean simply the thoughts we have in our heads about ourselves and one another; the shape and feel of our daily, moment-to-moment relations. Will institutionalizing assisted suicide equip us to be better human beings for each other, or will it unequip us?

A Lesson Learned in Kenya

When I was twenty I lived for a time in Kenya. One hot afternoon found me at a grade school in Nairobi, helping out at a fair for handicapped children. The event was understaffed, and when after games and lunch the children started having to go to the bathroom, things got hectic. A clamorous line of kids in leg braces and primitive wheelchairs formed outside the single outhouse. They needed help getting in, help going and cleaning up afterward. I did what I could, but I was young and singularly unschooled in this kind of neediness. Vividly I recall a boy of ten who walked with two crutches, dragging useless legs behind him. During the long wait he had defecated in his pants, and as I helped him to the outhouse door I retched, despite myself,

> *"If we make assisted suicide widely available, will we end up virtually eliminating that phase of life in which people are not whole, 'not there'?"*

at the stench and the stifling heat. Seeing my distress, another organizer, a thirtyish guy named Dennis, picked up the boy and swiftly carried him into the outhouse. I followed, watching as Dennis squatted before the boy, cleaning him with a towel, the boy looking up with a calm and patient expression.

That memory comes back to me whenever an acquaintance of mine—a man in his mid-sixties and in good health—outlines his game plan for old age. For him, goal number one is never, ever to become a helpless burden. "Once I start shitting my pants," he says, "that's it. Take me out and shoot me." I share his dread of becoming vulnerable, dependent, smelly; who doesn't? Yet at the same time I find myself looking back to that moment in the outhouse in Kenya, years ago. Helplessness was there, of course, and burden too, but beauty as well, so much so that I have never forgotten it—the helper and the helped joined in a mutual courage I could only hope some day to possess.

My point is that we experience a profound aspect of our humanity precisely in our intimate and awful knowledge of each other's physical neediness; and further, that what we draw from this knowledge constitutes not only a spiritual good but a social good. If, following the quality-of-life, take-me-out-and-shoot-me principle, we end up using assisted suicide to preempt the infirmities of old age and terminal illness, how well equipped will we be to encounter infirmity elsewhere? How to become fluent in help if we have banished helplessness from our vocabulary? I'm thinking of the way we treat people in wheelchairs, people who can't feed themselves, whose bodies don't look or work "right." Taken together with prenatal genetic testing and selective abortion, might not assisted suicide further a gradual drift toward functionalism in our attitude to life? Societies that drift in this direction, as Germany did under the Nazis, instill in their citizens a visceral sense of the handicapped as a drain or drag on the healthy body of the rest of us: a pointless deformity; an un-luck; an un-person. Such attitudes are not spontaneous manifestations of evil. You have to train people to feel this way; but if you do, they will.

Gretchen's Illness

A few years ago, my mother's lifelong best friend died at sixty of lung cancer. The last phase of Gretchen's life involved multiple surgeries, long hospital stays that sapped the will, and the disorienting pressures of pain and medication. For my mother, there was the anguish of watching a person she loved being overwhelmed by illness—an especially hard kind of sorrow. ("She's not there anymore," my mother would say after a bad visit.) But then came moments of joy—a visit or a phone call or a handwritten note in which, suddenly, Gretchen was there again, emerging by some grace from the fog of her illness to share with my mother an affirmation of how much they had loved and enjoyed each other through the decades of their friendship.

My mother has a bulletin board in her kitchen where she tacks up cards, favorite maxims, snapshots, and the like. But she doesn't display the last few notes she got from Gretchen. Instead, she keeps them taped to the inside of a cabinet high over the stove. I suspect they are still too highly charged for her; too much suffering and beauty attach to them.

Gretchen's illness is the kind on which Kevorkianism makes its core appeal—a remorseless, irreversible disease that steals a person from us bit by bit. Assisted suicide offers a way, in effect, to manage death so that it arrives before this insidious larceny has begun. As such it is an attempt to do people dignity—and our memories of them, too—by enabling them to go out whole. It's an option I imagine Gretchen might well have availed herself of; my mother, for her part, came away from her friend's death with a firm belief in the rightness of assisted suicide.

> *"Should laws, can laws, have a stake in our complexity—in the quality of our togetherness as well as the fact of our separateness?"*

And yet I think about those notes in her cabinet. It's hard to say this, but I believe that part of what makes them so profoundly meaningful to my mother is that they came from such a dark and pressured place, where Gretchen was not always the "same" Gretchen she had known. Finding her way back from that place to write those notes fashioned an understanding of courage which my mother carries with her today: the last of Gretchen's many gifts to her.

Rights Are Not Enough

One needs to tread very softly here. Taken to extremes, the notion of a vested interest in each other's suffering becomes barbaric; and I don't want anyone to think I'm questioning the correctness of relieving misery and pain. In fact, it's not assisted suicide per se I'm questioning, which in other forms has long been practiced unofficially by physicians informing the gravely ill about lethal doses, turning off ventilators to "let nature take its course," and so on. It's the institutionalizing of the practice I'm wondering about, and its effect on our relation to the *idea* of suffering. If we make assisted suicide widely available, will we end up virtually eliminating that phase of life in which people are not whole, "not there"? If so, will we be a better, richer, more humane society for having done so?

I'm aware many will consider this a pernicious basis for discussing the legality of assisted suicide. The notion that our laws should promote virtues as well as protect rights is anathema to modern American political thought. But the idea of rights alone can't capture the complexity of our connectedness to one another, and anyone who insists exclusively on them can end up sounding weirdly hollow. It is the hollowness, in fact, of Jack Kevorkian himself. I watched him not long ago on *60 Minutes*. Asked by Mike Wallace to discuss the ethics of abortion—he is vehemently prochoice—Kevorkian mulled it over for a moment, then responded in this way: "The autonomy of the fetus can never supersede the autonomy of the mother." Whatever you may think of Kevorkian, or of abortion, I think you'll agree that these are exceptionally arid terms with which to encounter complex human dilemmas. But in purest form they are the terms of rights.

Current debates about welfare reform, about drug policy, violence on TV, the legality of youth curfews and school uniforms: all suggest a growing urge in America, across the political spectrum, to move beyond *laissez-faire* liberalism—what political theorist Michael J. Sandel has called our modern "aspiration to neutrality"—toward some vision of the good. Whether you call this impulse communitarianism, republicanism, statecraft as soulcraft, or a concern for civic texture, what it means is making connections not only between laws and rights, but between laws and character—the kind and quality of citizen laws inevitably help produce. Where does assisted suicide fit in? Is it possible that accompanying and consoling those we love through grievous terminal illness constitutes one of the core experiences we need to have? That part of us, some quality of pity and compassion and terror and love, is reachable only by taking that awful journey? And if so, does the law have a role to play? Should laws, can laws, have a stake in our complexity—in the quality of our togetherness as well as the fact of our separateness?

Death Affects the Living

For the last few months of her very long life, my grandmother lay in a nursing home, floating in and out of consciousness, largely unable to eat. She wasn't in pain, but clearly she no longer possessed the active, vigorous perception which I believe institutionalizing assisted suicide may ultimately lead us to establish as the bottom-line criterion for meaningful life among the aged and the ill. For my part, I'd been fearing my visits to her, worrying that these last images of her diminished and helpless would later greedily elbow out other, happier memories. But this fear proved groundless. As it turns out, even those deeply unsettling moments when she looked more dead than alive and I barely recognized her, or when she unexpectedly squeezed my hand, as if sending a last, bodily message from some strange place between being and not-being—all of that forms part of the story of my grandmother that I carry with me; and I feel I am the richer for all of it, endowed with a more expansive vocabulary of body and spirit; and also a more intimate acquaintance with death, in all its mystery and terribleness.

Anyone who has accompanied someone through a terminal illness knows the solitariness of mortality—"the unknown," wrote English poet Edward Thomas shortly before his own death in World War I, "I must enter, and leave, alone." A sense of this deep privacy drives the right-to-die movement in America today. And yet to step outside the rights framework is to ask how institutionalizing assisted suicide will affect not only those who die, but those who live on; not only individuals, but society. The fact is, our deaths are both solo journeys toward an ultimate mystery and strands in the tapestries of each other's lives. Which side of this reality will we emphasize? Whose death is it, anyway? The debate about assisted suicide should begin at the place where that question ceases to be a rhetorical one.

Assisted Suicide Will Be Encouraged for Economic Reasons

by Don Sloan

About the author: *Don Sloan is a contributor to* Political Affairs, *a monthly magazine published by the Communist Party USA.*

The debate over doctor-assisted suicide almost suggests that Americans are preoccupied with death in that we seem to be constantly arguing the pros and cons over things that involve dying or killing in some way. Abortion, an issue that just will not go away, has transcended all aspects of law, science, politics, religion and morals. Doctors who legally perform this medical chore have been labeled "murderers" by anti-choice proponents. The crux of abortion has somehow filtered down to where life starts and ends.

The death penalty has been in the forefront of our thinking way beyond and before the Supreme Court turnaround in 1972. Since then, nearly 350 men, mostly African Americans, have been put to death. In some states like Florida and Texas, it has almost been a growth industry. Along with permitting guns in the general civilian population, we are the only industrialized nation in the world that has retained the death penalty and its proponents seem stronger than ever.

The Enigmas of Doctor-Assisted Suicide

Now, to that we can add doctor-assisted suicides, an issue that has added to our death preoccupation, but one that has presented us with many enigmas. The awaited court decision that is to be handed down in 1997, will do little to settle the matter. [On June 26, 1997, the U.S. Supreme Court ruled that the Constitution does not guarantee a "right to die." However, states are not precluded from passing laws that would establish this right.] As expected, the debate will rage on. Interestingly, subscribers and opponents seem to cross over both political and ethical lines. People from all sorts of social lines, religious groups and

Reprinted from Don Sloan, "The Politics of Doctor-Assisted Suicide: A Class Approach," *Political Affairs*, May 1997, by permission of the publisher.

sects, economic classes, and genders have gone against the tenets of their groups, almost to the point of heresy. Many legal authorities who are on record as being opposed to the death penalty because, they claim, no one, not even the state, has a right to take a human life, have joined the right-to-die bandwagon. Church officialdom, with emotional arguments in favor of life, somehow manage to accept the doctor-assisted suicide argument. Inconsistencies are very much the rule of the day.

> *"In a real sense, all patients under a doctor's care become captive audiences."*

It is also something of an enigma that many who have clamored that the American medical community has already been vested with an undeserved power are willing to give their doctors even more, this time over death as well as life. In a real sense, all patients under a doctor's care become captive audiences. It is almost as though a doctor takes on an immortality and can do no wrong—or at least that is what we like to think. After all, our lives are in their hands, and to think of the doctor as someone fallible puts us at risk. We tend to believe that our doctor doesn't get sick, doesn't lose control, won't ever be crazy or neurotic—and likely won't ever die.

Thanatology, the science of death, then, comes to have a special meaning for the patient. The doctor will always be able to cope and make the right decision, even when that decision is so final. Death has always been poorly understood by scientist and moralist alike. Maksim Gorky, the great Russian writer, in *On The Good Life,* wrote that we spend our energies just speculating on its secrets; we have developed Gods and idols and rituals to either worship it or fight it off. We have formed an image of "the other world," with names like Paradise or Hell.

Does death have a purpose? Or is it nature's imperfection? Whatever the answer its ombudsman certainly has made mistakes. It has taken the gifted and left us with fools, snatched away valued animals and left us with pests, felled our heroes and left us with villains. It would take more than Gorky to have us fully understand its meaning and intent. Karl Marx touched on the meaning of life and especially the role of humans in an animal world. His conclusions, brief as they were, noted that we homo sapiens were unique in having the brain power and verbal skill capacity to surpass the rest of the animal kingdom. It followed that such powers gave us a covenant to stay alive and care for our world.

Death and Health Care

To all this we must now add doctor-assisted suicide to the equation. American medicine is like no other in the developed world; we remain the world's only industrialized nation without a comprehensive health care plan for its citizens. Therefore, since doctor-assisted suicide is now a part of that equation, it, too, must be viewed in a special light. For if we are devoid of a schema to have us life with "dignity," that phrase often used by doctor-assisted suicide supporters, how can we ever consider a plan that allows for our "dying with dignity"?

A health care package was not on the agenda in the 105th Congress. Instead, the poor and underprivileged fight to keep Medicaid, their abysmal but only available health care plan, from being destroyed. The elderly, still settling for the opprobrium that is Medicare, are seeing their benefits and hopes for their futures slashed with every Congressional session. Since the New Deal of Franklin Delano Roosevelt in the '30s, just about every social program has either been gutted or eliminated: the minimum wage, unemployment benefits, special hospital procedures, welfare, and now, even that rather elegant prototype, America's security blanket, Social Security, is under the threat of severe reduction or privatization which are in essence the same thing. Children in America are still dying from ordinary household measles only for lack of proper funding for universal inoculations. Even the Richard Nixon Maternal Infant Care program that dramatically helped lower U.S. maternal and perinatal mortality in the 1970s, and was one of our proudest moments, has been reduced to its barest services, so that Black mortality in newborns is now twice that of the white population in America, a dubious claim if ever there were one.

The Power of Insurance Companies

Comparisons have often been made by the supporters of doctor-assisted suicide that in other places, such as the Netherlands and Australia, the recipe has been neither abused nor misapplied. What is not added to that conclusion is that every Dutch citizen and every Australian has the benefits of a fully funded health care program. What has our answer been to that burning demand? Tragically, we have resorted to one of capitalism's most egregious industries—private insurance and its newly-formed tentacle—the Health Maintenance Organization, the HMO. If [Speaker of the House] Newt Gingrich and the Contract on America, with [President Bill Clinton's] support, has its way, even Medicaid and Medicare will come under the yoke of HMOs in the private sector. Some states have already started their conversions and more are underway.

We are being told that this way is more "efficient," or more "prudent." These euphemisms are applied as the insurance cabal uses and exerts more of its power in Washington.

> *"American medicine is like no other in the developed world; we remain the world's only industrialized nation without a comprehensive health care plan for its citizens."*

Today each and every diagnosis has been assigned a dollar value and treatment and time schedule, and reimbursements to both doctor and hospital are preset. Diagnostic Related Groups (DRG) are playing a major role in setting these standards. You can imagine what has already happened, especially to the elderly when their pathologies tend to be more chronic and time and care demanding. Revolving door treatments, already in vogue for childbirth and breast surgery, are becoming the habit. Hospitals are finding ways of eliminating or transferring those patients who present them with what could become a more tedious disease or health need.

It gets worse. Doctor and hospital profiles are closely kept by the insurance statisticians, and penalties are meted out if either wanders too far. Hospitals are denied reimbursements through "carve outs" if patients are kept too long past the DRG designations, and physicians are dropped out of the loop and denied future referrals if their profiles suggest they use too many facilities as compared to their colleagues. There is a frequent conflict between patient care and the end-of-the-month profit-and-loss sheet, and I leave it to your imagination which one will take precedence in a service-for-profit capitalist system.

> *"Under our health-for-profit system, it is only a matter of time before market-oriented pharmaceutical firms conjure up clever names and ads for their 'pills that kill.'"*

How will doctor-assisted suicide fit in? It is only a matter of time before doctors and their health care professional assistants, with their newly assigned power to kill, will put that into the treatment formula and even make that decision based on economy rather than science. How could anything else be expected? If the faculty to kill is given legality, it then becomes a consideration in the management of patients who are deemed applicable. And how will that decision be made? That is a question never even addressed.

Under our health-for-profit system, it is only a matter of time before market-oriented pharmaceutical firms conjure up clever names and ads for their "pills that kill," and it will all be done up in the name of "dignity" or that other euphemism "humaneness." New brands of poisons will be devised with a pleasant taste, or in a nicely done up package. Eventually, the specialty of thanatology will have its board-certified specialist—the thanatologist—and each hospital unit will have one in waiting. Wannabe Jack Kevorkians will take their places in the American medical community. And how long will it take before lawyers, doctors, and estate planners form a combine that will even make it that much easier to use that pragmatic "die with dignity"?

There are even more fundamental problems with a doctor-assisted suicide program in a medical care system that is based on profit instead of patient need. In so many ways we all have subpar care if only because the insurance group remains firmly in charge and along with its technocrats, dictate our medical futures. We all view death as surely eventually inevitable, but also certainly postponable, at least for a time. When it finally is upon us, it is then seen as a technical failure, and when it is determined that that technology has failed we throw in the towel. It is assumed that all means have been spent and since it is not very cost-effective to maintain life with dignity, why not kill with dignity? The right-to-die movement has admittedly been experiencing a dilemma of sorts, one that reflects its widespread concerns about our health care failures and how America, despite its affluence and development, has failed so many of its people.

Shrinking Horizons

Allowing for the exception that makes the rule, the vast majority of the American people who ever come to the point of considering the right-to-die and doctor-assisted suicide are mired down within a system that has shamefully not made much of a priority of life. Nursing homes, with rare exception, are notoriously the worst American medicine has to offer. They are serviced by poorly trained and underpaid health care workers. They tend to then identify very little with the patient, a hallmark for optimal care, and the absentee ownership has been frequently associated with extortion, embezzlement and scandal. Poorly regulated by governmental authority, they are forced upon many of the elderly at a time in their lives when they have so little reserve to protest.

What is happening to the dying? Their horizons are shrinking; shrinking because they dare not think beyond what their compromised intellect allows. They feel sometimes only pain or fear, but they also want to spare their loved ones from the anguish of a terminal existence, and to suggest that there is such a thing as informed consent at that time is oxymoronic. If Sigmund Freud, Marx, Gorky and the others are right, and life is a drive, how can death, under any system, be a permissible alternative?

To pave the way to die in the throes of our present health care failures is only adding to those failures and is denying the real problems facing American health care delivery today, starting with the fact that we have none. The courts and the legislatures should not give the American medical community and its patients the awesome power to end our lives, before it provides us with the means to live them to the fullest. Then, at least, that decision which may someday have a place, will be made not out of fear and weakness and insecurity, but from strength, courage and conviction.

Assisted Suicide Would Respect the Rights of the Terminally Ill

by Robert C. Horn III

About the author: *Robert C. Horn III is professor emeritus of political science at California State University at Northridge. He is the author of* How Will They Know When I'm Dead? Transcending Disability and Terminal Illness.

In the national debate on doctor-assisted suicide, we have heard from judges and lawyers, doctors and clergymen, ethicists and editorial writers, politicians and pundits. The one group conspicuously absent so far from the discussion is the one most affected by its outcome: the terminally ill.

The Terminally Ill Deserve Autonomy

I am one of the terminally ill. In 1988, I was diagnosed as having amyotrophic lateral sclerosis, commonly known as Lou Gehrig's Disease. ALS is a degenerative neuromuscular disease that swiftly robs the victim of voluntary muscle control, including those necessary for breathing. The average life expectancy after diagnosis is two to four years. ALS does not affect the mind, so one is perfectly aware of his or her physical deterioration. By the end, the individual typically is unable to move, talk above a whisper, eat without choking or breathe without difficulty.

ALS is a terminal disease. It is progressive, unrelenting, merciless. Its endgame is inevitable. Shouldn't a person faced with such prospects have the legal right to choose whether to go on with life or end it with dignity? ALS victim Dennis Kaye, in his book *Laugh, I Thought I'd Die*, writes that he does not want to go on a ventilator when it becomes necessary. Why should he have to? In *This Far and No More*, another book about a personal struggle with ALS, Emily Bauer (a pseudonym) poignantly wrote in her diary: "I don't know how anyone with access to a normal life can expect me to accept such a limited one. That oth-

Reprinted from Robert C. Horn, "Choosing Life, Even on a Ventilator," *Los Angeles Times*, May 16, 1996, p. B-9, by permission of the author.

ers have accepted a drastically limited life does not mean that is the right course of action for me." Who has the right to tell Emily that she doesn't have a choice?

Life is about making decisions and choices. For the terminally ill, those choices should include when to die. This doesn't mean choice by doctors or family members or ministers or counselors or any person except the patient himself. Others can and should be consulted, but the decision must be up to—in the words of the U.S. Ninth Circuit Court of Appeals—the "mentally competent adult" patient. [The Ninth Circuit court's decision was overturned by the U.S. Supreme Court on June 26, 1997.]

Choosing Life

But the right to choose death necessarily must include the right to choose life. I was faced with that choice in February 1991. In less than three years, I had gone from a robust, physically active person to being completely disabled. I could barely squeeze out a sound, had lost more than a third of my body weight because I had trouble swallowing even mushy foods, was almost totally paralyzed and my breathing had become very labored. What to do?

I am fortunate in that I had a real choice. Two doctors separately offered me the option of ending my life painlessly. I didn't choose that option, but I deeply appreciate their compassion. I made a conscious decision to go on a ventilator and on with my life. I talked it over with several people close to me, especially my wife, who would take on the additional role of caregiver. But I alone made the decision. I chose life.

After five years of being tethered to a ventilator, "eating" via a tube in my stomach, "talking" with my eyebrows and operating the computer with my foot, did I make the right choice? You bet! What I have left is more valuable than what I have lost. The things I can do are more important than those that I can't. There is much more to life than physical ability. I am still a vibrant, healthy and independent person mentally, emotionally and spiritually. I can think, reason and analyze, remember, read, write, learn and communicate. I can love, feel happiness and sadness, be enthusiastic, get angry, feel joy. I can believe, hope and have faith. That adds up to an extensive list of things I can still "do" in spite of my disease.

Although I made the right decision for me, that is not to say that my choice would be appropriate for everyone. The personal struggles of people against life-threatening illnesses do not lend themselves to facile judgments. These are highly individual battles that depend on many factors, from personal outlook and philosophy to the specific circumstances and, significantly, to the nature of the illness itself. For instance, in ALS, the symptoms vary dramatically from patient to patient; one person's experience is no guide to someone else's.

> *"The right to choose death necessarily must include the right to choose life."*

Defending Both Choices

That said, I still would like to talk to those people who are seeking to end their lives—and would have liked to talk to those who did. What would I say? I would simply tell them that there is life on a ventilator. I have found that despite the difficult conditions of disability and terminal illness, life can be meaningful, productive, fulfilling, rewarding and valuable. I defend their right to die, but I also affirm their right to live.

For me, having a choice is the key. No one forced me to live. No one forced me to die. I chose. Because of that, I can cope with the negatives and "downs" as well as relish the positives and "ups" that my life presents. Choice makes all the difference; it's as simple and as complicated as that.

Assisted Suicide Would Respect the Rights of the Elderly

by Dudley Clendinen

About the author: *Dudley Clendinen is a former national correspondent for the* New York Times.

My cousin Florence Hosch finally died the Wednesday before Christmas 1995, about a thousand days after she had wished to.

Her Christmas card, mailed from the nursing home in Dunedin, Fla., came the following Tuesday. Florence herself didn't arrive for almost a month, but I knew she was en route.

A Death Delayed

After three years of hospitals, nursing homes, doctors, social workers, lawyers, accountants and real estate agents, the last employee of the last enterprise in charge of her long and exhausting death telephoned to say that it was over. "Hi, this is American Burial and Cremation calling, just to let you know that the cremains for Florence Hosch are being sent out today," the woman said.

Like so many others, Florence had been delayed by the snowstorm, as she had been delayed in dying—like so many others—by the System. Delayed against her principles. Against her wishes, oral and written. She was, in harboring the wish to die when life seemed over, ahead of her time.

Nursing homes are full of people like Florence, trapped in transit between retirement and death. They are the parents, the aunts and uncles of my generation—the boomers—and their number is going to grow and grow, because they are being cared for by a system that considers it irresponsible to let them die.

When Florence succumbed to lack of oxygen and increased morphine on Dec. 20, she was almost 93. She had had 90 good years and three wretched ones, the wretchedness relieved mainly by drugs, by the calls and visits of those who loved her, by her intermittent plotting of how to leave us all behind and, mainly, by her own splendid spirit.

No New Life

Her husband, Louie, had been dead for 10 years. They had no children. Her career had been in social work and she was devoutly atheistic, liberal and rational to a fault. She didn't think her life belonged to God or to anyone else. She thought it belonged to her. "You know, you can make a new life," she said to me when Louie died. "But I'm 83. I'm too old to make a new life. I have to live the one I have, or decide not to."

She wanted to leave gifts to the organizations she believed in and to the people she loved, and to leave their house and savings, as she and Louie had agreed, to her beloved sister-in-law and nephew in California. That was her plan, and she was perfectly prepared to put it in motion. She kept the pills in her bedside table drawer against the day when she decided that life had gone on too long. Her family knew it, her doctor and lawyer knew it, everyone knew it.

But she waited too long. One month she was a handsome, independent woman of 90, and the next, felled by a lung infection, she was breathless, bedridden, hospitalized.

She went home, then back to the hospital. Home. Hospital. Home. Her medical care at home, first with nurses' aides and eventually with registered nurses around the clock, went from $7,500 to $15,000 a month. She

> *"Nursing homes are full of people like Florence, trapped in transit between retirement and death."*

had been diagnosed with end-stage respiratory disease and was released to die in her own house under hospice care. If she had had her way, that would have taken about two hours. Back in her own bed again, with her bedside table and her pills, she called for a bourbon and water and swallowed as many as she could before she conked out. But she woke the next day to find herself still alive. "I botched it," she said.

Bedridden, tethered to an oxygen machine, trapped in a house staffed with witnesses, in a state whose laws could make a felon of anyone who tried to help her die, Florence pushed herself for months to recover the strength to walk again. She had gotten as far as the kitchen, where the nurses had moved her sleeping pills, when part of her spine, hollowed by osteoporosis, collapsed. She gave up and decided to wait for pneumonia.

The Pain of Lucidity

When I saw her last, on Thanksgiving weekend, her money had run out, her house and car and furniture had been sold to pay for her care, she no longer had the breath to do anything but breathe, and she was lying, panting, in her bed at the nursing home, four months past a bout of pneumonia that should have killed her. The nursing staff had given her antibiotics, and she had survived.

Her appearance was the perfect statement of her condition. Her complaint was that her mind stayed strong while her body declined, so that she was a horrified, captive, lucid witness to her own decay. Her wasted body lay under the sheet like a stick, like the stem of a rose, and at its head, lying on the pillow, glowing with spirit and intelligence, was Florence. She was all cheekbones, eyes, eyebrows and teeth.

In the bed next to her was a woman of 105 who lay perfectly still, her arms folded across her stomach, her white hair sprayed out across the pillow. Her mouth was open. "Help me," she kept saying. "Someone please help me." Her eyes were closed. Twice in the last year, the nurse told me later, she had gotten pneumonia. Twice, the nursing home had given her antibiotics. Twice the pneumonia had lost its grip. She did not seem happy about it.

I told Florence I didn't think she would have much longer now. "Oh?" she said, eyes brightening, eyebrows arching. "Do I have that phosphorescent glow?" I said I thought so. We went on to talk about death, about family and about my aunts Carolyn Smith and Bessie Clendinen in a nursing home across Tampa Bay. Florence always wanted to know how they were. They were terrible: deaf, crippled, incontinent. But they had also lost their minds years ago— Bessie's brain starved for oxygen from hardening of the arteries, Carolyn's withered by Alzheimer's. "They're the lucky ones," Florence said and smiled. She died three weeks later.

Heaven and Hell

Florence is in her burnished metal box in the bookshelf in the study now, behind the rosy clay bust of her that Louie made some years ago. Carolyn and Bessie are still in the Tampa nursing home. Carolyn is 87. Bessie is 90. I am responsible for them. Like Florence, they had signed living wills and powers of attorney. "I do not fear death as much as I fear the indignity of deterioration, dependence and hopeless pain," the will says. "If there is no reasonable expectation of my recovery from physical or mental disability, I wish to be allowed to die and not be kept alive by artificial means or heroic measures."

Bessie and Carolyn had a different reason from Florence for not wanting to linger. They were old-fashioned Southern Christian women. They believed that drinking, dancing, divorce, abortion and homosexuality were sins and that when they died they would go to heaven. Twice, pneumonia almost got Carolyn there. But each time, the Bay to Bay Nursing Center shipped her to the hospital, which, for $15,000, pumped her full of oxygen and antibiotics, cured her and shipped her back. Medicaid paid.

Before penicillin, most old people died from pneumonia. Now, giving antibiotics has become routine. "I'm not going to let her lie there and die," the head nurse said, when I protested. We have been at war ever since. I wrote them all a letter: No emergency room, no intravenous anything without my approval. I have not said no antibiotics, period. Maybe I should.

I last saw my aunts on Thanksgiving morning. Bessie, looking through her one eye—the other shattered when another patient pushed her and her head hit the tiled hall floor—didn't know me, and with Carolyn I did a stupid thing. I sat down, took one of her crippled hands in mine, and as she smiled at me in her glazed, gentle way, wished her a happy Thanksgiving. For a short, awful moment, her eyes lit with awareness, and she began to cry. Then, mercifully, the dementia closed in again, and her vacant look returned.

Carolyn and Bessie had always looked forward to heaven. Now they wouldn't know the difference if they got there. But if they still had their minds, they'd know where they are now. Florence did. "This is really hell," she said.

Voluntary Euthanasia Would Not Lead to Involuntary Killing

by Chris Hackler

About the author: *Chris Hackler is the director of the Division of Medical Humanities at the University of Arkansas College of Medicine.*

Consider the last years of Jonathan Swift, an Irish clergyman and one of the keenest satiric minds Britain has produced. This brilliant man of letters slowly lost all distinctly human qualities.

> His mind crumbled to pieces. It took him eight years to die while his brain rotted. He read the third chapter of Job on his birthday as long as he could see. "And Job spake, and said, Let the day perish when I was born, and the night in which it was said, There is a man-child conceived." The pain in Swift's eye was so acute that it took five men to hold him down, to keep him from tearing out his eye with his own hands. For the last three years he sat and drooled. Knives had to be kept entirely out of his reach. When the end came finally, his fits of convulsion lasted thirty-six hours. [Joseph Fletcher]

Swift's case is unusually dramatic, but it illustrates vividly the two conditions under which active euthanasia could be justified: (1) intolerable and uncontrollable suffering, and (2) the disintegration of personality.

Controlling Pain

Suffering. Very few people these days have to die the way Swift did. . . . Great advances in pain control have significantly reduced the suffering that accompanies ravaging diseases. But . . . available techniques are not fully employed. Too few physicians are sufficiently concerned with or knowledgeable about effective pain control. This is a serious problem that is finally being addressed in the literature of medical ethics. But until adequate palliative care is universally available, relief from pain will continue to be a compelling argument for euthanasia.

From Chris Hackler, "Euthanasia and the Red Herring of Totalitarianism." This article appeared in the March 1993 issue, and is reprinted with permission from, the *World & I*, a publication of The Washington Times Corporation; copyright ©1993.

Disintegration of personality. Even if pain can be controlled, death may be preferable to personal disintegration. Many diseases erode the mental faculties, producing amnesia and confusion and eventually destroying the capacity for personal relationships and distinctly human activities. Many people would prefer nonexistence to a subhuman existence. The Stoic sage Seneca expressed such a preference:

> I will not relinquish old age if it leaves my better part intact, but if it begins to shake my mind, if it destroys my faculties one by one . . . I will depart from the putrid or tottering edifice. I will not escape by death and disease so long as it may be healed and leaves my mind unimpaired. I will not raise my hand against myself on account of pain, for so to die is to be conquered, but if I know I must suffer without hope of relief, I will depart, not through fear of pain itself, but because it prevents all for which I would live.

A patient suffering from a painful and degenerative terminal illness may be able to avoid some of its worst consequences by refusing life-prolonging treatment, but sometimes the disease withholds its mortal threat. Swift is a dramatic example of a person for whom being allowed to die was not enough. The disease would not take him until it had tortured him beyond human endurance and slowly but relentlessly destroyed his humanity. Such extreme cases are no doubt rare, but pointless suffering and personal disintegration still occur and warrant the option of actively commuting a painful and degrading death to one that is relatively painless and dignified.

Justifying Euthanasia

A fairly simple way to legalize voluntary euthanasia would be to recognize it, like self-defense, as a legitimate defense against a charge of homicide. It would be up to a prosecutor, first of all, to decide whether a reported case of euthanasia were justified. If it appeared questionable, an investigation could be launched, and if the results supported the suspicions, criminal charges could be brought. It would then be up to the defendant to prove innocence. We would trust judges and juries to make the same sort of judgment that they make concerning pleas of self-defense.

It seems to me there are four conditions that would define justifiable euthanasia: (1) The condition from which the patient suffers must be irreversible. (2) The patient must freely authorize euthanasia while clearly competent. (3) All reasonable steps must have been taken to control pain and suffering. And (4) the act must be done for the benefit of the patient alone. They are not conditions that must be certified by some committee; they are simply the conditions that a physician or family member must be prepared to argue were satisfied. For example, anybody who assists in an act of voluntary euthanasia

> *"Many people would prefer nonexistence to a subhuman existence."*

had better be able to convince a prosecutor or jury that it was indeed an act of mercy for the patient, not for the patient's family or caregivers. As case law is developed, the criteria of justification will no doubt become filled out in greater detail, but the principals will still be kept honest in the knowledge that they must "sweat out" the judgments of prosecutors or juries.

> **"It seems impossible that involuntary active euthanasia would ever be a problem in a liberal society such as the United States."**

A common objection to legalizing euthanasia is that it will take the pressure off of the movement to perfect pain control. I believe the opposite to be true. If the proposed legal change were adopted, physicians would have to show that they did all they could to control pain and suffering before euthanasia was even considered. It is entirely plausible that the consequence of such legislation would be that fewer people would be in need of lethal relief than at present. I fully agree with Dr. Cicely Saunders that what is known already about pain relief "should be developed and extended and that terminal care everywhere should become so good that no one need ever ask for voluntary euthanasia." At least not for pain.

No Slippery Slope

The most common objection to legalizing euthanasia is the danger of the slippery slope. We might expect this slope, if it were justly feared, to be well worn. In fact we find only one account of a society that supposedly slid in this manner into moral obloquy: Nazi Germany. It is true that voluntary euthanasia was allowed by the Nazis, and that later they began killing the insane, the defective, and other "useless eaters," as Hitler called them, and even practiced genocide against their own minorities. But . . . the analogy is specious. It was the racist and nationalist and militarist basis of Nazism that made its unspeakable crimes possible. There simply is no good evidence that legalizing voluntary euthanasia was the key that unlocked the Nazi closet of horrors. Surely it is wrong to deny relief from palpable suffering for such speculative reasons.

It seems impossible that involuntary active euthanasia would ever be a problem in a liberal society such as the United States. If ever there were a strongly held moral consensus, it is that killing innocent people against their wishes is wrong. What we need to consider is the possibility of nonvoluntary active euthanasia. I believe this further step could be justified, perhaps after some experience with strictly voluntary euthanasia. We currently allow family members to request passive euthanasia when it would provide merciful release from suffering. We place careful restrictions on the practice to ensure that the decision is consistent with the best interests of the patient and what we know about his or her preferences. I would want my family to be able to decide for me that my suffering had become pointless, degrading, and unbearable and to request an end to it. Hence I would favor eventually amending the second condition I formulated above to allow appropriate proxies to authorize euthanasia, subject of course to the restrictions expressed in the other conditions. I see no more potential for abuse than currently exists with passive euthanasia, since they cover the same kinds of hopeless cases. The step we rightly reject—involuntary killing—would never be taken in a free society. Our proper fear is not euthanasia but totalitarianism. Surely the former will not lead to the latter.

Some Individuals
Have a Duty to Die

by John Hardwig

About the author: *John Hardwig teaches medical ethics and social and political philosophy at East Tennessee State University in Johnson City.*

When [former Colorado governor] Richard Lamm made the statement that old people have a duty to die, it was generally shouted down or ridiculed. The whole idea is just too preposterous to entertain. Or too threatening. In fact, a fairly common argument against legalizing physician-assisted suicide is that if it were legal, some people might somehow get the idea that they have a duty to die. These people could only be the victims of twisted moral reasoning or vicious social pressure. It goes without saying that there is no duty to die.

A Crucial Question

But for me the question is real and very important. I feel strongly that I may very well some day have a duty to die. I do not believe that I am idiosyncratic, morbid, mentally ill, or morally perverse in thinking this. I think many of us will eventually face precisely this duty. But I am first of all concerned with my own duty. I write partly to clarify my own convictions and to prepare myself. Ending my life might be a very difficult thing for me to do. . . .

Because a duty to die seems such a real possibility to me, I wonder why contemporary bioethics has dismissed it without serious consideration. I believe that most bioethics still share in one of our deeply embedded American dreams: the individualistic fantasy. This fantasy leads us to imagine that lives are separate and unconnected, or that they could be so if we chose. If lives were unconnected, things that happened in my life would not or need not affect others. And if others were not (much) affected by my life, I would have no duty to consider the impact of my decisions on others. I would then be free morally to live my life however I please, choosing whatever life and death I prefer for myself. The way I live would be nobody's business but my own. I certainly would have no duty to die if I preferred to live.

Reprinted from John Hardwig, "Is There a Duty to Die?" *Hastings Center Report*, March/April 1997, by permission of the author and the *Hastings Center Report*.

Within a health care context, the individualistic fantasy leads us to assume that the patient is the only one affected by decisions about her medical treatment. If only the patient were affected, the relevant questions when making treatment decisions would be precisely those we ask: What will benefit the patient? Who can best decide that? The pivotal issue would always be simply whether the patient wants to live like this and whether she would consider herself better off dead. "Whose life is it, anyway?" we ask rhetorically.

> *"Most of us are affiliated with particular others and most deeply, with family and loved ones."*

But this is morally obtuse. We are not a race of hermits. . . .

Most of us are affiliated with particular others and most deeply, with family and loved ones. Families and loved ones are bound together by ties of care and affection, by legal relations and obligations, by inhabiting shared spaces and living units, by interlocking finances and economic prospects, by common projects and also commitments to support the different life projects of other family members, by shared histories, by ties of loyalty. This life together of family and loved ones is what defines and sustains us; it is what gives meaning to most of our lives. We would not have it any other way. We would not want to be all alone, especially when we are seriously ill, as we age, and when we are dying.

But the fact of deeply interwoven lives debars us from making exclusively self-regarding decisions, as the decisions of one member of a family may dramatically affect the lives of all the rest. The impact of my decisions upon my family and loved ones is the source of many of my strongest obligations and also the most plausible and likeliest basis of a duty to die. . . .

High Costs for Families

The lives of our loved ones can be seriously compromised by caring for us. The burdens of providing care or even just supervision twenty-four hours a day, seven days a week are often overwhelming. When this kind of caregiving goes on for years, it leaves the caregiver exhausted, with no time for herself or life of her own. Ultimately, even her health is often destroyed. But it can also be emotionally devastating simply to live with a spouse who is increasingly distant, uncommunicative, unresponsive, foreign, and unreachable. Other family members' needs often go unmet as the caring capacity of the family is exceeded. Social life and friendships evaporate, as there is no opportunity to go out to see friends and the home is no longer a place suitable for having friends in.

We must also acknowledge that the lives of our loved ones can be devastated just by having to pay for health care for us. One part of the recent Study to Understand Prognoses and Preferences for Outcomes and Risks of Treatments (SUPPORT) documented the financial aspects of caring for a dying member of a family. Only those who had illnesses severe enough to give them less than a

50 percent chance to live six more months were included in this study. When these patients survived their initial hospitalization and were discharged about one-third required considerable caregiving from their families; in 20 percent of cases a family member had to quit work or make some other major lifestyle change; almost one-third of these families lost all of their savings; and just under 30 percent lost a major source of income.

If talking about money sounds venal or trivial, remember that much more than money is normally at stake here. When someone has to quit work, she may well lose her career. Savings decimated late in life cannot be recouped in the few remaining years of employability, so the loss compromises the quality of the rest of the caregiver's life. For a young person, the chance to go to college may be lost to the attempt to pay debts due to an illness in the family, and this decisively shapes an entire life. . . .

Families Do Have Obligations

I am not advocating a crass, quasi-economic conception of burdens and benefits, nor a shallow, hedonistic view of life. Given a suitably rich understanding of benefits, family members sometimes do benefit from suffering through the long illness of a loved one. Caring for the sick or aged can foster growth, even as it makes daily life immeasurably harder and the prospects for the future much bleaker. Chronic illness or a drawn-out death can also pull a family together, making the care for each other stronger and more evident.

> *"The lives of our loved ones can be seriously compromised by caring for us."*

If my loved ones are truly benefiting from coping with my illness or debility, I have no duty to die based on burdens to them.

But it would be irresponsible to blithely assume that this always happens, that it will happen in my family, or that it will be the fault of my family if they cannot manage to turn my illness into a positive experience. Perhaps the opposite is more common: a hospital chaplain once told me that he could not think of a single case in which a family was strengthened or brought together by what happened at the hospital.

Our families and loved ones also have obligations, of course—they have the responsibility to stand by us and to support us through debilitating illness and death. They must be prepared to make significant sacrifices to respond to an illness in the family. I am far from denying that. Most of us are aware of this responsibility and most families meet it rather well. In fact, families deliver more than 80 percent of the long-term care in this country, almost always at great personal cost. Most of us who are a part of a family can expect to be sustained in our time of need by family members and those who love us.

But most discussions of an illness in the family sound as if responsibility were a one-way street. It is not, of course. When we become seriously ill or debilitated, we too may have to make sacrifices. . . .

To my mind, the most serious objections to the idea of a duty to die lie in the effects on my loved ones of ending my life. But to most others, the important objections have little or nothing to do with family and loved ones. Perhaps the most common objections are: (1) there is a higher duty that always takes precedence over a duty to die; (2) a duty to end one's own life would be incompatible with a recognition of human dignity or the intrinsic value of a person; and (3) seriously ill, debilitated, or dying people are already bearing the harshest burdens and so it would be wrong to ask them to bear the additional burden of ending their own lives.

> *"Death—or ending your own life—is simply not the greatest evil or the greatest burden."*

These are all important objections; all deserve a thorough discussion. Here I will only be able to suggest some moral counterweights—ideas that might provide the basis for an argument that these objections do not always preclude a duty to die.

An example of the first line of argument would be the claim that a duty to God, the giver of life, forbids that anyone take her own life. It could be argued that this duty always supersedes whatever obligations we might have to our families. But what convinces us that we always have such a religious duty in the first place? And what guarantees that it always supersedes our obligations to try to protect our loved ones?

Certainly, the view that death is the ultimate evil cannot be squared with Christian theology. It does not reflect the actions of Jesus or those of his early followers. Nor is it clear that the belief that life is sacred requires that we never take it. There are other theological possibilities. In any case, most of us—bioethicists, physicians, and patients alike—do not subscribe to the view that we have an obligation to preserve human life as long as possible. . . .

Secondly, religious considerations aside, the claim could be made that an obligation to end one's own life would be incompatible with human dignity or would embody a failure to recognize the intrinsic value of a person. But I do not see that in thinking I had a duty to die I would necessarily be failing to respect myself or to appreciate my dignity or worth. Nor would I necessarily be failing to respect you in thinking that you had a similar duty. There is surely also a sense in which we fail to respect ourselves if in the face of illness or death, we stoop to choosing just what is best for ourselves. . . .

The Greater Burden

A third objection appeals to the relative weight of burdens and thus, ultimately, to considerations of fairness or justice. The burdens that an illness creates for the family could not possibly be great enough to justify an obligation to end one's life—the sacrifice of life itself would be a far greater burden than any involved in caring for a chronically ill family member.

But is this true? Consider the following case:

> An 87-year-old woman was dying of congestive heart failure. Her Acute Phys-
> iology and Comprehensive Health Evaluation (APACHE) score predicted that
> she had less than a 50 percent chance to live for another six months. She was
> lucid, assertive, and terrified of death. She very much wanted to live and kept
> opting for rehospitalization and the most aggressive life-prolonging treatment
> possible. That treatment successfully prolonged her life (though with increas-
> ing debility) for nearly two years. Her 55-year-old daughter was her only re-
> maining family, her caregiver, and the main source of her financial support.
> The daughter duly cared for her mother. But before her mother died, her ill-
> ness had cost the daughter all of her savings, her home, her job, and her career.

This is by no means an uncommon sort of case. Thousands of similar cases occur each year. Now, ask yourself which is the greater burden:

a) To lose a 50 percent chance of six more months of life at age 87?

b) To lose all your savings, your home, and your career at age 55?

Which burden would you prefer to bear? Do we really believe the former is
the greater burden? Would even the dying mother say that (a) is the greater burden? Or has she been encouraged to believe that the burdens of (b) are somehow morally irrelevant to her choices?

I think most of us would quickly agree that (b) is a greater burden. That is the
evil we would more hope to avoid in our lives. If we are tempted to say that the
mother's disease and impending death are the greater evil, I believe it is because we are taking a "slice of time" perspective rather than a "lifetime perspective." But surely the lifetime perspective is the appropriate perspective
when weighing burdens. If (b) is the greater burden, then we must admit that
we have been promulgating an ethics that advocates imposing greater burdens
on some people in order to provide smaller benefits for others just because they are ill and thus gain our professional attention and advocacy.

> *"A duty to die is more likely
> when you have already
> lived a full and rich life."*

A whole range of cases like this
one could easily be generated. In
some, the answer about which burden is greater will not be clear. But in many it
is. Death—or ending your own life—is simply not the greatest evil or the greatest burden. . . .

A Family Decision

Suppose, then, that there can be a duty to die. Who has a duty to die? And
when? To my mind, these are the right questions, the questions we should be
asking. Many of us may one day badly need answers to just these questions.

But I cannot supply answers here, for two reasons. In the first place, answers will have to be very particular and contextual. Our concrete duties are often situated, defined in part by the myriad details of our circumstances, histories, and relationships. . . .

Second and perhaps even more importantly, I believe that those of us with family and loved ones should not define our duties unilaterally, especially not a decision about a duty to die. It would be isolating and distancing for me to decide without consulting them what is too much of a burden for my loved ones to bear. That way of deciding about my moral duties is not only atomistic, it also treats my family and loved ones paternalistically. They must be allowed to speak for them-

> *"If our society were providing for the debilitated, the chronically ill, and the elderly as it should be, there would be only very rare cases of a duty to die."*

selves about the burdens my life imposes on them and how they feel about bearing those burdens.

Some may object that it would be wrong to put a loved one in a position of having to say, in effect, "You should end your life because caring for you is too hard on me and the rest of the family." Not only will it be almost impossible to say something like that to someone you love, it will carry with it a heavy load of guilt. On this view, you should decide by yourself whether you have a duty to die and approach your loved ones only after you have made up your mind to say good-bye to them. Your family could then try to change your mind, but the tremendous weight of moral decision would be lifted from their shoulders.

Perhaps so. But I believe in family decisions. Important decisions for those whose lives are interwoven should be made together, in a family discussion. Granted, a conversation about whether I have a duty to die would be a tremendously difficult conversation. The temptations to be dishonest could be enormous. Nevertheless, if I am contemplating a duty to die, my family and I should, if possible, have just such an agonizing discussion. It will act as a check on the information, perceptions, and reasoning of all of us. But even more importantly, it affirms our connectedness at a critical juncture in our lives and our life together. Honest talk about difficult matters almost always strengthens relationships.

However, many families seem unable to talk about death at all, much less a duty to die. Certainly most families could not have this discussion all at once, in one sitting. It might well take a number of discussions to be able to approach this topic. But even if talking about death is impossible, there are always behavioral clues—about your caregiver's tiredness, physical condition, health, prevailing mood, anxiety, financial concerns, outlook, overall well-being, and so on. And families unable to talk about death can often talk about how the caregiver is feeling, about finances, about tensions within the family resulting from the illness, about concerns for the future. Deciding whether you have a duty to die based on these behavioral clues and conversation about them honors your relationships better than deciding on your own about how burdensome you and your care must be.

When Is There a Duty to Die?

I cannot say when someone has a duty to die. Still, I can suggest a few features of one's illness, history, and circumstances that make it more likely that one has a duty to die. I present them here without much elaboration or explanation.

1) A duty to die is more likely when continuing to live will impose significant burdens—emotional burdens, extensive caregiving, destruction of life plans, and, yes, financial hardship—on your family and loved ones. This is the fundamental insight underlying a duty to die.

2) A duty to die becomes greater as you grow older. As we age, we will be giving up less by giving up our lives, if only because we will sacrifice fewer remaining years of life and a smaller portion of our life plans. After all, it's not as if we would be immortal and live forever if we could just manage to avoid a duty to die. To have reached the age of, say, seventy-five or eighty years without being ready to die is itself a moral failing, the sign of a life out of touch with life's basic realities.

3) A duty to die is more likely when you have already lived a full and rich life. You have already had a full share of the good things life offers.

> *"If I end my life to spare the futures of my loved ones, I testify in my death that I am connected to them."*

4) There is greater duty to die if your loved ones' lives have already been difficult or impoverished, if they have had only a small share of the good things that life has to offer (especially if through no fault of their own).

5) A duty to die is more likely when your loved ones have already made great contributions—perhaps even sacrifices—to make your life a good one. Especially if you have not made similar sacrifices for their well-being or for the well-being of other members of your family.

6) To the extent that you can make a good adjustment to your illness or handicapping condition, there is less likely to be a duty to die. A good adjustment means that smaller sacrifices will be required of loved ones and there is more compensating interaction for them. Still, we must also recognize that some diseases—Alzheimer or Huntington chorea—will eventually take their toll on your loved ones no matter how courageously, resolutely, even cheerfully you manage to face that illness.

7) There is less likely to be a duty to die if you can still make significant contributions to the lives of others, especially your family. The burdens to family members are not only or even primarily financial; neither are the contributions to them. However, the old and those who have terminal illnesses must also bear in mind that the loss their family members will feel when they die cannot be avoided, only postponed.

8) A duty to die is more likely when the part of you that is loved will soon be gone or seriously compromised. Or when you soon will no longer be capable of giving love. Part of the horror of dementing disease is that it destroys the capacity to nurture and sustain relationships, taking away a person's agency and the emotions that bind her to others.

9) There is a greater duty to die to the extent that you have lived a relatively lavish lifestyle instead of saving for illness or old age. Like most upper-middle-class Americans, I could easily have saved more. It is a greater wrong to come to your family for assistance if your need is the result of having chosen leisure or a spendthrift lifestyle. I may eventually have to face the moral consequences of decisions I am now making.

These, then, are some of the considerations that give shape and definition to the duty to die. . . .

The Duties of the Incompetent

Severe mental deterioration springs readily to mind as one of the situations in which I believe I could have a duty to die. But can incompetent people have duties at all? We can have moral duties we do not recognize or acknowledge, including duties that we never recognized. But can we have duties we are unable to recognize? Duties when we are unable to understand the concept of morality at all? If so, do others have a moral obligation to help us carry out this duty? These are extremely difficult theoretical questions. The reach of moral agency is severely strained by mental incompetence. . . .

> *"If I am correct, death is so difficult for us partly because our sense of community is so weak."*

If a formerly competent person can no longer have a duty to die (or if other people are not likely to help her carry out this duty), I believe that my obligation may be to die while I am still competent, before I become unable to make and carry out that decision for myself. Surely it would be irresponsible to evade my moral duties by temporizing until I escape into incompetence. And so I must die sooner than I otherwise would have to. On the other hand, if I could count on others to end my life after I become incompetent, I might be able to fulfill my responsibilities while also living out all my competent or semi-competent days. Given our society's reluctance to permit physicians, let alone family members, to perform aid-in-dying, I believe I may well have a duty to end my life when I can see mental incapacity on the horizon.

There is also the very real problem of sudden incompetence—due to a serious stroke or automobile accident, for example. For me, that is the real nightmare. If I suddenly become incompetent, I will fall into the hands of a medical-legal system that will conscientiously disregard my moral beliefs and do what is best for me, regardless of the consequences for my loved ones. And that is not at all what I would have wanted!

The claim that there is a duty to die will seem to some a misplaced response to social negligence. If our society were providing for the debilitated, the chronically ill, and the elderly as it should be, there would be only very rare cases of a duty to die. On this view, I am asking the sick and debilitated to step in and accept responsibility because society is derelict in its responsibility to provide for the incapacitated.

> *"A death motivated by the desire to spare the futures of my loved ones might well be a better death for me."*

This much is surely true: there are a number of social policies we could pursue that would dramatically reduce the incidence of such a duty. Most obviously, we could decide to pay for facilities that provided excellent long-term care (not just health care!) for all chronically ill, debilitated, mentally ill, or demented people in this country. We probably could still afford to do this. If we did, sick, debilitated, and dying people might still be morally required to make sacrifices for their families. I might, for example, have a duty to forgo personal care by a family member who knows me and really does care for me. But these sacrifices would only rarely include the sacrifice of life itself. The duty to die would then be virtually eliminated. . . .

A duty to die seems very harsh, and often it would be. It is one of the tragedies of our lives that someone who wants very much to live can nevertheless have a duty to die. It is both tragic and ironic that it is precisely the very real good of family and loved ones that gives rise to this duty. Indeed, the genuine love, closeness, and supportiveness of family members is a major source of this duty: we could not be such a burden if they did not care for us. Finally, there is deep irony in the fact that the very successes of our life-prolonging medicine help to create a widespread duty to die. We do not live in such a happy world that we can avoid such tragedies and ironies. We ought not to close our eyes to this reality or pretend that it just doesn't exist. We ought not to minimize the tragedy in any way.

And yet, a duty to die will not always be as harsh as we might assume. If I love my family, I will want to protect them and their lives. I will want not to make choices that compromise their futures. Indeed, I can easily imagine that I might want to avoid compromising their lives more than I would want anything else. . . .

Finding Meaning in Death

We do not even ask about meaning in death, so busy are we with trying to postpone it. But we will not conquer death by one day developing a technology so magnificent that no one will have to die. Nor can we conquer death by postponing it ever longer. We can conquer death only by finding meaning in it.

Although the existence of a duty to die does not hinge on this, recognizing such a duty would go some way toward recovering meaning in death. Paradoxically, it would restore dignity to those who are seriously ill or dying. It would also reaffirm the connections required to give life (and death) meaning. I close now with a few words about both of these points.

First, recognizing a duty to die affirms my agency and also my moral agency. I can still do things that make an important difference in the lives of my loved ones. Moreover, the fact that I still have responsibilities keeps me within the community of moral agents. My illness or debility has not reduced me to a mere moral patient (to use the language of the philosophers). Though it may not be the whole story, surely Immanuel Kant was onto something important when he claimed that human dignity rests on the capacity for moral agency within a community of those who respect the demands of morality.

By contrast, surely there is something deeply insulting in a medicine and an ethic that would ask only what I want (or would have wanted) when I become ill. To treat me as if I had no moral responsibilities when I am ill or debilitated implies that my condition has rendered me morally incompetent. Only small children, the demented or insane, and those totally lacking in the capacity to act are free from moral duties. There is dignity, then, and a kind of meaning in moral agency, even as it forces extremely difficult decisions upon us.

Second, recovering meaning in death requires an affirmation of connections. If I end my life to spare the futures of my loved ones, I testify in my death that I am connected to them. It is because I love and care for precisely these people (and I know they care for me) that I wish not to be such a burden to them. By contrast, a life in which I am free to choose whatever I want for myself is a life unconnected to others. A bioethics that would treat me as if I had no serious moral responsibilities does what it can to marginalize, weaken, or even destroy my connections with others.

But life without connection is meaningless. The individualistic fantasy, though occasionally liberating, is deeply destructive. When life is good and vitality seems unending, life itself and life lived for yourself may seem quite sufficient. But if not life, certainly death without connection is meaningless. . . .

But as we age or when we become chronically ill, connections with other people usually become much more restricted. Often, only ties with family and close friends remain and remain important to us. Moreover, for many of us, other connections just don't go deep enough. As [the late senator] Paul Tsongas has reminded us, "When it comes time to die, no one says, 'I wish I had spent more time at the office.'"

If I am correct, death is so difficult for us partly because our sense of community is so weak. Death seems to wipe out everything when we can't fit it into the lives of those who live on. A death motivated by the desire to spare the futures of my loved ones might well be a better death for me than the one I would get as a result of opting to continue my life as long as there is any pleasure in it for me. Pleasure is nice, but it is meaning that matters.

Bibliography

Books

Michael Betzold	*Appointment with Doctor Death*. Troy, MI: Momentum Books, 1993.
Donald W. Cox	*Hemlock's Cup: The Struggle for Death with Dignity*. Buffalo, NY: Prometheus Books, 1993.
David Cundiff	*Euthanasia Is Not the Answer: A Hospice Physician's View*. Totowa, NJ: Humana Press, 1992.
Ronald M. Dworkin	*Life's Dominion: An Argument About Abortion, Euthanasia, and Individual Freedom*. New York: Knopf, 1993.
Herbert Hendin	*Seduced by Death: Doctors, Patients, and the Dutch Cure*. New York: Norton, 1997.
James M. Hoefler and Brian E. Kamoie	*Deathright: Culture, Medicine, Politics, and the Right to Die*. Boulder, CO: Westview Press, 1994.
Robert C. Horn III	*How Will They Know if I'm Dead? Transcending Disability and Terminal Illness*. Del Ray Beach, FL: Gr/St. Lucie Press, 1997.
Derek Humphry	*Lawful Exit: The Limits of Freedom for Help in Dying*. Junction City, OR: Norris Lane Press, 1993.
Stephen Jamison	*Final Acts of Love: Families, Friends, and Assisted Dying*. New York: Putnam, 1995.
Brian P. Johnston	*Death as a Salesman: What's Wrong with Assisted Suicide*. Sacramento, CA: New Regency, 1997.
John Keown, ed.	*Euthanasia Examined: Ethical, Clinical, and Legal Perspectives*. Cambridge: Cambridge University Press, 1995.
Rita Marker	*Deadly Compassion: The Death of Ann Humphry and the Truth About Euthanasia*. New York: Morrow, 1993.
William F. May	*Testing the Medical Covenant: Active Euthanasia and Health Care Reform*. Grand Rapids, MI: Eerdmans, 1996.
Gary E. McCuen	*Doctor Assisted Suicide and the Euthanasia Movement*. Hudson, WI: McCuen Publications, 1994.
Jonathan D. Moreno, ed.	*Arguing Euthanasia: The Controversy over Mercy Killing, Assisted Suicide, and the "Right to Die."* New York: Simon & Schuster, 1995.

M. Scott Peck	*Denial of the Soul: Spiritual and Medical Perspectives on Euthanasia and Mortality*. New York: Harmony Books, 1997.
Timothy E. Quill	*Death and Dignity: Making Choices and Taking Charge*. New York: Norton, 1993.
Lonny Shavelson	*A Chosen Death: The Dying Confront Assisted Suicide*. New York: Simon & Schuster, 1995.
Wesley J. Smith	*Forced Exit: The Slippery Slope from Assisted Suicide to Legalized Murder*. New York: Times Books, 1997.
Howard M. Spiro, Mary G. McCrea Curnen, and Lee Palmer Wandel, eds.	*Facing Death and Dying*. New Haven, CT: Yale University Press, 1996.

Periodicals

Jay Branegan	"I Want to Draw the Line Myself," *Time*, March 17, 1997.
Barbara Dority	"A Quantum Leap for the Right to Die," *Humanist*, January/February 1995.
Mark A. Duntley Jr.	"Moral Authority and Assisted Suicide," *Sojourners*, May/June 1995.
Peter Fish	"A Harder Better Death," *Health*, November/December 1997.
Linda Ganzini and Melinda A. Lee	"Psychiatry and Assisted Suicide in the United States," *New England Journal of Medicine*, June 19, 1997. Available from 10 Shattuck St., Boston, MA 02115-6094.
Robert P. George and William C. Porth Jr.	"Death, Be Not Proud," *National Review*, June 26, 1995.
Lawrence O. Gostin	"Deciding Life and Death in the Courtroom: From *Quinlan* to *Cruzan, Glucksberg*, and *Vacco*—a Brief History and Analysis of Constitutional Protection of the 'Right to Die,'" *JAMA*, November 12, 1997. Available from Subscriber Services Center, American Medical Association, 515 N. State St., Chicago, IL 60610.
Judy Harrow	"Coup de Grace: Neo-Pagan Ethics and Assisted Suicide," *Gnosis*, Winter 1997. Available from PO Box 14217, San Francisco, CA 94114-0217.
Herbert Hendin	"Scared to Death of Dying," *New York Times*, December 16, 1994.
Herbert Hendin	"Selling Death and Dignity," *Hastings Center Report*, May/June 1995.
Leon R. Kass and Nelson Lund	"Courting Death: Assisted Suicide, Doctors, and the Law," *Commentary*, December 1996.
Robert Lipsyte	"It's Life or Death: Who Can You Trust?" *New York Times*, January 12, 1997.

Bibliography

Robert Marquand	"Supreme Court Weighs Whether Suicide Is a Right," *Christian Science Monitor*, January 9, 1997.
Richard A. McCormick	*"Vive la Difference*! Killing and Allowing to Die," *America*, December 6, 1997.
Steven H. Miles	"Physicians and Their Patients' Suicides," *JAMA*, June 8, 1994.
Franklin G. Miller and Howard Brody	"Professional Integrity and Physician-Assisted Death," *Hastings Center Report*, May/June 1995.
Terence Monmaney	"The Morality of Dying," *Los Angeles Times*, November 14, 1996. Available from Reprints, Times Mirror Square, Los Angeles, CA 90053.
Elizabeth Morrow	"Attitudes of Women from Vulnerable Populations Toward Physician-Assisted Death: A Qualitative Approach," *Journal of Clinical Ethics*, Fall 1997. Available from 107 E. Church St., Frederick, MD 21701.
New York Times	"Excerpts from Decision That Assisted Suicide Bans Are Constitutional," June 27, 1997.
Nancy J. Osgood	"Assisted Suicide and Older People—a Deadly Combination: Ethical Problems in Permitting Assisted Suicide," *Issues in Law & Medicine*, Spring 1995.
Greg Pence	"Dr. Kevorkian and the Struggle for Physician-Assisted Dying," *Bioethics*, January 1995. Available from Blackwell Publishers, Journals Marketing Manager, 238 Main St., Cambridge, MA 02142.
Thomas A. Preston	"Professional Norms and Physician Attitudes Toward Euthanasia," *Journal of Law, Medicine & Ethics*, Spring 1994.
Mary Ruwart and Sue Woodman	"My Sister's Last Wish: To Die with Dignity," *McCall's*, February 1994.
David Schiedermayer	"Oregon and the Death of Dignity," *Christianity Today*, February 6, 1995.
Wesley J. Smith	"Better Dead than Fed?" *National Review*, June 27, 1994.
Sheryl Gay Stolberg	"The Good Death: Embracing a Right to Die Well," *New York Times*, June 29, 1997.
Daniel P. Sulmasy	"End-of-Life Care," *JAMA*, June 18, 1997.
Peter B. Terry and Karen A. Korzick	"Thoughts About the End-of-Life Decision-Making Process," *Journal of Clinical Ethics*, Spring 1997. Available from 107 E. Church St., Frederick, MD 21701.
James M. Thunder	"Assisted Suicide: The Violation of the Inalienable Right to Life," *Vital Speeches of the Day*, May 1, 1997.
Paul Wilkes	"Dying Well Is the Best Revenge," *New York Times Magazine*, July 6, 1997.
Richard L. Worsnop	"Assisted Suicide Controversy," *CQ Researcher*, May 5, 1995. Available from 1414 22nd St. NW, Washington, DC 20037.

Organizations to Contact

The editors have compiled the following list of organizations concerned with the issues debated in this book. The descriptions are derived from materials provided by the organizations. All have publications or information available for interested readers. The list was compiled on the date of publication of the present volume; the information provided here may change. Be aware that many organizations take several weeks or longer to respond to inquiries, so allow as much time as possible.

American Foundation for Suicide Prevention (AFSP)
120 Wall St., 22nd Fl., New York, NY 10005
(212) 363-3500, fax: (212) 363-6237
e-mail: mtomecki@afsp.org, web address: http://www.afsp.org

Formerly known as the American Suicide Foundation, AFSP supports scientific research on depression and suicide, educates the public and mental health professionals on how to recognize and treat depressed and suicidal individuals, and provides support programs for those coping with the loss of a loved one to suicide. It opposes the legalization of physician-assisted suicide. AFSP publishes a policy statement on physician-assisted suicide, the newsletter *Crisis*, and the quarterly *Lifesavers*.

American Life League (ALL)
PO Box 1350, Stafford, VA 22555
(540) 659-4171

ALL is a pro-life organization that provides information and educational materials to organizations opposed to physician-assisted suicide and abortion. Its publications include pamphlets, reports, the monthly newsletter *ALL About Issues*, and books such as *Choice in Matters of Life and Death* and *The Living Will*.

American Medical Association (AMA)
515 N. State St., Chicago, IL 60610
(312) 464-4818, fax: (312) 464-4184
web address: http://www.ama-assn.org

Founded in 1847, the AMA is the primary professional association of physicians in the United States. It disseminates information concerning medical breakthroughs, medical and health legislation, educational standards for physicians, and other issues concerning medicine and health care. It opposes physician-assisted suicide. The AMA operates a library and offers many publications, including its weekly journal *JAMA*, the weekly newspaper *American Medical News*, and journals covering specific types of medical specialties.

American Society of Law, Medicine, and Ethics (ASLME)
765 Commonwealth Ave., 16th Fl., Boston, MA 02215
(617) 262-4990, fax: (617) 437-7596
e-mail: aslme@bu.edu, web address: http://www.aslme.org

The society's members include physicians, attorneys, health care administrators, and others interested in the relationship between law, medicine, and ethics. The organization has an information clearinghouse and a library, and it acts as a forum for discussion of issues such as euthanasia and assisted suicide. It publishes the quarterlies *American Journal of Law and Medicine* and *Journal of Law, Medicine, and Ethics;* the newsletter *ASLME Briefings;* and books such as *Legal and Ethical Aspects of Treating Critically and Terminally Ill Patients.*

Center for the Rights of the Terminally Ill
PO Box 54246, Hurst, TX 76054
(817) 656-5143

The center opposes euthanasia and assisted suicide and maintains that these practices threaten the rights of the elderly, handicapped, sick, and dying. Its publications include pamphlets such as *Living Wills: Unnecessary, Counterproductive, Dangerous* and *Patient Self-Determination Act of 1990: Problematic, Dangerous.*

Choice in Dying
200 Varick St., New York, NY 10014
(212) 366-5540, (800) 989-WILL, fax: (212) 366-5337
e-mail: cid@choices.org, web address: http://www.choices.org

Choice in Dying educates medical professionals and the public about the legal, ethical, and psychological consequences of decisions concerning the terminally ill. For example, it provides physicians with information about the consequences of assisting in a patient's suicide or taking part in euthanasia. It publishes the quarterly newsletter *Choices* and the Question & Answer series, which includes the titles *You & Your Choices*, *Medical Treatments & Your Advance Directives*, *Advance Directives & End-of-Life Decisions*, and *Dying at Home.*

Compassion In Dying
410 E. Denny Way, Suite 111, Seattle, WA 98122
(206) 624-2775, fax: (206) 624-2673
web address: http://www.compassionindying.org

Compassion In Dying believes that terminally ill adults who are mentally competent have the right to choose to die without pain and suffering. The organization does not promote or encourage suicide, but it does offer moral support to those who choose to intentionally hasten death. It publishes the quarterly newsletter *Compassion In Dying.*

Dying With Dignity
188 Eglinton Ave. East, #706, Toronto, ON M4P 2X7 CANADA
(416) 486-3998, fax: (416) 489-9010
web address: dwdca@web.apc.org

Dying With Dignity seeks to improve the quality of dying for all Canadians. It educates Canadians about their end-of-life health care options and provides counseling when requested. In addition, the organization offers living wills, works to legalize advanced directives in Canada, and seeks public support to legally permit voluntary physician-assisted dying. It publishes a quarterly newsletter, *Dying With Dignity,* and the pamphlet *Dying With Dignity: A Canadian Society Concerned with the Quality of Dying.*

Euthanasia Research and Guidance Organization (ERGO)
24829 Norris Ln., Junction City, OR 97448-9559
phone and fax: (541) 998-1873
e-mail: ergo@efn.org, web address: http://www.finalexit.org

ERGO advocates the passage of laws permitting physician-assisted suicide for the advanced terminally ill and the irreversibly ill who are suffering unbearably. To accomplish its goals, ERGO offers research data, works to increase public awareness, and helps to raise campaign funds. The organization also provides the manual *Final Exit*, drug information, technique advice, and moral support to terminally ill individuals contemplating suicide.

The Hastings Center
Garrison, NY 10524-5555
(914) 424-4040, fax: (914) 424-4545
e-mail: mail@thehastingscenter.org

Since its founding in 1969, the center has played a central role in responding to advances in medicine, the biological sciences, and the social sciences by raising ethical questions related to such advances. It conducts research and provides consultations on ethical issues. The Hastings Center does not take a position on issues such as euthanasia and assisted suicide, but it offers a forum for exploration and debate. The center publishes books, papers, guidelines, and the bimonthly *Hastings Center Report*.

The Hemlock Society
PO Box 101810, Denver, CO 80250-1810
(303) 639-1202, (800) 247-7421, fax: (303) 639-1224
e-mail: hemlock@privatei.com, web address: http://www.hemlock.org/hemlock

The society believes that terminally ill individuals have the right to self-deliverance and to physician-assisted dying. The society publishes books on suicide, death, and dying, as well as its quarterly newsletter *Timelines*.

Human Life International (HLI)
4 Family Life, Front Royal, VA 22630
(540) 635-7884, fax: (540) 622-2838
e-mail: hli.@hli.org, web address: http://www.hli.org

The pro-life Human Life International is a research, educational, and service organization. It opposes euthanasia, infant euthanasia, and assisted suicide. It publishes the monthly newsletter *HLI Reports*, the monthly dispatch *Special Report*, and the monthly report *HLI Update*.

International Anti-Euthanasia Task Force (IAETF)
PO Box 760, Steubenville, OH 43952
(614) 282-3810, fax: (614) 282-0769
e-mail: info@iaetf.org, web address: http://www.iaetf.org

IAETF opposes death-with-dignity laws. It maintains an extensive and up-to-date library devoted solely to the issues surrounding euthanasia. IAETF publishes position papers and fact sheets on euthanasia-related topics, as well as the bimonthly *IAETF Update* and the report *When Death Is Sought*.

National Hospice Organization
1901 N. Moore St., Suite 901, Arlington, VA 22209
(703) 243-5900, (800) 658-8898, fax: (703) 525-5762
e-mail: drsnho@cais.com, web address: http://www.nho.org

The organization works to educate the public and health care professionals about the benefits of hospice care for the terminally ill and their families. It promotes the idea that, with proper care and pain medication, the terminally ill can live out their lives comfortably and in the company of their families. The organization opposes euthanasia and assisted suicide. It publishes the quarterlies *Hospice Journal* and *Hospice Magazine,* as well as books and monographs.

National Right to Life
419 Seventh St. NW, Suite 500, Washington, DC 20004-2293
(202) 626-8800, fax: (202) 737-9189
e-mail: nrtlc@aol.com, web address: http://www.nrlc.org

National Right to Life opposes euthanasia, physician-assisted suicide, and abortion because it believes these practices disregard the value of human life. It launches educational campaigns and publishes educational materials to help inform the public about issues such as abortion, euthanasia, and physician-assisted suicide. Its *National Right to Life News* is published twice each month.

Park Ridge Center
211 E. Ontario, Suite 800, Chicago, IL 60611-9398
(312) 266-2222, fax: (312) 266-6086

The Park Ridge Center explores the relationship between health care, religious faith, and ethics. It also facilitates discussion and debate about topics such as euthanasia and assisted suicide. The center publishes monographs, including *Active Euthanasia, Religion, and the Public Debate*, and the quarterly journal *Second Opinion*.

The Right to Die Society of Canada
532 Montreal Rd., Suite 200, Ottawa, ON K1K 4R4 CANADA
(416) 535-0690, fax: (604) 386-3800
e-mail: rights@islandnet.com, web address: http://www.rights.org/deathnet

The society respects the right of any mature individual who is chronically or terminally ill to choose the time, place, and means of his or her death. It helps patients throughout the dying process. It publishes informational pamphlets, brochures, and the periodic serial *Last Rights*.

Suicide Information and Education Centre (SIEC)
1615 Tenth Ave. SW, #201, Calgary, Alta., T3C OJ7 CANADA
(403) 245-3900, fax: (403) 245-0299
e-mail: siec@nucleus.com, web address: http://www.siec.ca

SIEC serves as a resource center and clearinghouse of materials related to suicide and suicidal behavior. It offers various materials on suicide, including books, self-help suicide prevention kits, the bimonthly magazine *SIEC Alert,* and the video "Reach Out with Hope."

Index

Index

Index

SUPPORT, 160, 200–201
surrogate decision making, 118–19
Swift, Jonathan, 195

technology, medical. *See* medical science
terminally ill
  are treated poorly, 160
  care of
    destroys families, 200–201
    strengthens families, 182, 201
  children, 43
    deciding fate of, 24, 25
    deserve right to die, 82, 188–90
    deserve right to life, 189
    need compassion, 41
thanatology, 184, 186
This Far and No More (Bauer), 188–90
Thomas, Clarence, 75
Thompson, Richard, 172
Toffler, William L., 49, 50
Tonti-Filippini, Nicholas, 31, 33
Tuskegee project, 164

Uhlmann, Michael M., 89
underclass, 50, 175

United States
  Constitution, 77, 96
    14th Amendment of, 56, 67
  Supreme Court, decision of 6/26/97
    did not grant right to die, 37–38
    excerpt from, 84–88
    legal logic behind, 89–97, 100–103,
      104–12

Vacco v. Quill, 37–38, 72, 99, 101–102

Wantz, Marjorie, 152
Washington ban on assisted suicide. *See*
  *Compassion in Dying v. State of
  Washington*
Washington v. Glucksberg
  did not grant right to die, 37–38
  excerpt from, 84–88
  legal logic behind, 89–97, 100–103,
    104–12
withdrawal of treatment, 48, 131
  see also refusal of treatment
women, duty to die and, 136–37

Youngberg v. Romeo, 66